"The delivery of policing in any democratic s〈...〉 of those democratic systems and civic instit〈...〉 security for citizens and to protect those who ar〈...〉 *Criminology for the Police* is the first book to interrogate this enduring tension and competing interpretations of the relationship between crime and policing in the context of the College of Policing's Police Education Qualifications Framework. The book introduces key ideas and concepts that underpin our understanding of crime as well as the design and delivery of twenty-first century policing and assesses their implications for those tasked with front-line policing. The book also outlines the growing importance of data and knowledge generation to the contemporary policing landscape and introduces readers to the basic skills required to use research and data to understand dynamic and complex challenges and improve the delivery of policing."

Baroness Helena Kennedy

"The relationship between academic and policing is not new, but the introduction of the PEQF is a game changer and thousands of new recruits into the police are already finding themselves engaged in academic studies of policing that they might not have expected to be part of their role. This book helps these officers navigate their way through various theories and concepts by drawing out the different ways in which criminology informs our understanding of policing. Importantly, the authors remind us that criminology encompasses a diverse range of perspectives, and they focus on making the appropriate links between different criminological voices and the relevant aspects of policing."

Dominic Wood
*Head of the School of Law, Policing and Social
Sciences at Canterbury Christ Church University*

Criminology for the Police

This book offers an applied approach to criminology suitable for prospective police officers. It covers the fundamentals of criminological knowledge, theory and research, and their relevance to policing. The book is split into two parts, the first introducing the basics of criminology, and the second connecting criminological research to police practice. It focuses on the principles of evidence-based practice and encourages students to think critically about the issues covered. Core content includes the following:

- A history of policing in England and Wales, through a criminological lens.
- An overview of the literature on police culture, bias, and discretion.
- A review of the challenges of applying criminological insights to policing, and the impact of the College of Policing code of ethics on police practice.
- An exploration of the challenges of contemporary policing, including complex crime, transnational investigation, and digital and organised crime.
- A critical overview of evidence, and public sources of evidence.
- An examination of the contested definitions and perspectives on Evidence-Based Policing.
- An introduction to criminological research, including quantitative, qualitative, and mixed methods.
- A review of problem-solving in policing, including SARA and ATLAS models.

This book is essential reading for all students studying degrees in Professional Policing, as well as students of criminology engaged in criminal justice knowledge and practice.

Craig Paterson is a Principal Lecturer at the Department of Law and Criminology, Sheffield Hallam University, UK.

Ed Pollock is a Senior Lecturer in Criminology at the Department of Law and Criminology, Sheffield Hallam University, UK.

Routledge Advances in Police Practice and Knowledge

Series Editors
Dr Tom Cockcroft, Leeds Beckett University, UK, and
Dr Martin Wright, Canterbury Centre for Policing Research, UK

Routledge Advances in Police Practice and Knowledge is a new series of books which brings together established academics and authors in the field of police studies to provide themed textbooks that will support students engaging with professional police studies within higher education. The focus of the series is to provide academically rigorous accounts of research and knowledge and to contextualise them in the practical and applied context of policework. In doing so, the books that make up the series will provide an invaluable resource to students studying policing through a variety of academic and vocational routes.

The Editors, Dr Tom Cockcroft and Dr Martin Wright dedicate this series to the memory of Professor PAJ (Tank) Waddington who believed policing to be an honourable profession, and whose career's work embodied the values that inform the direction of the series.

Policing Structures
Colin Rogers

Improving Intelligence Analysis in Policing
Stuart Kirby and Scott Keay

Criminology for the Police
Craig Paterson and Ed Pollock

Criminology for the Police

Craig Paterson and Ed Pollock

Routledge
Taylor & Francis Group

LONDON AND NEW YORK

Cover image: anyababii

First published 2022
by Routledge
4 Park Square, Milton Park, Abingdon, Oxon OX14 4RN

and by Routledge
605 Third Avenue, New York, NY 10158

Routledge is an imprint of the Taylor & Francis Group, an informa business

British Library Cataloguing-in-Publication Data
A catalogue record for this book is available from the British Library

Library of Congress Cataloging-in-Publication Data
Names: Paterson, Craig (Lecturer in criminology), author. | Pollock, Ed, author.
Title: Criminology for the police / Craig Paterson and Ed Pollock.
Description: Milton Park, Abingdon, Oxon; New York, NY: Routledge, 2022. |
Includes bibliographical references and index. |
Identifiers: LCCN 2021053870 | ISBN 9780367532291 (hardback) |
ISBN 9780367532307 (paperback) | ISBN 9781003081012 (ebook)
Subjects: LCSH: Criminology–Great Britain. | Police ethics–Great Britain. |
Law enforcement–Great Britain.
Classification: LCC HV6025. P416 2022 |
DDC 364.942–dc23/eng/20211115
LC record available at https://lccn.loc.gov/2021053870

ISBN: 978-0-367-53229-1 (hbk)
ISBN: 978-0-367-53230-7 (pbk)
ISBN: 978-1-003-08101-2 (ebk)

DOI: 10.4324/9781003081012

Typeset in Times New Roman
by Newgen Publishing UK

MIX
Paper | Supporting
responsible forestry
FSC
www.fsc.org   FSC™ C013985

Printed in the United Kingdom
by Henry Ling Limited

Contents

Figures

Tables

Chapter 1

Introduction

A Criminology for the Police?

Introduction

Welcome to *Criminology for the Police!*

The main objective of this book is to introduce prospective police officers and students of policing to the two fundamental components of criminological knowledge: theory and research. The book is split into two parts with the first part providing an introduction to the underpinning ideas that have dominated criminology as an academic discipline and the linkages with changing perspectives of police amongst the public and key policing stakeholders as well as police policy and practice itself. The book thus offers an introduction to criminological thought that should have practical use for those interested in police. The book does not offer a comprehensive state of the art picture of criminology across the globe, but it provides introductory nudges to this literature via a curated gallery of academic and policy sources that have been selected specifically for those attempting to understand what police do through a criminological analytical lens.

The second part of the book introduces applied contemporary criminological challenges to connect criminological research and theory to police practice. The book does this by focusing upon principles of evidence-based practice, which are commonplace in many professions but relatively new to the field of police, and encourages students to think critically about the knowledge that they will encounter, access, and use in their future professional domain. The book explores the influence of the ever-changing social world that surrounds the world of professional practice and uses a myriad of case studies and problem-based tasks to get you to think about how academic criminology can help you to address real-world police problems. For those of you who are new to criminology, you will see that we utilise a range of literature from different academic disciplines (sociology, psychology, geography, law, and many others) to try to understand why crime happens and to explore how these insights might influence how you respond to the social problems you see around you. Criminology is a broad discipline, so we will be focusing

DOI: 10.4324/9781003081012-1

upon the bits which are most closely aligned to the College of Policing's Police Education Qualifications Framework (College of Policing, 2020) whilst also providing links to other literature that you may want to investigate in the future.

As the title states, this book is an introduction to *Criminology for the Police*, so whilst much of the book will address issues related to front-line policing to assist those who are interested in joining the police and those who have recently joined as police officers, the book also covers the contextual issues that might inform the development of policing policies so that it will be useful for police officers, managers, and civilian staff in a wide variety of roles. The book is essentially about problem-solving and how introducing police to a wider variety of analytical tools can help to improve individual and organisational responses to changing landscapes of crime, deviance and disorder as well as public (in)tolerance of different issues.

Most importantly for us as authors, the book draws on our experiences of working with those involved in police training and education. This includes the students we have met over 15 years of working together, new recruits to the police, police staff, trainers, and educators in England and Wales and across the world. The book thus engages directly with the content of the pre-join undergraduate degree (BA Hons in Professional Policing), the police constable degree apprenticeship, and the degree holder entry programme curricula to introduce police-relevant criminological knowledge in alignment with the College of Policing's Police Education Qualification Framework (College of Policing, 2020). The book has a primary focus upon police work in England and Wales to align with the demands of the College of Policing's education framework, but it is also contextualised and informed by recognition that the local impact of crime is influenced by national, global, and transnational forces.

The College of Policing curriculum has introduced a new focus upon digital crimes, vulnerability, and social scientific research that can be interrogated using criminological analysis, and we address these issues in the middle and latter parts of the book. Thus, while the book seeks to support those who are encountering criminology through their interest in police, we will extend the scope of our analysis beyond the police curriculum to engage with new and often contentious subject matter and the multiple critiques of police and policing that you will encounter in your personal and professional lives.

This introductory chapter addresses the most obvious yet potentially complex question, "what is the point of criminology for police"? The chapter explores the potential benefits that degree-level study offers to the police officer role using evidence from a range of international jurisdictions and connects this evidence to theoretical critiques of the role and function of the police as an institution. The chapter discusses the benefits and challenges of the new

Policing Educational Qualification Framework and points readers in the direction of appropriate further reading to help understand the advantages to police officers of understanding criminology as an applied discipline and the benefits of engaging with criminological literature more generally to support your own future development.

Before we proceed any further, we are required to ask some simple questions with hugely complex answers. First, we need to ask what do the police actually do? This question provides some baseline context for our second question (and the one most commonly raised by public and politicians at times of crises), what should the police be doing? This discussion will take up the next couple of thousand words of this introductory chapter, so if you want to look at specific information, then please just use the contents and index to navigate your way around this book. If you're happy with the chronological approach, then the next thing we will do is introduce some context surrounding what the police do. In this section, we will introduce you to criminological theory for the first time.

In the workshops we run with students and police professionals, we tend to find that the word "theory" is quite off-putting, but it is an essential component of the analytical framework which we will use throughout the rest of the book. Theories are just ways of explaining things. They help us to explore and challenge our underpinning assumptions about the world that surrounds us. An everyday example of a theory could be taken from what we choose to buy to eat and how we interpret which foods are best for us (is it the most tasty, or the most nutritional?). We try to provide logic to our decision-making by providing explanations about why we eat so healthily (or not!). In academic language, this is an explanatory theory. In this book, our questions focus upon what makes the best police and policing, and we use theory to explain the thinking that underpins these different criminological theoretical perspectives. It will come as no surprise to you that there are lots of different theories and perspectives about what makes the best police and what the police should do. We will turn to this issue now.

Reflective Task

What do you think are the main roles and function of the Police Service in England and Wales? The College of Policing's website (www.college. police.uk/) provides you with an introduction to the many and varied responsibilities of the twenty-first century police.

Now, have a look for your local police force's website and look for their mission or values statement. To what extent does this correspond with your expectations of the police role?

What Do the Police Do?

The core function of what the police do is often presented to the public as a balance between crime-fighting and order maintenance although the day-to-day functions of police work could be more simply described as peace-keeping. Criminological pioneers from the United Kingdom and United States such as Banton (1964) and Skolnick (1966) have illustrated how the police undertake an essential social role in keeping the peace through the deterrent value of the Police Service's uniformed presence on the streets and the coercive, and most commonly unused, threat of their legal power to use force (Bittner, 1970). This publicly visible presence is highly valued in England and Wales with approximately 75% of the British public indicating support for the police role and demands for more police officers being a recurrent discourse in political election campaigns (Office of National Statistics, 2021). This debate about what the police should be doing and how many police we need, when placed in a political and economic context, is essentially a discussion about what is the best use of finite government funds and police resources.

The 2011 Her Majesty's Inspectorate of Constabulary assessment of police demand identified that 61% of the police workforce could be described as working on the front-line in a mixture of visible patrol and specialist roles (this figure increases to 70% in some forces). Yet, studies in the United States and the United Kingdom have consistently shown that less than 25% of calls for service to the police involve crime directly, and this figure has regularly decreased to between 15% and 20% (Bayley, 1994). There are some logical reasons for this. A phone call to report a crime may turn out to be inaccurate, the disturbance or situation may have been resolved prior to police attendance and support may be required from another agency. Thus, contrary to much public belief, crime is a relatively minor part of everyday patrol work (Morris and Heal, 1981). But, and it is a significant but, police visibility is directly linked to levels of public confidence in the police in England and Wales (Bradford et al., 2009; Mesko and Tankebe, 2015), so even without the productivity of resolving crime problems, there is a strong argument to maintain visible police patrols. Everyday policing is thus relatively mundane and, as Banton acknowledged many years ago, often made up of "waiting, boredom and paperwork" (1964: 85).

There is longstanding consistency in this depiction of everyday policing. In a similar 1996 Audit Commission report entitled *Streetwise: Effective Foot Patrol*, it was identified that 75% of police resources were taken up with front-line roles that included patrolling by foot or car and criminal investigation. This resource-intensive and reactive approach to policing is driven by the public who are the most significant influencers of what the police do. Members of the public make the 999 and 101 calls that determine how police officers are deployed, and in cities across the world, these emergency calls have historically generated around 90% of patrol work (Bayley, 1994). It is this reactive mandate and the position of police as the sole 24/7 emergency responses service that stretches the police role beyond crime and into public nuisance, anti-social behaviour, public health management, and other social issues.

Once the police engage with the public, the police role is most commonly interpreted through their legal authority to use force, to stop and search, and to remove a person's liberty as well as their role as investigators of crime. This legal authority provides police officers with a formal role as gatekeepers to the criminal justice system and a more blurred social authority to make judgements about individual and/or collective behaviour and to decide where it is appropriate to exercise some form of regulatory control. These regulatory controls serve a range of purposes that incorporate diffuse elements of order maintenance (Marenin, 1982; Wilson and Kelling, 1982), public protection (Bajpai, 2013; Bittner, 1970), and crime prevention (Alderson, 1979; Farrell, 2001). Despite law being the tool that the police use to administer justice, justice itself is mentioned on only rare occasions (Manning, 2010). These different visions of the purpose of policing highlight the complex and contested nature of developing, configuring, and implementing policing strategies but also the partial lens through which the purpose of policing is conceptualised. There is little discussion of the ways in which policing compounds existing inequalities, the blind eye that is turned to crimes of the wealthy, or the impact upon over-policed populations' conceptions of democracy and social justice (Manning, 2010; Sklansky, 2005; Tyler, 2006).

The police are also often defined in news stories and fictional characterisations by their legal authority to use violence and coercion (Bittner, 1970). This definition tends to shift focus onto formal uniformed police agencies rather than the much broader networks of, often informal or at least non-uniformed, policing that exist within any society. It is thus worthwhile to outline the main functions of the police before we move on any further. The three core functions that are highlighted here are by no means exhaustive and represent a simplification of the myriad of tasks policing agencies are asked to undertake. But... they are at least a starting point.

The American academic Egon Bittner remains the most influential articulator of the role and function of policing in western Anglophone societies. In his classic text, *The Functions of Police in Modern Society* (1970), Bittner describes the role of the police officer as emerging out of situations that people face and where something needs to be done about a problem and the selected response is required with urgency. This loose description captures the role of police in many societies as the only 24/7 emergency service that is available to manage social problems and maintain order. The maintenance of order is thus a key symbolic function of the police officer.

Order Maintenance

In simple terms, the police order maintenance function can be likened to that of the scarecrow with the primary purpose being to provide a visible presence that deters threats from a defined geographical location. The most well-known modern articulation of this view is Wilson and Kelling's (1982) Broken Windows which uses the metaphor of the broken window as a sign of public decay and an absence of deterrence that attracts opportunists who perceive they can commit crime without risk of being caught. This deterrence-based thinking, grounded in the idea that we are all rational thinkers that respond to positive and negative stimuli in predictable ways, informs much of the public discussion about the role of the police, but it often fails to capture the complex origins of police and the multiplicity of tasks that police officers undertake.

The conceptual links between policing and order hark back to the work of La Mare (1719) in France who conceived the idea of "police" as generated by local and central government plus civil society with the purpose of the generation and maintenance of good social order. Prior to the advent of professional police in England and Wales in 1829, good order was oriented around ideals of victim and community protection, although this changed with the establishment of professional police who were tasked with the pursuit of offenders (Bajpai, 2013). In contemporary democratic societies order maintenance is enacted through a variety of organisations beyond the state police that operate under a broad conceptualisation of the police term, policing. Key policing actors include formal police agencies, commercial security such as bouncers and private investigators, local government officials, and voluntary organisations, amongst many others. Recourse to police often only takes places after other informal policing interventions have failed.

Skolnick, and many others since, point to the importance of dispute resolution at the local level that takes place in the shadow of the law and without formal recourse to official sanctions (Skolnick, 1966). The informality of everyday order maintenance through a diversity of policing providers challenges the everyday assumption that the police are policing and that policing is done by the police. As Bittner (1970) notes, the public police are differentiated from other members of society due to their state-sanctioned monopoly over the use of violence and coercive force but that does not necessarily mean that they are the sole providers of policing and order maintenance. When people feel that order has been maintained, they feel safe and confident in the police as the primary providers of policing. When this is not the case, other policing providers may be sought out from the private sector or the local community. Perceptions of the threat posed by crime are thus critical to the public's interpretation of the type of protection it needs.

Public Protection

The priority for all nation states should be to protect its citizens. This priority is captured in the Universal Declaration of Human Rights and was first published by the United Nations General Assembly on 10 December 1948 (United Nations, 2020). The formal priority for most democratic police agencies is thus to provide public protection, but this relatively uncomplicated starting point quickly becomes contested when questions are raised about which members of the public are being protected and from whom. As there are limited police resources available, political decisions have to be made about the priority targets for these resources. Police officers therefore have to make decisions on a day-to-day basis that are informed by their managers, organisations, and political overseers to direct them to those who are understood to be in most need of protection. Simple? Well...

There is recognition from across the globe that the distribution of the police protection of citizens is inherently unequal (Bowling et al., 2019; Manning, 2010), and some people are more vulnerable to specific types of crime. Police policy-makers and strategists therefore need to recognise that some people hold less power and resources than others and subsequently may need more protection. In many instances, police agencies and police officers will not know who is in the most vulnerable or potentially harmful situations and their job becomes an interrogation of unclear circumstances to try and ascertain who is at risk and who presents a threat. There is a high profile to these areas of police work as they often produce the most challenging circumstances in the form of providing protection for children, investigating domestic abuse, and attempting to uncover those who present the most serious and persistent threats to the public.

Given that police intervention is often morally problematic, there is longstanding agreement that liberal models of policing should be founded upon a principle of minimal intervention (Manning, 2010) to maximise public trust and legitimacy (Mesko and Tankebe, 2015). Furthermore, as Sklansky (2005) notes, in a democratic society, policing should be underpinned by fundamental principles of equality, security, and opportunity which means that wherever the police serve to amplify inequality and insecurity then their role and function should be minimised. This perspective provides a normative position for the police's public protection purpose whereby all police activity should be subject to the principle of minimal intervention and where police activity is harmful it should be stopped or handed over to alternative agencies who will be tasked with ensuring security and order.

Crime Prevention

Since 1829, the primary purpose of police organisations has been crime prevention with success often measured through the absence of visible crime.

Immediately prior to Peel's establishment of the London Metropolitan Police, Patrick Colquhoun (1800/2012) referred to police as a new science that would focus on the prevention and detection of crime to generate good order. Colquhoun's work drew on La Mare and others who viewed "police" as a new science of government administration. The emergence of Peel's professional police was, at least in part, a response to anxiety from the privileged classes about working-class criminality, hence the focus on visible crime in public areas. Similarly, the rise of commercial crime prevention from the early 1980s was a response to public and political dissatisfaction with the police's response to three decades worth of rising crime. The 2008 economic crisis encouraged a further re-evaluation of the configuration of policing as the impunity of the financial elite was followed by a run of scandals involving politicians, the media and police officers which led to a questioning of the police's suitability to investigate crimes of the powerful, the advent of democratically elected police and crime commissioners and a decade of fiscal retreat that has re-moulded the shape of police forces in England and Wales. The new policing degrees have thus arrived at the same time as the police workforce has been slimmed down and is being re-shaped for twenty-first century challenges.

With similar roots to La Mare, the origins of the term "police" can be found in Boucher d'Argis's (1765) "art of providing a comfortable and quiet life (Boucher d'Argis, 1765)." Thus, any emphasis upon crime prevention in democratic societies needs to be envisaged as a bottom-up process through which trust in policing and other modes of social control are built up in societies (Loader and Walker, 2007) rather than the more authoritarian leanings of order maintenance strategies. It was this argument that led to Peel's successful introduction of the new police in 1829 as he contrasted his vision of civilian police attached to local administrative structures in comparison to the more authoritarian state police that were found in our revolutionary neighbours in France (Brodeur, 2010).

Therefore, the basis for the emergence and success of any formal or informal locally democratic policing structure is trust in impersonal authority (Manning, 2010: 9) and institutional structures that credibly maintain the public peace as well as symbolic and culturally accepted forms of order (Loader and Mulcahy, 2003). Any police or policing organisation which fails to achieve this trust will be challenged by internal and/or external forces as we have seen across the western democracies in protests about racialised policing and the inadequate protection of women and children. Thus, the purpose of democratic policing is not just to prevent crime and to reproduce the existing order (Ericson, 1982), but to re-distribute social order with an emphasis on equity and social justice (Manning, 2010). It is this latter issue that is most problematic for police forces and has led to a renewed focus upon targeted forms of crime prevention that recognise social inequity and the specific vulnerabilities of a range of groups who are at more risk of serious harm than the rest of the population.

Patterns of crime constantly change and policing responses need to change in response to these patterns of crime. The slower the police adaptation, the more likely that people will be exposed to harm and trust in police will fall. Furthermore, any sense of inequity or an absence of trust in police action, governance, or accountability generates the space for other, potentially more just, modes of policing to emerge (Tyler, 2006). We, as individuals and societies, are thus constantly required to re-engage with and re-visit these questions about what the police should be doing as the world around us changes.

Reflective Task

What do you think should be the core functions of the police?
How would you describe the roles that you think the police should prioritise?

What Should the Police Do?

violence is considered at the same time to be the prime expression of evil and the necessary instrument of peace and order.

(Brodeur, 2010: 39)

Brodeur's quote captures the contradictions that lie at the heart of policing. Police are expected to both respond with the threat of coercive force where it is deemed necessary but at the same time accept that perceived misuse of this force challenges their position in the accepted social order. In diverse globalised societies, police thus sit between communities that experience conflict and in democratic societies must both respect basic rights of individuals and groups whilst providing adequate and equitable protection. We will therefore endeavour to answer this question, *What should the police do*, throughout this book. Having outlined what the traditional police role and function has been, we can start to develop our understanding of police and policing and their relationship with twenty-first century societies. It is essential that you, as practitioners, students, and future leaders are at the heart of this discussion.

As we have already acknowledged, policing in England and Wales is undergoing radical shifts. Individual and collective vulnerability have become prominent concerns and accelerated changes in the purpose of policing that have been evident since the re-emergence of community policing as a policing policy goal in the late 1980s. The language of community policing emerged in response to failures in the crime control/law enforcement model of policing in England and Wales and led to almost three decades of experimentation in ways to re-connect police organisations with communities, re-build public confidence and police legitimacy, and contribute to reductions in recorded crime through proactive engagement with crime and other social problems. This process stretched the remit of policing, without any formal government reviews of the police role, to include partnership responses to social problems, proactive community crime prevention, and the management of public fear.

This broadening and lengthening of the police role had led to a belated recognition that policing has always, although to varying extents, involved the everyday management of a broad range of social problems (Bittner, 1970). A failure to recognise the blurred boundaries between public health, local government, and policing perhaps explains the failure to provide appropriate safety nets for the most vulnerable people in societies and the subsequent use of law enforcement methods to manage some of the most complex social challenges related to migration, mental ill health, domestic abuse, and the exploitation of young people by organised crime groups.

Yet, it is in the peculiar evolution of our governing institutions that we may find our solution to these problems. Prior to the establishment of a professional police force in England and Wales, there were a range of different responders tasked with social problems. It was only with the establishment of a police force "to prevent crime, protect property etc." that vulnerable people were re-conceptualised as the property of the police (Foucault, 1969). This reflection on the evolution of policing as the management of public health and social order aligns with the current re-emergence of vulnerability as a core responsibility of police agencies. Yet police agencies have not grown sufficiently to properly resource a response to the myriad of tasks that they are faced with. Instead, police officers are required to engage with partner agencies to undertake partnership, or plural, policing of social problems.

As you can see, there are multiple different perspectives on what the police should be doing and how they should fit in with other forms of policing and social control processes. Criminological theories provide us with analytical tools that help us to understand a range of different perspectives, interpretations, and understandings of the role of police in society, and in the following section, we introduce the most prominent theories that we will be focusing upon throughout this book. This section just provides short introductions to the theories which will be interrogated in more detail later in the book but keep an eye out for ideas that align with your world view as well as those which you think are a load of rubbish!!

Sociological Positivism and Social Disorganisation

Emile Durkheim (1858–1917) developed the first fully sociological explanation of crime and his ideas inspired a generation of sociologists of juvenile delinquency in the United States, known as the Chicago School. While Durkheim's core concepts of "anomie," a "collective conscience," and "mechanical solidarity" first came to the fore in the late nineteenth century, they continue to be of relevance to policing today. Using Durkheim's theoretical perspective, it is possible to analyse the relationship between police, crime, and society as a product of social changes. The police institution was established during a period of social and political unrest in the early to mid-nineteenth century, and subsequent policing crises have similarly occurred at times of rapid social change and conflict that produce new forms of crime and/or rises in crime rates. Rapid social change can also provide challenges for the notion of policing by consent that underpins policing in the UK.

Reflective Task

Which new crime problems have the police had to face over the past decade as a consequence of social changes? How have the police responded to these new crime problems?

The Chicago School of Sociology developed Durkheim's ideas and created an understanding of crime as a consequence of social conditions and the influence of the surrounding environment. Robert Park identified "human ecology" (or, environmental criminology, as it is now known) as the core focus of analysis with the extent of social organisation or disorganisation in an area influencing the quality of the relationships between people and the character of the area. In their book, *The City*, Park and Burgess (1925) developed this concept further and pointed towards the high levels of crime and deviance in disorganised geographical areas with transient populations and an absence of social integration. The most vulnerable area was described as a "zone of transition" which would often experience high rates of immigration, infant mortality, mental ill health, school exclusions, and crime (Shaw and McKay, 1942). These conditions encouraged individuals and families with the economic means to move out of these geographical areas which, in turn, could lead to the area suffering from sustained patterns of social deprivation.

The idea that the social environment influences individual and group dynamics is widely known as sociological positivism and is discussed in more detail in the next chapter. This social environment perspective continues to inform our understanding of crime patterns in urban areas and has led to crime analysis techniques such as crime mapping and policing strategies such as hotspot policing. From a practical policing perspective, this theory of crime causation raises the question of how high levels of crime in urban areas should be regulated or policed. Environmental criminology has had a strong influence over forms of crime prevention that can be used in crime hotspots and the idea that architects, town planners, and housing officers all play a key policing role in designing-out crime from urban areas.

The focus on new forms of crime prevention from the 1980s onwards was underpinned by this environmental design approach to urban areas to nudge or discourage criminal and disorderly behaviour which led to the proliferation of urban crime prevention techniques such as improved surveillance with CCTV, additional street lighting in areas of vulnerability, and better locks for houses and cars. Most police forces now employ crime analysts who identify concentrations of specific types of criminality to inform problem-oriented policing responses to these crime problems.

Reflective Task

Is there a "zone of transition" where you live?
Do you think that ideas such as "human ecology" and "social disorgan-
    isation" are still relevant to the world we live in today?

Robert Merton carried on the Chicago School of Sociology tradition by taking Durkheim's concept of "anomie" and applying it to the experience of poor American citizens in the 1930s Depression. Merton used the term "strain" to explain challenges to the existing social structure that emerged when pre-viously culturally accepted goals and expectations could not be met. Merton argued that people were socialised towards the shared aim of "The American Dream" in the United States but that these dreams and aspirations were not realisable for many people. The failure of these dreams and aspiration led to a social strain which, in turn, could lead to deviance, disorder, and crime (Merton, 1938: 672). Merton's ideas about social strain inspired what became known as subcultural theory which was used to explain what was perceived to be a rise in delinquent groups and gangs in the period after the Second World War (Cohen, 1955; Downes, 1966; Matza, 1964) and retains its influence over criminology through a range of cultural analyses of specific types of crime and disorder.

Reflective Task

Why do young people commit such a high proportion of recorded criminal offences?

Surveillance, Deterrence, and Right Realism

Ahead of the arrival of Peel's 1829 London Metropolitan Police Act, social reformers such as Henry Fielding (1707–1754) and Patrick Colquhoun (1745–1820), were developing the ideas of La Mare and Boucher d'Argis into a new police science which would provide an "unremitting gaze" over newly urbanised towns and cities. The new police would provide general deterrence through a permanent visible presence in urban areas that were understood to present a threat to social order. The unremitting gaze of the new police science drew on the influential work of Jeremy Bentham (1748–1832) who sought to mould social structures in a way that would guide individuals to act in a more self-disciplined and pro-social manner that would help to reproduce a civilised social order.

Bentham had been inspired by Cesare Beccaria (1738–1794), one of the key European criminological thinkers, to pursue the utilitarian aim of achieving "the greatest happiness for the greatest number" through the generation of good social order, or *policie*. Together, Beccaria and Bentham established the classical school of criminology which interpreted human behaviour through an economic lens where rationally motivated individuals sought pleasure and avoided pain. Interpreting human behaviour through this simple economic calculus generated a vision of how individuals and society could be subtly shaped through consensual modes of policing, a precursor to the idea of policing by consent. If the aim of the law and the role of the police could be to protect society from mutually agreed harms, then populations would understand that compliance with the law was in both their own individual interest and that of society too.

This enlightenment era philosophy was re-born in the last quarter of the twentieth century as the concept of the free-willed, rational thinking actor drove criminal justice policy in the UK Home Office (Clarke and Mayhew, 1980). A renewed focus upon influencing the economic calculus of the deviant and law abiding supported the development of situational crime prevention where criminal behaviour would be understood as a normal aspect of human behaviour (Garland, 1996) that could be regulated and controlled through situational and environmental influences.

This new form of administrative criminology, underpinned by rational choice theory, prioritised a view of crime as being driven by opportunity (Clarke and Mayhew, 1980). In the United States, Cohen and Felson (1979) were developing a complementary routine activity theoretical perspective that identified three inter-linked causal factors that would lead to a criminal act taking place:

- A motivated offender
- A potential victim/target
- The absence of a capable guardian

An intersection of each of these factors provides the situation in which a crime event takes place and determines the where, when, and how of criminal activity. It is often known simply as the crime triangle which provides a simple visualisation of this useful theoretical tool.

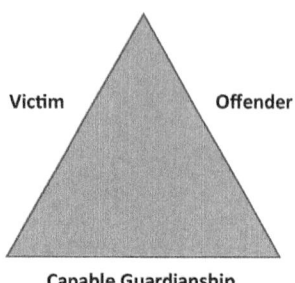

Figure 1.1 The Crime Triangle.

This theoretical framework will help you identify how different forms of situational crime prevention and policing strategies could reduce the likelihood of crime events taking place and, once again, highlights the importance of the unremitting gaze in providing a visible police presence that provides forms of general deterrence in areas with high levels of crime and disorder.

There are similarities between rational choice and routine activities theories and the "broken windows" argument put forward by Wilson and Kelling (1982) in the United States and, collectively, these perspectives became known as right realist theories of criminology. Wilson and Kelling interpreted "broken windows" as precursors to crime that must be fixed to stop crime and disorder from flourishing. Controversially, Wilson and Kelling proposed that police should increase their intervention with subcriminal behaviour that provided signs of disorder, such as gatherings of young people, homeless populations, littering, and derelict properties. The Broken Windows argument was politically popular in the United States and is frequently cited in public discussion about policing in the United Kingdom, but it does not have the strong theoretical and scientific underpinning of the work produced by Clarke, Mayhew, and Felson. Indeed, the Broken Windows perspective is now more closely associated with the problem of racialised and discriminatory policing (Vitale, 2017), so please make sure you have your critical radar turned on when this language appears in media discussions.

The 1970s and 1980s bore witness to a polarisation of Marxist conflict theories from the left wing of politics and right wing economic theories that focused upon individual free will, but a new theoretical perspective would soon emerged which would combine elements of both conflict and consensus perspectives and which would provide the theoretical underpinning for a less ideological and more pragmatic or "realistic" approach to our understanding of crime and policing that has endured until the present day.

Left-Realism

Left-realism integrates the sociological positivist focus upon the social environment and its links to crime causation with the rational choice emphasis upon general deterrence to provide a more balanced approach to managing social problems and criminal behaviour. Left-realist criminologists, such as John Lea and Jock Young (1984), had originally developed their academic work from a Marxist perspective of criminology that understood state tools such as police and prisons as a threat to working-class communities but were in the process of revising these ideas to incorporate the need to combat the very real threat of crime in working-class communities. Hence, left-realism:

- Left = tough on the causes of crime
- Realism = tough on (the reality of) crime (problems)

Left-realists took on the challenge of providing a credible crime control response that also recognised the need to simultaneously alleviate the deprivation, economic insecurity, and poor living conditions that people experienced in high-crime areas. Left realists drew upon a range of existing criminological theory to expand the scope of investigation to include four intersecting factors which provided "a square of crime":

- The police and other agencies of social control
- The public
- Offenders
- Victims

We will look at these theories in more detail throughout the book, but the reason for highlighting them now is due to the influence they have had on the contours of criminal justice policy. Rational choice theory and routine activities theory underpin the use of situational crime prevention that is a core element of contemporary policing. Similarly, left-realism influenced the development of proactive policing strategies that seek to reduce harm in communities and demand on police forces. We will use these theories throughout this book to help explain how specific policing strategies and tactics might work and will also bring in other influential theories that have shaped policing policy and its contemporary emphasis upon situating vulnerability and harm reduction at the heart of policing policy.

The Structure of This Book

So far, this chapter has provided an outline of the context that has informed the development of this book. From this point onwards, the book is split into two distinct parts that can be read chronologically or as discrete collections of chapters. Part 1 provides an overview of the evolution of the academic disciplines of criminology and its application to the police profession. As the subject matter of this book seeks to align itself with the police education qualifications framework, the coverage of the criminological discipline is partial. A much more comprehensive overview of the relationship between criminology and policing is provided in our overview of these two subjects that was published a decade earlier (Paterson and Pollock, 2011). You can also find interesting multi-disciplinary theoretical critiques of policing policy and practice in some of the references at the end of this chapter (Brodeur, 2010; Manning, 2010 are both highly recommended).

Chapter 2 provides a historical account of policing developments in England and Wales viewed through a criminological lens. As we have started to do in this chapter, Chapter 2 introduces different perspectives on the origins and evolution of police and policing and identifies the implications of these insights for the twenty-first century police officer. Indicative content includes the shifts in methods of policing and social control before and after the emergence of the modern professional police in 1829 and the more contemporary shifts towards victim-oriented approaches in policing and criminal justice. The chapter provides a chronological historical account of changing perspectives on the causal underpinnings of crime and the influence of these theoretical perspectives upon crime prevention and policing interventions. Illustrative examples include the right and left realist theoretical underpinnings of reactive and proactive interventions and the emergence of administrative criminology, situational crime prevention, and responsibilisation strategies.

Chapter 3 provides an overview of the subject discipline of criminology and introduces relevant theory that will be of practical use to police officers. The theoretical content focuses upon sociological and environmental criminology which address, in turn, the social and environmental causes of crime and simultaneously identify opportunities for police and other agencies to apply interventions that deny opportunities for crimes to take place. The chapter draws on theories such as communitarianism and authoritarianism and situates older communitarian theories (such as Durkheim's Mechanical Solidarity) in their contemporary context. The chapter draws on these perspectives to explain contemporary shifts in the forms of intervention demanded of policing strategies, such as changes from reactive to proactive policing, the growth of inter-agency co-operation, and the myriad forms of community and problem-oriented policing that can be found across England and Wales as well as further afield.

Chapter 4 focuses upon contemporary crime, risks, and threats and the challenges they pose to policing strategies. The chapter assesses the challenges of managing rising demand with fewer resources and the broadening role of the wider policing family. The chapter draws on the decision-making processes involved in determining policing strategy and encourages the reader to cast a critical eye over the strengths and weaknesses of some commonly used strategies and tactics to analyse and understand their suitability for use in particular contexts and situations. The chapter draws on a criminological disciplinary underpinning to provide an academically informed rationale for decision-making in practice. Although the chapter will focus on decision-making and strategy generally, priority will be given to existing contemporary and emerging crime problems in England and Wales and beyond and the requirements for effective multi-agency collaboration. A key focus of this chapter will be the tensions associated with a myriad of often competing police reforms and legislative developments such as the Crime and Disorder Act 1998, Police Reform Act 2002, Police Reform and Social Responsibility Act 2011, and the Police and Crime Act 2017.

Chapter 5 focuses upon the rise in importance of an appreciation of individual and collective vulnerabilities and the impact this has had upon police interpretations of what constitutes a victim or offender. The chapter introduces several contributions made by criminologists on the subject of police culture and assesses how useful these theories are in making sense of how police use their discretionary powers and the impact this has in a diverse society with complex and often conflicting demands and needs. Consideration is given to the challenge faced by the Police Service in delivering fair and just policing services that generate and maintain the public legitimacy of police officers and organisations. The chapter addresses the ongoing challenge of policing by consent in societies with an ever-increasing diversity of demands. Key content includes contentious debates around racialised and gendered policing as well as assessing the potential for genuinely democratic policing with those individuals and communities most commonly subjected to policing controls. The chapter summarises the extensive literature on police culture alongside contemporary social psychological insights on bias and discretion to draw out the most important criminological insights for police practice and assesses future implications upon the police role and function.

It is at this juncture that the book moves on from theoretically grounded criminological analysis to a focus upon criminological research, data generation and analysis, and an assessment of the role research, data, and intelligence will have upon future forms of police accountability. Chapter 6 sets the tone for the second half of the book with a focus upon the role of social scientific and criminological analysis in supporting police problem-solving. This chapter encourages the reader to think about ethical and practical problem-solving strategies and uses case studies to support this work. The National Decision Model (NDM) is used to illustrate how research can be embedded into practice to address risks, minimise harm, and reduced associated costs and harms to individuals and communities in an evidence-based way. The SARA and ATLAS models are introduced in this chapter and linked to relevant theory (rational choice theory, routine activities theory, and social crime prevention) from the first half of the book. Part 2 makes much more explicit links between theory, research, and the insights they can provide to support practical police interventions.

Chapter 7 moves from analysis of evidence for the purpose of problem-solving to the subject of evidence-based policing. Evidence has also always played a central role in policing through criminal investigations to the preparation of cases for presentation at court, but the global development of the evidence-based policing movement has made the links between police, policing, and criminology more explicit. The chapter critically appraises what we consider to be evidence and identifies key public sources of evidence that students can use. The chapter will encourage the reader to focus upon how to use research and data alongside their professional knowledge and provides an introduction to key terminology such as effectiveness, impact, and evaluation. It is through the concept of evidence-based policing that the College of Policing are driving change in the new police education framework to embed thinking about research, data, and criminology into the initial preparation of police officers for their role. Evidence-based policing is not a British concept but a new way of thinking about professional policing which is taking root across the globe. It is also a contested concept, and this chapter will introduce different perspectives and definitions of evidence-based policing to illustrate how different scholars and police officers interpret these developments.

Chapter 8 encourages you to develop your own skills as a researcher by doing research on crime and policing. Doing research need not be difficult. All we are doing is collecting data in a systematic manner about things we, or others, have done. Once you have learnt these basic skills, you can spend a lifetime refining them and developing ways of making research useful in your future career. This chapter aims to de-mystify the research process with brief introductions to different ways of doing research. The chapter introduces different forms of research and evaluation such as systematic reviews, rapid evidence assessment, and open source intelligence research. As always, lots of further reading will be included for those who are interested in a specific aspect of the research process. The chapter will help you to construct a logical argument and select appropriate strategies for exploring research problems. You will learn how to develop research design skills to justify the collection of new empirical data and also to analyse secondary data that has been collected by others.

Chapter 9 brings the substantive chapters to a close with a road map that guides you through the process of doing your own research. The chapter takes you through each of the steps involved in developing your own empirical research project with guidance on how to generate your research design and advice on your selection of data collection tools. This content includes introductions to quantitative and qualitative approaches to research as well as slightly more complicated mixed methods approaches. Readers will be introduced to research philosophies and research design and will identify, justify, and use methodological knowledge to create a framework for research analysis. The chapter introduces you to some fundamental research techniques as well as aspects of sampling, data analysis and research ethics. Collectively, Chapters 6 to 9 introduce you to the value of understanding research and data for the purpose of improving your understanding of policing problems and your personal and organisational agility in developing new responses to rapidly changing or evolving social problems.

The book concludes with a chapter that reviews key learning points from the book and then points the criminological analytical lens into the future to see what sort of crime and policing challenges we should expect to see next. A future-focused police research agenda is set out for you to engage with in your career as increased demands are made upon police officers and organisations by the enhanced complexity of twenty-first century societies and policing problems. The future is always fuzzy and hazy and much more easily understood with hindsight. Yet, we can state with conviction that once theory and research have been embedded into professions, they do not leave. Evidence has been a core focal point for critical decision-making and problem-solving in medicine, education, law, and the social professions (probation and social work) for many decades and, in some instances, centuries. Now, it's over to you to shape what happens next.

References

Alderson, J. (1979) *Policing Freedom: A Commentary on the Dilemmas of Policing in Western Democracies*. Plymouth: McDonald and Evans.

Audit Commission (1996) *Streetwise: Effective Foot Patrol*. London: HMSO.

Bajpai, G. S. (2013) *Locating the Crime Victim in Criminal Procedure Ideologies*. Available at: Locating the Crime Victim in Criminal Procedure Ideologies by G. S. Bajpai :: SSRN

Banton, M. (1964) *The Policeman in the Community*. London: Tavistock.

Bayley, D. (1994) *Police for the Future*. Oxford: Oxford University Press.

Bittner, E. (1970) *The Functions of Police in Modern Society*. Washington: National Institute of Justice.

Boucher d'Argis. (1765) Police. In D. Diderot and J. d'Alembert (eds.) *Encyclopedie ou Dictionnaire Raisonne des Sciences, des Artes et des Metiers*, 12–905. Neufchastel: Samuel Faulche.

Bowling, B., Reiner, R. and Sheptycki, J. (2019) *The Politics of the Police* (Fifth Edition). Oxford: Oxford University Press.

Bradford, B., Jackson, J. and Stanko, E. (2009) Contact and confidence: Revisiting the impact of public encounters with the police. *Policing and Society*. 19(1): 20–46.

Brodeur, J. P. (2010) *The Policing Web*. Oxford: Oxford University Press.

Clarke, R. and Mayhew, P. (1980) *Designing-Out Crime*. London: Home Office.

Cohen, A. (1955) *Delinquent Boys: The Culture of the Gang*. New York: MacMillan.

Cohen, L. and Felson, M. (1979) Social inequality and predatory criminal victimization: An exposition and test of a formal theory. *American Sociological Review*. 44(4): 588–608.

College of Policing (2020) *Policing Education Qualification Framework*. Available at: www.college.police.uk/career-learning/learning/PEQF

Colquhoun, P. (1800/2012) *A Treatise on the Police of the Metropolis*. Cambridge: Cambridge University Press.

Downes, D. (1966) *The Delinquent Solution*. London: Hutchinson.

Ericson, R. (1982) *Reproducing Order: A Study of Police Patrol Work*. Toronto: University of Toronto Press.

Farrell, G. (2001) How victim-oriented is policing? *International Symposium on Victimology, Montreal*. Available at: www.researchgate.net/publication/28575311_How_victim-oriented_is_policing

Foucault, M. (1969/2001) *Madness and Civilisation: A History of Insanity in the Age of Reason*. London: Routledge.

Garland, D. (1996) The limits of the sovereign state. *British Journal of Criminology*. 36(4): 445–471.

Her Majesty's Inspectorate of Constabulary (2011) *Demanding Times: The Frontline and Police Visibility*. Available at: www.justiceinspectorates.gov.uk/hmicfrs/media/demanding-times-062011.pdf

La Mare, N. (1719) *Traite de la Police*. Paris: Biblioteque Nationale de France. Available at: https://data.bnf.fr/fr/12450313/nicolas_de_la_mare_traite_de_la_police/

Lea, J. and Young, J. (1984) *What Is to be Done About Law and Order? Crisis in the Eighties*. London: Penguin.

Loader, I. and Mulcahy, A. (2003) *Policing and the Condition of England: Memory, Politics and Culture*. Oxford: Clarendon Press.

Loader, I. and Walker, N. (2007) *Civilizing Security*. Cambridge: Cambridge University Press.

Manning, P. (2010) *Democratic Policing for a Changing World*. Boulder: Paradigm Publishing.

Marenin, O. (1982) Parking tickets and class repression: The concept of policing in critical theories of criminal justice. *Contemporary Crises*. 6: 241–266.

Matza, D. (1964) *Delinquency and Drift*. New York: John Wiley and Sons.

Merton, R. (1938) Social structure and anomie. *American Sociological Review*. 3(5): 672–682.

Mesko, G. and Tankebe, J. (2015) *Trust and Legitimacy in Criminal Justice*. Geneva: Springer International Publishing.

Morris, P. and Heal, K. (1981) *Crime Control and the Police: A Review of Research*. Home Office Research Study No.67. London: HMSO.

Office of National Statistics (2021) *Crime Survey for England and Wales: Year Ending December 2020*. Available at: www.ons.gov.uk/peoplepopulationandcommunity/crimeandjustice/bulletins/crimeinenglandandwales/yearendingdecember2020

Park, R. and Burgess, E. (1925) *The City*. Chicago: Chicago University Press.

Paterson, C. and Pollock, E. (2011) *Policing and Criminology*. London: Sage (Learning Matters).

Shaw, C. and McKay, H. (1942) *Juvenile Delinquency in Urban Areas*. Chicago: Chicago University Press.

Sklansky, D. (2005) *Police and Democracy*. Available at: https://papers.ssrn.com/sol3/papers.cfm?abstract_id=710701

Skolnick, J. (1966) *Justice without Trial: Law Enforcement in a Democratic Society*. New York: Wiley.

Tyler, T. (2006) *Why People Obey the Law*. Princeton: Princeton University Press.

United Nations (2020) *Universal Declaration of Human Rights*. United Nations. Available at: www.un.org/en/about-us/universal-declaration-of-human-rights

Vitale, A. (2017) *The End of Policing*. New York: Verso.

Wilson, J. Q. and Kelling, G. (1982) *Broken Windows: The Police and Neighbourhood Safety*. The Atlantic. Available at: www.theatlantic.com/magazine/archive/1982/03/broken-windows/304465/

Chapter 2

Disciplinary Criminology and the Police

Introduction

This chapter provides an introduction to criminology as a subject discipline with particular relevance to a policing practice context drawing on the knowledge base required by the College of Policing syllabus and the Police Educational Qualifications Framework. The opening section of this chapter explores criminology in its disciplinary context explaining the origins of the discipline and of the police force before discussing the role and function of the modern police force, including the role of police officers as front-line administrators of the rule of law. The chapter then takes a detailed look at policing and crime reduction with reference to the key criminological theoretical perspective of Left Realism and how it informs policing as a form of intervention in and wider important issues related to policing. First, the discussion offers an understanding of the importance of crime victims to policing and discusses issues crucial to victimology such as harm caused by criminal behaviour, repeat victimisation, victim support, and the police role in supporting victims of crime including use of the Code of Practice for Victims. The chapter then ends with a discussion of Left Realism as applied to crime reporting and recording and offers a discussion of Recoded crime and the Crime Survey of England and Wales as well as a critique of crime statistics more generally.

Criminology in Its Disciplinary Context

Criminology is a multi-disciplinary social science grounded in, according to David Garland and Richard Sparks, crime, criminals, crime control, crime rates, crime policy and policies and practices of policing, prevention, and punishment (Garland and Sparks, 2000). Garland and Sparks also contend criminology is inscribed within the spheres of academia (scholarly discourse), government (crime control and criminal justice), and culture (mass media and popular culture). Contemporary criminology is most entwined within

DOI: 10.4324/9781003081012-2

these first two spheres. Modern policing is most closely tied to the second – Government and issues of crime control and justice.

As a multi-disciplinary area of study, criminology has been described by David Downes and Stan Cohen as a rendezvous (Downes, 1988) and parasitic (Cohen, 1988) discipline in that it was born out of and "feeds off" already-established ideas and existing academic disciplines. Garland and Sparks (2000) argue that ever since its emergence, Criminology has sought to be a contemporary, timely worldly subject which depends on the ideas of other disciplines to progress. Hence, criminology is a subject that constantly reconstitutes itself (Garland and Sparks, 2000) and has evolved as an academic multi-discipline, rather than an autonomous or self-standing subject. Academic influences on the development of criminological thought include traditional subjects such as biology, sociology and class, political and cultural studies, psychology and psychiatry, gender and race, geography, and medicine as well as more contemporary areas such as environmental studies (under labels such as Green and Species Criminology) and Postmodern Criminology with a focus on risk reduction and management. Ever more recently, influences have been in some of the more lesser-known areas such as Southern Criminology (see, e.g., Carrington et al., 2016), Anarchist Criminology and Abolitionist and Convict Criminology (see Hopkins Burke, 2020). Hence, the roots of criminological study are many and constantly changing, reflecting that crime is dynamic with constantly changing processes, relationships, and dynamics between offenders, victims, targets, causes, motives, methods, and impacts on individuals and wider society. It is important for police officers to understand these important dynamics in dealing with offenders, caring for victims, deciding on strategy, gathering evidence, promoting prevention, and, ultimately, keeping communities safe.

Most criminological interest in crime causation has been centred on exploring offenders and individual risk factors (such as age, psychological composition and well-being, and levels of intelligence) and social risk factors (such as educational attainment, employment status, and previous and current family background). Other research has focused more on places, environmental criminology, and crime mapping whereby offenders use their "cognitive map" and commit crimes in their "awareness space" (see, for example, Brantingham and Brantingham, 1981) – areas they know well and where they feel safe, where they feel comfortable offending, where they are aware of escape routes to evade capture and arrest, and where they can dispose of stolen goods or weapons. This awareness space is developed through their lifestyle and anchored around travelling points influenced by their lifestyle and routine activities (such as leaving home to attend work, school, leisure activity, and visit friends).

Interest in environmental criminology has also focused on differences in crime problems in urban and rural areas and as to why inner-city areas are more Criminogenic (crime attracting) than rural areas and the differences in crime type committed in various locations; for example, burglary or violent crime in inner-city areas and livestock or machinery theft in rural locations (National Farmers Union, 2021). Criminological attention also focuses on temporal aspects of crime with, for example, well-established research findings around the likely time of day for a burglary to occur (Ratcliffe, 2002) and crime in what is referred to as the Night-time Economy (Hadfield et al., 2009). A key focus of criminological enquiry has centred around motives for criminal behaviour (for example, poverty or financial need, financial gain, conflicts and gang violence, or peer influence or the need to prove status). Finally, more recent interest has focused on impacts of criminal behaviour on places and victims through recognition of the place of the victim in policing and the criminal justice process.

In addition to forming around dimensions of causation, Criminology, as an academic discipline, has been formed around "dimensions of intervention" (Hopkins Burke and Pollock, 2004). The first dimension is the criminal law. The second dimension, Situational Crime Prevention, is concerned with changing the situations in which crime occurs and reducing the opportunity to offend (Hopkins Burke and Pollock, 2004). The third, social crime prevention, is an approach that "aims to prevent people drifting into crime by improving social conditions, strengthening community institutions and enhancing recreational, educational and employment opportunities" (Bright, 1987: 62). The role and function of modern policing requires, in some form, incorporation of these (and more) "dimensions" of intervention and will be discussed in later chapters, and keeping communities safe and maintaining social control has remained a crucial function of policing since the emergence of the professional police force in 1829 and before.

Policing Before the Police

According to Robert Reiner, "there is an ideological assumption within modern societies that the police are a functional pre-requisite of social order and that without the police, chaos would ensue" (Reiner, 2010: 3). Before the first professional police force was established in 1829 social control was enforced by the community through strong social bonds, community cohesion and high levels of social and economic homogeneity. Policing and social control relied on community cohesiveness and public compliance and citizens' endorsement of reciprocal positive attitudes, beliefs customs, norms, and values – what Emile Durkhiem termed "mechanical solidarity" (Durkheim, 1933). Durkheim proposed that earlier more simple forms of society comprised high levels of "mechanical" solidarity characterised by a likeness and similarity between individuals, invariably from the same ethnic group, who held common and rigid attitudes, beliefs, consciences, and morals reinforced by religious conviction (Durkheim, 1915). In a Mechanical Society, the level of social control depends on the social relationship and level of co-operation between individuals and extent to which they are prepared to obey the rules of behaviour and respect the norms and values of that community. In such a homogenous, undifferentiated society, anti–social and deviant acts offend the strong cohesiveness and social conscience of the people and perform the important function of delineating the boundaries between those who supported and those who transgressed social values (Hopkins Burke and Pollock, 2004). Hence, crime control is dependent on peoples' observance of the rules of behaviour and co-operation and respect for those who enforce social control. Hence, there emerged an early form of policing legitimacy and "policing by consent."

Another concept crucial to early policing and that remains important in contemporary policing and crime control was what was later termed by David Garland as "Responsibilisation" whereby responsibility for crime control rests, not with Central Government, but with other partner agencies including community citizens (Garland, 1996). Garland's theoretical ideas can be seen in policy application in the Police Reform and Social Responsibility Act 2011 and then Prime Minister David Cameron's idea of building what he called the Big Society where, according to Cameron:

> people, in their everyday lives, in their homes, in their neighbourhoods, in their workplace......don't always turn to officials, local authorities or central government for answers to the problems they face...but instead feel both free and powerful enough to help themselves and their own communities.
>
> (Cameron, 2010)

Prior to the establishment of the professional police force, members of the community served as police constables on a voluntary basis alongside their paid employment (similar to the modern special police constable). In addition to the responsibility of community citizens to undertake policing functions, there was a legal obligation on those who witnessed a crime to apprehend those responsible and notify a constable or justice of the peace (similar to a modern "citizens' arrest"). The first publicly funded police officers replaced voluntary police constables during the eighteenth century when the Bow Street Patrols were established under authority of Middlesex Magistrates and eventually expanded to other London neighbourhoods. By the early nineteenth century, professional "Watches" had been established across the UK, and patrol officers were employed with established pay, working conditions and jurisdiction with more freedom to operate and use discretionary power than Watches who were restricted to beat patrol of a certain area. This diverse mixture of policing agencies caused confusion around which agencies and individuals had legal authority to discharge policing duties and their jurisdiction (Emsley, 1991). Thus, there came a need for codification of legal power and responsibility of policing agents. The most significant move to this and the formation of a professional police force was the appointment of Sir Robert Peel as Home Secretary in 1822 who implemented the Metropolitan Police Act in 1829, establishing the first professional police force.

Policing and the Rule of Law

The Metropolitan Police Act 1829 provided the first legal formalisation of the powers necessary for the police to discharge their duties effectively and legitimately. Before this, a mixture of municipal organisations, private agencies, and citizen groups assumed a policing role to generate and maintain social control in local neighbourhoods (Emsley, 1991). According to Bowling et al. (2019), if policing agencies cannot achieve or maintain full legal legitimacy to discharge their power, the moral legitimacy of their role in the community is undermined and questioned. Here, Bowling et al. draw on the important distinction between moral and legal legitimacy. Unlike moral legitimacy, which depends on reciprocal values between the police and public, such as those followed in a Mechanical Society, legal legitimacy draws on statutory and common law, and cannot be subjective meaning all actions by the police must be consistent with the Rule of Law. Legal Philosopher Joseph Raz set out four fundamental principles of the Rule of Law: that the law should be *Clear*, so citizens can understand it; *Stable,* so frequent changes are avoided; *Prospective*, so citizens are judged on current rather than previous actions; and *Open*, meaning easily accessible (Raz, 1979). Since the enactment of the Metropolitan Police Act 1829, all police powers have been underpinned by legislative provision to ensure police officers act legally in discharging their duties and functions.

Practical Task

Have a go at answering the following questions: consider how clear, stable, prospective, and open the rule of law is in each of your answers.
   What are the legal implications presented by:

> Exceeding the speed limit while driving your car?
> Being caught with stolen goods?
> Being caught carrying a wooden plank on a pavement?
> Shooting the Welsh from inside the walls of Chester after midnight?

The answers to these questions are in the appendices of this book, and, as you will see (spoiler alert!), some laws are more clear, stable, prospective, and open than others. It is this ambiguity that makes the police officer's application of the law such a complicated task. Faced with multiple transgressions of the law, a police officer must use discretion in applying the law in line with such considerations as legal requirements, policing priorities and changing expectations, needs and demands of the public. Therefore, to fully understand the role and function of the police and appreciate the public's understanding of it, we need to look closely at the moral legitimacy of the police, police–societal relations and the influencing societal changes and, finally, understand the combination of legal, sociological, and environmental interrogations and explanations of crime and policing. And it is to this that we now turn.

The Role and Function of Modern Policing

The police have a range of roles and responsibilities primarily centred on local policing, crime prevention, public protection, and offender management alongside multi-agency working (National Police Chiefs Council, 2019). A range of agencies contribute to the setting of policing priorities including the College of Policing, National Police Chiefs Council, National Crime Agency, and Policing and Crime Commissioners. Alongside functions set out by formal agents, academic works have been influential in forming our knowledge of the role and functions of the police. Paul Brodeur, for example, divides policing functions into High Policing (the work of the intelligence community) and Low Policing (front-line uniformed police officers) (Brodeur, 1983). The term "front-line" policing is commonplace and refers to "those who are in everyday contact with the public and who directly intervene to keep people safe and enforce the law" (HMIC, 2011: 6). Policing operations have also been classified in terms of Reactive (responding to public calls) and Proactive (community visibility and engagement). In her maiden speech as Home Secretary to the Conservative Party Conference in October 2019, Priti Patel appeared to focus the policing role very much around law and order maintenance in focusing the role of the police around keeping the country safe from danger and pledging to back the police as a force of law and order (Patel, 2020).

So, policing encompasses various "routine" policing duties such as apprehending suspects, stopping and searching or managing minor or non-criminal conduct such as antisocial behaviour. Policing strategies, therefore, encompasses wide-ranging duties some of which may be defined as "hard" (order maintenance, risk management and public protection) and "soft" (crime prevention and community-orientated policing). These opposite approaches to policing, as a form of "intervention," are grounded in the opposing criminological theoretical perspectives of "Right" and "Left" Realism. As these names suggest, both are underpinned by opposing political standpoints with "Left" Realism more associated with the political Left Wing (Marxism, Socialism, and, usually, Liberal) with Right Realism more associated with the political Right Wing (Conservative), reflecting the penal ideology and approach to sentencing and criminal justice of each political "Wing" (Conservative "punitivism" and Labour "welfarism").

The term "Realism" developed from the views of 1970s Criminological scholars that responses to crime and interventions were ill-informed, sporadic, and ineffective due to a lack of an evidence base. Hence, "Realism" denotes the call to find "real" or "genuine" interventions. The key difference is the emphasis on crime causation. For Left Realists, it is not possible to deal with crime effectively if interventions are not informed by and do not respond to causes of crime. Right Realists, on the other hand, do not attach any importance to understanding crime causation, regarding it as insignificant to effective punishment and instead, focusing on punitive interventions arguing that severity of punishment is more effective in deterring future offending and, therefore, reducing crime.

The discipline of criminology is primarily clustered around the political Left due to the enduring influence of sociology and the view that crime is not a product of individual choice but of social context and disadvantage and intervention should, therefore, be focused on rehabilitation, reformation, and "softer" policing methods. The influence of the political Right is manifested in Conservative ideology whereby crime is a product of individual choice and intervention is focused on punishment and "hard" policing such as reactive policing, stopping and searching, arresting, detaining, questioning, and prosecuting rather than softer approaches of community-orientated and neighbourhood policing, or restorative approaches to dealing with suspects. Policing from a Left Realist perspective must be focused on community orientation and addressing crime causation (which the police can only achieve to a minimal level without contributions and support from other agencies and government).

In order to understand crime, its impacts and intervention from a "real" perspective, as is the central tenet of Realist theorists, it is important to collect empirical data from those closest to a crime problem be that offenders if, for example, we want to find out about causes, criminal justice professionals if we want to find out about effectiveness of interventions and victims if we want to find about impacts. And interest in the real impacts of crime through the eyes of the victim became an important focus for Left Realist criminologists during the 1970s which led to the emergence of Victimology – a branch of Criminology focused on the study of victims and victimisation which it was hoped, would lead to a better and more comprehensive understanding of crime and find a place for the study of the victim, as well as the offender, in criminological study.

Left Realism and Victimology

Just as there are a range of crime types that lead to victimisation, so too are there a range of impacts upon the victim including psychological, emotional, physical, and financial, all of which will lead to different needs of support from a range of agencies including the police. Carrabine (2014) refers to the "hierarchy of victimisation" whereby some groups do not feel their victimisation is taken seriously and who feel under-protected. At the bottom of this hierarchy are those who are homeless who experience anti-social behaviour and violence and the elderly who experience more psychological and physical abuse. In terms of victims support, some shorter term needs may be provided by the police such as reassurance, practical assistance to secure property, information on the progress of the case and, if the suspect is found guilty and sentenced, information about the release of the offender from sentence. Other longer term needs such as counselling, medical assistance, financial assistance, and assistance in completing forms for compensation may be provided by health services, victims support and others.

Part of the support for victims also includes advice on court processes and what the victim can expect to experience in court during the prosecution process. The UK has an "adversarial" criminal justice system – meaning the primary focus is on building a case around seeking to prosecute offenders or, what is commonly termed "bringing the offender to justice" and so requiring the police to build a case against a suspect and presenting that evidence in court as part of the prosecution case. However, in an Adversarial system, the victim is also required to give evidence in court against a suspect which can sometimes be a traumatic and intimidating experience. Hence, another key focus for Victimology is the care and rights of victims.

The Youth Justice and Criminal Evidence Act 1999 aims to make giving evidence in court a less traumatic and intimidating experience for victims – particularly those who are, in some way, vulnerable in respect of, for example, their age or physical or psychological disorder. It is by way of this legislation that police officers may see people giving evidence in court via video link from another room in the court building or another location or from behind a screen in the court room and hidden from view of others. These provisions are designed to make giving evidence less traumatic and intimidating particularly in cross-examination. Some of the provisions of the Youth Justice and Criminal Evidence Act 1999 are particularly crucial in assisting young victims of crime giving evidence in court such as the requirement of lawyers, judges, and other personnel to remove their wigs during witness testimony and giving evidence in private in sexual abuse cases. These provisions reflect the increasing recognition over more recent years that the victim ought to have a place at the heart of the criminal justice system and are in addition to provisions set out in earlier legislation such as abolishing the need for corroboration of unsworn evidence of a child (in the Criminal Justice Act 1988) and the introduction of video recorded testimony (Criminal Justice Act 1991).

Victim Support

The Home Office produced the Victims Charter in 1996 detailing certain provisions for victims before, during, and after victimisation, the police investigation, and the prosecution and courts process. The Charter also makes provision for supporting the victim in applying for compensation for criminal injuries and entitling them to explain to the court how the victimisation has affected them. The Victims Charter was the precursor to the national Victim Personal Statement Scheme (Home Office, 2001) which gives victims of crime the opportunity to explain the impact that the crime has had on themselves, including the impact of any injuries sustained, (Victim Support, nd) and express their concerns regarding any bail arrangements of the suspect or offender and voice any fears of intimidation or vulnerability arising from racial, cultural, or disability issues (Roberts and Manikis, 2013). The victim may write a Victim Personal Statement (VPS) at the same time as their witness statement to the police, to express a view of what sentence ought to be imposed, for the sentencer to take into account at the time of sentencing. Offering victims of crime the opportunity to make a VPS is part of the Code of Practice for Victim Care (see below) although the number of victims that choose to make one varies, and they are more likely to be submitted by victims of serious crime, particularly those that are personal to them such as domestic violence (Roberts and Manikis, 2013).

Code of Practice for Victims of Crime

The Code of Practice for Victims of Crime (also known as the Victims Code) sets out the services and a minimum standard that must be provided to victims of crime by organisations (referred to as service providers), including the police, in England and Wales (Ministry of Justice, 2020). Under the Code victims are entitled to:

- Be able to understand and be understood
- Have details of the crime recorded without unjustified delay
- Be provided with information when reporting a crime
- Be referred to services that support victims and have services and support tailored to their needs
- Be provided with information about compensation
- Be provided with information about the investigation and prosecution
- Make a Victim Personal Statement

- Be given information about the trial, trial process and the victims role as a witness
- Be given information about the outcome of the case and any appeal
- Be paid expenses and have property returned
- Be given information about the offender following a conviction
- Make a complaint if their rights are not being met

All police forces and Police and Crime Commissioners (PCCs) are required to contribute to deliver these rights to victims under the Code and as the police are involved with the victim at almost every stage of the criminal justice process from the point of a victim reporting a crime to providing evidence in court as part of the prosecution process, responsibility for fulfilling the Code weighs heavily on them and PCCs who are responsible for commissioning many of the services that support victims under the Code (Ministry of Justice, 2020). However, some parts of the Code are particularly key for the police in areas such as crime reporting and recording, referral to victim support services (including Restorative Justice Services – see below), interviewing crime victims, requesting witness statements, and assisting victims with making VPSs. Under the Code, the police also have a duty to give victims an update on the investigation process and police decision-making (particularly where the case is discontinued or where further action is not taken against the suspect). In the case of bereavement following the death of a close family member, the victim has a right to a Family Liaison Officer (FLO) under the Victims Code. FLOs are experienced police officers who have chosen to train to undertake the role. They provide an investigation and support role to families of victims of crime, particularly serious crimes involving fatality. The FLO is assigned to gather evidence and information to contribute to the investigation and provide support and information to the family in a sensitive and compassionate manner (College of Policing, 2021).

The Code of Practice for Victims of Crime follows several initiatives, policies, and academic research papers designed to improve the rights of and support for victims of crime from the Criminal Justice Act 1988 to the Victims Charter 1996.

At around the same time as the publication of the Victims Charter, academic works were emerging into the problem of repeat victimisation – when a person or place is repeatedly targeted for crime or disorder (Tseloni et al., 2005).

Repeat Victimisation

Scholarly research into repeat victimisation over the past three decades has found past victimisation to be one of the best predictors of future victimisation. As many offence types are repeat offences, repeat victimisation contributes significantly to crime rates and preventing it can, therefore, be significant for crime reduction. Numbers of repeat offences depend on the crime type because some crimes are more likely to be repeat offences than others, but in terms of offenders, estimates suggest that between 7% and 10% of offenders are responsible for 50% of all crime committed (Garside, 2004; Home Office, 2001). In terms of repeat victims, Ken Pease provides a useful estimate – that 1% of victims experience 59% of personal crimes and 2% of victims experience 41% of non-vehicle related property crime (Pease, 1998). Hence, because reducing repeat victimisation means targeting a small number of offenders (7% to 10%) and victims (1% to 2%) targeting policing and crime reduction resources towards repeat offenders and repeat victims may be efficient in terms of resource allocation and effective in reducing crime levels.

Thirty years of research and scholarship on repeat victimisation has enabled improvements in policing of repeat offences beginning with burglary in the 1980s (see Forrester et al., 1988) and racial hate crime (see Sampson and Philips, 1992) and, a little time later, domestic violence (Lloyd et al., 1994). Understanding the dynamics of crime remains important to policing in cases where people or targets are particularly vulnerable to victimisation.

Crime Recording and Reporting

The government and police have recorded crime statistics since the nineteenth century, but procedures for crime reporting started during the 1700s when Middlesex Magistrates would sit in "rotation offices" at specific times of the day for victims to report crime. Crime statistics measuring levels and trends are now published annually by the Office for National Statistics (ONS) from two main sets of crime statistics: the Crime Survey for England and Wales (CSEW) – a self-report victimisation study and Recorded Crime – crime reported to and recorded by the police. Both surveys have strengths and limitations, but it is argued that together, they provide a more comprehensive picture of crime than using just one (ONS, 2020) Crime statistics are also recorded by other agencies such as the National Society for the Prevention and Cruelty to Children (NSPCC), Royal Society for the Protection of Animals (RSPCA), and HM Revenue and Customs (HMRC) and published in specific reports such as business surveys (which record crime specifically against businesses rather than households). The broadest picture of crime against households and individuals is recorded on the CSEW. The most recent crime data from the CSEW and police Recorded statistics combined to 30 September 2020 show that 11.7 million offences were recorded, with police recorded crime decreasing by 6% to 5.7 million offences including, to the 12 months to the end of June 2020, a 4% decrease in recorded crime including reductions in firearms offences and offences using a knife or sharp object. Other crimes increased such as violence against the person and homicide (ONS, 2020). However, amongst the 7% rise in homicides was the Grays lorry incident in October 2019 where 39 Vietnamese migrants died from lack oxygen and over-heating in the back of a refrigerated lorry in Grays in Essex (ONS, 2020). When single and very unpredictable incidents such as this occur, data can become distorted and skewed, making it difficult to make comparisons with data collected during a common counting year where these unusual events have not occurred. Hence, it is important not to take crime statistics at face value but to deconstruct them into individual component crime types, not only to avoid anomaly data due to, for instance, the occurrence of an unusual event such as the Grays incident, but also to see which offence types are increasing or falling and, therefore, where policing and crime reduction policies may need to be focused.

Such data are seen as crucial to policing and crime reduction because crime figures can be taken as an indication of how effective the police are in. Crime data can also help us to understand the types of harm caused and so inform us about victims and targets (particularly repeat victims and targets) to aid the police and other crime reduction agencies in understanding where crime prevention advice may be appropriate and where crime reduction initiatives should be directed. For example, the 16% increase in drugs offences between April and June 2020 is said to be driven by more effective policing in "hotspot" areas (Office for National Statistics, 2020: 4). Hence, crime statistics can also indicate the effectiveness of current interventions and responses.

Deeper analyses of crime conducted for other official reports can inform us of the levels of specific types of crime and also the broader costs. It is estimated that the costs of crime where there is a recognisable personal victim is in the region of 50 billion pounds (Heeks et al., 2018: 6). Costs of crime are split into three areas: first, costs in anticipation. These are money that is spent on crime prevention and detection (e.g. crime prevention technology). Second, as a consequence of crime (e.g. cost of stolen property, any damage caused, reduced output and productivity from victims taking time off work, health services, and victims services costs). The final area of cost of crime is the responses to crime. This category includes the costs of crime to policing and other Criminal Justice agencies such as courts services, legal services, and offender management services (Heeks et al., 2018). These costs are important to policy-makers in deciding appropriate policing and crime reduction measures and ensuring cost efficiency and effectiveness. However, figures pertaining to crime costs and crime rates can only ever be an estimate, and their usefulness is debated due to issues of under-reporting, leading to concerns about what is referred to as the "dark figure" of crime. This chapter now turns to look at each of these crime surveys in a little more detail.

Crime Survey for England and Wales

A self-report victimisation survey, the CSEW (formerly the British Crime Survey until 2018), records people's experiences of crime and fear of crime during the preceding 12 months of their answering the survey. The first sweep of the survey in 1977 coincided with calls from criminologists that crime reduction policies ought to be evidence-based and reflective of the "real" social and personal impact of crime. The CSEW is now conducted annually with 46,000 randomly selected households asking occupants about their experience and fear of "personal" and "household" offences during the previous 12 months. According to the CSEW for 2018/2019, the general population has a 21% risk of crime victimisation with a 16% risk of being a victim of household crime and a 3% risk of being a victim of violent crime (ONS, 2019).

However, these broader figures mask the varying risk of crime of different social groups and demographics such as age, gender, sexual orientation, race, employment, socio-economic status, and education. The survey does not cover crime known as "victimless" – where illegal acts lack a complainant either because no-one is harmed or where harm is negated by the informed consent of a willing participant (Veneziano and Veneziano, 1993). It also does not cover group residences, hence excluding those who live in student halls of residences and care homes. It has been argued that the CSEW provides a more accurate picture of the extent of crime in the UK and long-term trends as it includes offences that may not be reported to or recorded by the police. There are some plausible reasons as to why crime is not recorded by the police, and these are discussed below. Although the CSEW does contribute to building a picture of the extent of crime and crime trends, the delay, in some cases, a year before crime is reported to the CSEW may make it ineffective in contributing to immediate community safety or in building confidence in the police. Those who report crime to the police have experienced victimisation at that specific point in time and, therefore, expect the police to act immediately in investigating it. Failure to do so leads to public confidence in the police diminishing and, in the case of repeat victimisation particularly, criminal behaviour continuing. Hence, the CSEW does not allow for immediate preventative action or police investigation.

Recorded Crime (Police Statistics)

Recorded crime refers to crime reported to the police, usually by either a victim or someone who has witnessed or has reason to believe a crime has taken place. Crime recording must comply with the policing values that are set out in the College of Policing's Code of Ethics. To ensure crime is recorded accurately, to a consistent standard, with a victim orientated approach and to foster public trust, all police forces must record crime according the Counting Rules set out in the National Counting Recording Standards (Home Office, 2020) and all crime data recorded by police forces are inspected as part of Her Majesty's Inspectorate of Constabulary and Fire and Rescue Services (HMICFRS) inspection processes.

Whilst crime statistics can inform us of how much crime has been committed, they also underline the most common crime types and locations of offences and, so can assist in the use of intelligence-led policing through crime mapping and building intelligence on crime and criminal behaviour. Crime statistics can also ensure victims are placed at the core (Home Office, 2020) by highlighting the number of crime victims and indicating their needs from the police (such as the need for a criminal investigation or crime prevention advice) and other agencies (such as victim support). The Standard directs a victim-centred approach where a victim is believed and that belief is sufficient to justify recording the incident as a crime, and the victim benefits from the statutory entitlements under the Code of Practice for the Victims of Crime (Home Office, 2020).

Hence, the victim is key in the decision as to whether or not to record a suspected crime as a crime incident or notifiable offence. So,

> where there are grounds to suspect that a 'victim related' crime i.e. a crime requiring victim confirmation may have taken place but no victim, (or person reasonably assumed to be acting on behalf of the victim), can immediately be found or identified, then subject to the exceptions of what is termed 'recording without victim confirmation', the matter must be recorded as a crime related incident until such time as the victim is located or comes forward to provide an account.
>
> (Home Office, 2020: 4)

An incident will be recorded as a crime (notifiable offence) for "victim-related offences" if, on the balance of probability:

> the circumstances of the victim's report amounts to a crime defined by law (the police will determine this, based on their knowledge of the law and counting rules) and there is no credible evidence to the contrary immediately available. Once recorded, a crime will remain recorded unless additional verifiable information is found and documented which determines that no notifiable crime has occurred or crimes are transferred or cancelled.
>
> (Home Office, 2020: 4)

As there needs to be a recognisable victim for an offence to be Notifiable, a significant number of routine offences that the police may deal with day to day, such as summary driving offences or drugs offences, are not notified as crimes in the official statistics.

Some may be sceptical as to whether crime statistics are a true measure of crime. Lewis suggests there is very little evidence that crime figures are fiddled (Lewis, 2013) and the Home Office counting rules are intended to ensure crime is recorded accurately and consistently. In fact, the Counting Rules were established after some police forces were found to be incorrectly recording crime, inappropriately encouraging victims to retract allegations in order to record a "no crime" rather than having to leave a crime recorded as unsolved, to improve clear-up rates and meet government-set targets. Lewis also reports pressure from government to massage crime figures to present a more positive picture to the public (Lewis, 2013). Police and government should now be a little more relaxed about the picture that crime figures are painting to the public given crime, particularly involving vehicle theft and burglary, has fallen sharply since the mid-1990s (Maguire and McVie, 2017). However, the problem of under-reporting remains with some crime types, particularly very personal offences such as domestic violence or sexual offences, commonly under-reported (Maguire and McVie, 2017). In these instances, victims may feel too frightened to report, may be intimidated into not reporting, perceive the crime as too personal, or fear they will not be believed. It is likely some of these offences will skew crime data due to multiple-victimisation and because the CSEW caps the number of offences of any one kind recorded per victim at five (Maguire and McVie, 2017: 174). Offences perceived as "victimless" such as drug use are also typically under-reported (notwithstanding the harm caused to communities – see Chapter 3).

Conclusion

To conclude, this chapter introduced criminology as a subject discipline with particular relevance to policing practice. The chapter introduced the two opposing disciplinary theories – Right and Left Realism – that can underpin the role and function of the modern police force in order maintenance and community-focused policing strategies. The discussion of Left Realism provided the criminological base for an examination of victimology and victims issues including harm caused by criminal behaviour, repeat victimisation, victim support, and the important role of the police in supporting victims of crime including use of the Code of Practice for Victims. The chapter concluded with a discussion of crime reporting and recording drawing on the importance of counting rules and consistency in recording and critical discussion of crime surveys and crime statistics more generally. The next chapter moves away from discussing theories of intervention to a discussion of crime causation and policing.

References

Bowling, B., Reiner, R. and Sheptycki, J. (2019) *The Politics of the Police: Fifth Edition.* Oxford: Oxford University Press.

Brantingham, P. J. and Brantingham, P. L. (1981) *Environmental Criminology.* Beverly Hills: Sage.

Bright, J. (1987) Community safety, crime prevention and the local authority. In P. Wilmot (ed.) *Policing in the Community.* London: Policy Studies Institute.

Brodeur, J. (1983) High and low policing: Remarks about the policing of political activities. *Social Problems.* 30(5): 507–520.

Cameron, D. (2010) *Big Society Speech.* Available at: www.gov.uk/government/speeches/big-society-speech

Carrabine, E. (2014) *Criminology; A Sociological Introduction* (Third Edition). London: Routledge.

Carrington, K., Hogg, R. and Sozzo, M. (2016) Southern criminology. *British Journal of Criminology.* 56(1): 445–471.

Cohen, S. (1988) *Against Criminology.* Oxford and New Brunswick, NJ: Transaction Books.

College of Policing (2021) *Family Liaison Officer.* Available at: https://profdev.college.police.uk/professional-profile/family-liaison-officer-flo/

Downes, D. (1988) The sociology of crime and social control in Britain 1960–1987. *British Journal of Criminology.* 28(2): 45–57.

Durkheim, E. (1915) *The Elementary Forms of the Religious Life.* London: Allen and Unwin.

Durkheim, E (1933, originally 1893) *The Division of Labour in Society.* Glencoe: Free Press.

Emsley, C. (1991) *The English Police: A Political and Social History.* Essex: Pearson Education.

Forrester, D., Chatterton, M. and Pease, K. (1988) *The Kirkholt Burglary Prevention Project.* Rochdale. London: Home Office.

Garland, D. (1996) The limits of the sovereign state. *British Journal of Criminology.* 36(4): 445–471.

Garland, D. and Sparks, R. (2000) Criminological social theory and the challenge of our times. *British Journal of Criminology.* 40(2): 189–204.

Garside, R. (2004) *Crime, Persistent Offenders and the Justice Gap.* London: Crime & Society Foundation.

Hadfield, P., Lister, S. and Traynor, P. (2009) This town's a different town today: Policing and regulating the night time economy. *Criminology and Criminal Justice.* 9(4): 465–485.

Heeks, M., Reed, S., Tafsiri, M. and Prince, S. (2018) *The Economic and Social Costs of Crime. Research Report 99.* London: Home Office.

HMIC (2011) *Demanding Times: The Frontline and Police Visibility.* London: HMIC.

Home Office (2001) Criminal Justice: The Way Ahead. London: Home Office. Available at: https://assets.publishing.service.gov.uk/government/uploads/system/uploads/attachment_data/file/250876/5074.pdf

Home Office (2020) *Crime Recording General Rules*. Available at: https://assets. publishing.service.gov.uk/government/uploads/system/uploads/attachment_data/ file/940262/count-general-nov-2020.pdf

Hopkins Burke, R. and Pollock, E. (2004) A tale of two anomies: Some observations on the contribution of (sociological) criminological theory to explaining hate crime motivation. *Internet Journal of Criminology*. Available at: Internetjournalofcriminology.com

Hopkins Burke, R. (2020) *Contemporary Criminological Theory*. London: Routledge.

Lewis, C. (2013) The Truth about crime statistics. *The Police Journal: Theory, Practice and Principles*. 86(3): 220–234.

Lloyd, S., Farrell, G. and Pease, K. (1994) *Preventing Repeated Domestic Violence: A Demonstration Project on Merseyside*. London: Home Office Police Department.

Maguire, M. and McVie, S. (2017) Crime data and criminal statistics: A critical reflection. In A. Liebling, S. Maruna and L. McAra (eds.) *The Oxford Handbook of Criminology*, 163–189. Oxford: Oxford University Press.

Ministry of Justice (2020) *Code of Practice for Victims of Crime in England and Wales (Victim's Code)*. Available at: https://assets.publishing.service.gov.uk/government/ uploads/system/uploads/attachment_data/file/974376/victims-code-2020.pdf

Murphy, T. (2020) *Criminology: A Contemporary Introduction*. London: Sage.

National Farmers Union (2021) *Rural Crime. Available from Rural Crime*. Available at: nfuonline.com

National Police Chiefs Council (2019) *Policing Vision 2025*. Available at: www.npcc. police.uk/documents/Policing%20Vision.pdf

Office for National Statistics (2019) *Crime in England and Wales: Year Ending December 2018*. Available at: www.ons.gov.uk/peoplepopulationandcommunity/ crimeandjustice/bulletins/crimeinenglandandwales/yearendingdecember2018

Office for National Statistics (2020) *Crime in England and Wales: Year Ending September 2020*. Available at: www.ons.gov.uk/peoplepopulationandcommunity/ crimeandjustice/bulletins/crimeinenglandandwales/yearendingseptember2020

Patel, P. (2020) *Priti Patel 2020 Speech at Conservative Party Conference. The Speech Made by Priti Patel, the Home Secretary, on 4 October 2020*. Available at: www. ukpol.co.uk/priti-patel-2020-speech-at-conservative-party-conference/

Pease, K. (1998) *Repeat Victimisation: Taking Stock*. London: Home Office.

Ratcliffe, J. (2002) Burglary reduction and the myth of displacement. *Trends and Issues in Crime and Criminal Justice*, 232. Canberra: Australian Institute of Criminology.

Raz, J. (1979) *The Authority of Law: Essays on Law and Morality*. Wotton-Under-Edge: Clarendon Press

Reiner, R. (2010) *The Politics of the Police: Third Edition* (First Edition). Oxford: Oxford University Press.

Roberts, J. V. and Manikis, M. (2013) Victim personal statements in England and Wales: Latest (and last) trends from the witnesses and victims experience survey. Criminology and *Criminal Justice*. 13(3): 245–261. Available at: https://journals. sagepub.com/doi/pdf/10.1177/1748895812452281

Sampson, A. and Philips, C. (1992) *Multiple Victimisation: Racial Attacks on an East London Estate*. London: Home Office Police Department.

Tseloni, A., Knutsson, J. and Laycock, G. (2005) Repeat victimization: Introduction. *International Review of Victimology*. 12: 47–49.

Veneziano, L. and Veneziano, C. (1993) Are victimless crimes actually harmful? *Journal of Contemporary Criminal Justice*. 9(1): 1–14.

Victim Support (nd) *Victim Personal Statements*. Available at: www.victimsupport. org.uk/help-and-support/your-rights/victim-personal-statements/

Chapter 3

Criminology for the Police

Introduction

This chapter focuses on crime causation as relevant to policing. Beginning with a focus on Biological causation of crime, the chapter draws on theory and research relating to alcohol- and drug-related crime and policing. The chapter then discusses how key Sociological and Environmental influences may impact on contemporary policing and crime reduction beginning with an exploration of fragmented communities and social disorganisation where the discussion is around issues such as crime problems in deprived and disadvantaged communities in addition to the impact of the built environment on criminal behaviour before ending with a discussion of neighbourhood and urban renewal. The chapter then discusses unemployment, crime and strain, and gangs and youth subcultures and moral panics. Following this, the chapter discusses Labelling and deviancy amplification with particular attention to the progress made in policing young people. The chapter ends with a discussion of Psychological Criminology focusing initially on psychological disorder and influence on criminal behaviour and policing mental health with reference to the provisions of the Mental Health Act 1983 including the problems of policing those with mental health needs.

Biological Criminology

Biology refers to how "individual evolution" influences criminal behaviour. Early scholarly works on biological influences on crime focused on anthropology (the scientific study of human behaviour), geneticism, and "Atavism" (the idea that criminals are inherently evil) as causes of crime. The first person to suggest the link between biological and sociological perspectives and crime was Cesare Lombroso who made primitive links between biology and crime based upon the results of a postmortem of a thief whose indented skull, Lombroso argued, was similar to that of an ape (Lombroso, 1876). Similar results of other postmortems and findings of anthropometric studies

DOI: 10.4324/9781003081012-3

of criminals led Lombroso to conceive that criminals were "born" deviant and could be identified by particular physical characteristics.

Lombroso subsequently developed the theory of "criminal anthropology" whereby criminals were understood to be "throwbacks" to an earlier stage of human evolution and could be distinguished from non-criminals through certain physical "abnormalities" such as an asymmetric face, large jaw, and excessively long arms. Obviously, this early theoretical framework for crime causation is now discredited and irrelevant – but more modern biological explanations provide genuine explanations for crime and some are particularly relevant to policing. However, modern bio-criminological study involves genetic and neural explanations of offending through focusing on five biological influences on cognitive functioning: alcohol use (see, e.g., Squeglia et al., 2014), brain injury (see, e.g., Williams et al., 2018), diet and nutrition, (see, e.g., Benton, 2007) illegal drug use (see, e.g., Jorgensen et al., 2016), and genetics (see, e.g. Brunner et al., 1993). The most relevant to policing are alcohol and drug use, so the following discussion will focus on these.

Alcohol Use

Although no psychoactive drug is a "cause" of complex human behaviour, any drug is likely to modify that complex behaviour (Council of Europe, 2004). Alcohol consumption, even in moderate quantities, has an impact on cognitive function (Topiwala et al., 2017) (blurred vision, slowed reaction times, impaired memory, poor judgement about risks, increases in aggressive behaviour, and lowered inhibitions). Alcohol-related crime commonly relates to two types of offences. The first include offences that could not have been committed but for alcohol consumption (such as drunkenness offences and driving with excess alcohol). The second include offences committed because the offender was under the influence of alcohol (Institute of Alcohol Studies, 2017) (offences where offenders may lose their inhibitions or alcohol consumption has reduce their capacity for control).

The most common of these alcohol-related incidents involve a combination of criminal damage, drunk and disorderly offences, and other public order offences involving men between the ages of 18 and 30 years of age in a minimal, segmented entertainment area of a city or town centre (Deehan et al., 2002). Like drug use, alcohol, as the most widely used drug in the UK (Deehan et al., 2002), has long been associated with crime, and in particular with crimes of disorder and violence (Bennett, 2000). Despite this, alcohol has not been offered the same prominence in policing or harm reduction measures as drug use (Deehan et al., 2002) – probably due to its status as a legal "drug" and because the majority of people who drink alcohol do so sensibly and without causing harm to others.

The estimated cost to the police and criminal justice system of alcohol-related violent crime and other alcohol-related crimes is an estimated £1.6 billion (Institute of Economic Affairs, 2015, 6). Some victimisation surveys also cover offences that were perceived by the victim to have been alcohol-related. Of all offences reported to the police between March 2016 and March 2017, 47.6% of violent offences, 20.6% of criminal damages, 21.5% of hate crimes, and 12.4% of theft offences were perceived by the victim to be related to the offender's alcohol use (Crime Survey for England and Wales, 2017).

The main way of managing alcohol-related crime is through situational measures as a means of prevention, but lots of people will still come into contact with the police when under the influence of alcohol under the suspicion of having caused some form of disorder (drunk and disorderly) or criminal offences such as affray, public order violations, criminal damage, or an offence against the person. The majority of intoxicated people apprehended by the police pass through police custody suites between 10.30 pm and 3.30 am and are likely to be held for four to six hours, to sober up before being released (Deehan et al., 2002: 50). Very few people who are arrested, detained, and prosecuted for an offence under the influence of alcohol receive a custodial sentence, and many cases do not progress to court.

However, the duty of care on police officers to look after those under the influence of alcohol is significant given they are one of the most likely groups to die in police custody and handling them can be difficult given they may be aggressive and violent (Deehan, 2002). Deehan's research is useful in identifying the two groups of drinkers who usually make contact with the police. The first is the small number of habitual drinkers who are likely to have a problem with alcohol misuse to the point of dependency, often also having other physical and social problems (such as unemployment and homelessness) and usually drink in a group during the day in local areas. Their contact with the police is likely to be frequent, and for petty crime.

The second group is larger in number, usually males who are weekend binge drinkers and who consume large amounts on single occasions and are arrested for an offence of drunkenness, combined with an element of disorder such as urinating in the street. They are less likely than the habitual drunks to have had previous contact with the police (Deehan, 2002: 51). Given this group uses a significant amount of police resources at the weekends, a public health or situational crime preventative approach (see Chapter 4) may be beneficial to improve resource efficiency as it involves a minimal contribution from the police. Deehan (2002) suggests that this group also contribute to fear of crime in town centres late at night, but lifestyle theory informs us that this may only impact on those who frequent town and city centres in the later evening or night time and are also under the influence of alcohol. However, the significant rise in awareness of sexual harassment against young women is proving a different focus to the problem of alcohol-related offending in the night-time social environment.

Driving Under the Influence of Alcohol

Another group of offences that fall under the auspices of alcohol-related crimes are driving while unfit through drink or drugs regulated under the Road Traffic Act 1998 and the Road Traffic Offenders Act 1998. Section 4 (Subsection 1) of the Road Traffic Act 1998 makes it an offence to drive or attempt to drive a mechanically propelled vehicle (motor vehicle or bicycle) when unfit through drink or drugs. The offence is triable summarily (so in the Magistrates Court) and carries a penalty of up to six months in prison or a fine (or both) along with obligatory disqualification. Drink driving encompasses four offences. First, driving or attempting to drive while unfit through alcohol (so where a breathalyser test returns a "pass" result but the driver displays other indicators, such as slurred speech or swerving whilst driving, which may lead a police officer to judge driving is impaired through alcohol consumption); second, driving or attempting to drive while above the legal alcohol limit; third, causing death by careless driving when under the influence of alcohol (or drugs), and, finally, causing death by dangerous driving (where consumption of excess alcohol before driving will be an aggravating factor on sentencing).

A police officer in uniform who suspects a driver may be driving over the proscribed limit may undertake "preliminary testing" of a suspect at the scene involving either a breath or blood test to indicate the presence of excess alcohol in breath or blood or an impairment test (known as a Field Impairment Test), requiring a suspect to perform a specific task to a specified standard with their eyes closed (such as walking in a straight line or touching the tip of their nose with their finger). A positive result from a breathalyser test provides sufficient evidence for an officer to suspect that someone is driving whilst over the proscribed alcohol limit and is therefore grounds for arrest. A further evidential test (a further breath test or a urine or blood sample) may be taken at the police station or in a hospital if a suspect is admitted following a road traffic accident and can be used as evidence in court. There are specific rules and processes for taking an evidential test in a hospital setting. Although there are prescribed maximum alcohol limits, results of a preliminary breath test can be affected by factors such as the physiology of the suspect, length of time between drinking alcohol or eating a meal, and taking the breath test and substances such as food (eating a meal) or smoking tobacco.

Driving whilst under the influence of drugs is covered in Section 11 of the Road Traffic Act 1988 and includes any intoxicant other than alcohol. In a case of suspected drug driving, the police may take a swab sample of sweat or saliva from the suspect to test for the presence of tetrahydrocannabinol – the active ingredient in Cannabis or Cocaine. A police officer may also make an arrest on suspicion that a suspect has consumed other proscribed drugs that are not recognised by the test device if the driver displays other indicators.

Illegal Drug Use

Aside from driving whilst under the influence of drugs, there has long been a view that drug use is a key cause of other offence types – particularly acquisitive crime such as burglary and theft. It is difficult to estimate the annual cost of drug-related crime to society, but up to half of all acquisitive crime is understood to be drug-related, and the market value of goods stolen involved is estimated at between two to two-and-a-half billion pounds each year (Drugwise, 2017). Seddon suggests that the relationship between drug use and crime is due to a range of inter-relational factors such as social exclusion, disadvantage, and unemployment which means that problematic illegal drug use tends to blight the poorest communities and neighbourhoods (Seddon, 2006).

Goldstein suggests understandings of problematic illegal drug use can be formed around a threefold framework that includes:

- *Economic Compulsive* – where drug users commit economic crime to fund their drug habit,
- *Psychopharmacological* – drug use causes crime as a result of changes in cognitive functioning or loosening of inhibitions and, finally,
- *Systemic* – where drug use is inextricably linked to other crime problems such as violent crime by, for example, dealers seeking to eradicate competitor dealers (Goldstein, 1985).

The debate around the link between drug use and crime can be categorised into whether involvement in crime causes drug use, or illicit drug use causes crime or whether drugs and crime are intertwined in a more complex manner. The vast majority of drug use is short-lived, experimental, and trouble-free, often hidden from view and rarely attracts police attention but the focus on longer term illicit drug use by addicts in poorer communities is significant to policing as it is this, rather than drug use by the higher or richer classes, that is policed more readily due to the on-street presence of the users.

Lister et al. (2008) suggest on-street drug policing should involve a combination of proactive and reactive approaches as well as social and situational approaches. Obviously, the strategy deployed is dependent on context, and this will be discussed further in Chapter 4. However, in their research, Lister et al. (2008) identified that police–drug user contact involved informal and formal encounters.

Informal encounters are where neighbourhood policing teams encounter problem drug users on the street and check their well-being, which also causes them to know they are being monitored and potentially used as "informers" for the acquisition of information in either an impromptu manner or as part of an investigation. More formal encounters relate to the use of stop and account and stop and search. Towards the end of this chapter, we discuss the welfarist role of the police in dealing with those with mental health needs. Given the police are often the first emergency service to encounter on-street drug users, the police are often pushed into a similar public health role (Lister et al., 2008). It must also be recognised that drug use and drug crime is linked to other serious social problems such as gang membership, violent crime, and offences involving the use of weapons – all of which pose a challenge for policing. Drug use is also linked to urban decay which, in turn, is linked to crime and disorder (see the discussion of Broken Windows in Chapter 4 and the discussion of urban renewal later in this chapter).

Sociological and Environmental Criminology

Sociology analyses and explains important matters in individuals' personal lives, social environments, communities, and the world. At the personal level, sociology investigates the social causes and consequences of such things as personal interaction, racial and gender identity, family conflict, deviant behaviour, aging, and religious faith. At the societal level, sociology examines and explains matters such as crime and law, poverty and wealth, prejudice and discrimination, schools and education, social movements, and urban community (this is usually referred to as Environmental Criminology). At the global level, sociology studies such phenomena as population growth and migration, war and peace, and economic development. Sociologists emphasise the careful gathering and analysis of evidence about social life to develop and enrich our understanding of key social processes. The research methods sociologists use are varied. They may, for example, observe the everyday life of groups, conduct large-scale surveys, interpret historical documents, analyse census data, study video-taped interactions, interview participants of groups, and conduct laboratory experiments. The research methods and theories of sociology yield powerful insights into the social processes shaping human lives and social problems and prospects in the contemporary world.

For students of policing, the key area of focus is the role of different influences on individuals which shape offending behaviours. We can understand behaviours in the context of social processes, which relate to such things as our environment, community dynamics, and economic conditions. Early seeds were sown for connecting social processes to individuals early in the nineteenth century through the pioneering work of scholars such as Auguste Comte, Adolphe Quetelet, and Emile Durkheim. This way of thinking about crime and justice is usually labelled sociological positivism. Key ideas within sociological positivism include concepts such as anomie and strain, social disorganisation, and subcultures. Durkheim's concept of anomie was developed (1897/1993) and utilised (1925/2002) to describe how individuals' normative frameworks and thus their moral regulation can loosen and wane as the nature of society changes. One contemporary example of this might be differences in the way people behave and articulate themselves in digital as opposed to physical spaces.

Reflective Task

Have a think about your own experiences of crime and deviance in digital spaces. What are the most obvious changes in social behaviour that you see in digital spaces compared to physical spaces? You might want to think about your own actions and behaviour as well as others!!

We will use sociological ideas throughout the book to interrogate contemporary understandings and interpretations of crime and criminal behaviour. As criminologists or police officers, we are all particularly interested in how these social relationships and interactions cause crime. These insights provide us with our rationales for designing, developing, and implementing new and existing policing interventions. In the following sections, we will look at some of the most commonly studied and understood sociological relationships that are associated with crime and deviance. These are:

1   Fragmented Community Cohesion
2   Social Disorganisation
3   Unemployment, Crime, and Strain
4   Youth Subcultures
5   Labelling

Fragmented Community Cohesion

Durkheim's theory of Mechanical Solidarity was introduced in Chapter 2 and revolves around the idea that social control in older less developed communities was enforced by community cohesion and public compliance as well as citizens' endorsement of reciprocal positive attitudes, beliefs, customs, norms, and values. Another key focus of Durkheim's work is the notion of "functionalism." Durkheim argues that crime serves two functions in a Mechanical Society. First, because most people living in a Mechanical Society endorse reciprocal attitudes, beliefs, customs, norms, and values, it is easy to recognise those who do not. Hence, offenders can be easily recognised as distinct and different from everyone else. Second, punishment is "functional" because repressive and summary punishments used against those that transgress against the collective will function as a deterrent to other potential offenders.

Deterrence is a key aim of the sentencing framework in England and Wales, although Individual Deterrence (whereby punishment is aimed at deterring a specific offender from future offending) is preferred to the General Deterrence that Durkheim is describing. However, many people see a need for punishment to be public so that it makes a statement to other potential transgressors that certain forms of behaviour are not to be tolerated. For Durkheim, this public need to see punishment done is part of an expressive function within his idea of community cohesion and "collective consciousness" (Durkheim, 1893) discussed in Chapter 2. Visible policing strategies are part of the general deterrence function, but they require ongoing support from the public and the "collective consciousness" to function effectively.

Robert Park and Earnest Burgess developed this idea of the "collective consciousness" to explore the link between breakdowns in community cohesion and crime with their "concentric zone theory" (see Park and Burgess, 1925). Park and Burgess argued that as people moved to larger cities in search of work, they would have to move initially into the cheap and most freely available housing in the "Zone of Transition," characterised by transient populations, with often a prevalence of low economic status, ethnic heterogeneity, and family disruption. This, argued Park and Burgess, created community social disorganisation, causing high rates of criminal behaviour. The key argument here is that in a socially disorganised community, there is little social structure, no sense of common values and, therefore, as Durkheim argues, few means of maintaining effective social control (Sampson and Groves, 1989). Those who progressed in their jobs and became more successful quickly move out of the cheap and available housing in the "Zone of Transition" into the outer suburbs whilst others move into the city to find work and inhabit the unoccupied housing in the "Zone of Transition". Hence, the "Zone of Transition" remains in a state of constant flux without a stable environment due to the constantly changing population (see Park and Burgess, 1925). This model of the structure of Chicago in the 1930s has some replicability for most cities in most countries, including the UK, today. It is also the case that crime rates continue to be higher in inner-city areas rather than in the suburbs and that these inner-city areas are most likely to be the targets of policing strategies, tactics and resources.

Practical Task

Think about a large city close to where you live. Can you recognise the Chicago model whereby the city centre lies in the middle followed by an area characterised by cheaper housing, social deprivation, and maybe a little run down or neglected, followed by more affluent suburbs further out of Zone Two? Explore the key crime problems in your area by putting your postcode into www.ukcrimestats.com/

Local councils have spent significant sums of money gentrifying inner-city areas, replacing older and neglected housing and infrastructure with newer modern apartments and social spaces in order to create a more pleasant and less "criminogenic" environment. Environmental criminology focuses on changing environments to reduce opportunities for crime to take place. This is known as *Crime prevention through environmental design (CPTED)*. Jane Jacobs was one of the first scholars to recognise a link between the design of urban neighbourhoods and the occurrence of crime and anti-social behaviour (Jacobs, 1961). Jacobs was particularly critical of post war urban planning, which she claimed caused social disorder in neighbourhoods. In the UK, the high demand for social housing from the end of the Second World War to the 1960s led to the construction of many mass housing estates and high-rise buildings. These now aging estates have since gained a social stigma as troublesome or criminogenic (Dean and Hastings, 2000) with the Institute for Public Policy Research describing them as, "... some of the country's worst failures in urban planning ..." (Pearce, 2005).

Oscar Newman (1972) argued that such mass housing estates promote "indefensible" space including anonymous walkways, underpasses, lifts, stairwells, long dark corridors and, importantly, no personal space for which any individual takes responsibility for looking after. In the UK, Alice Coleman (1985) identified a number of design disadvantages with mass housing estates, which she also correlated with high levels of anti-social behaviour. Both Newman and Coleman advocated changing the environment of such estates in order to "design out" crime. This environmental intervention is necessary for those areas where deprivation, unemployment, anti-social behaviour, and drug use have escalated so considerably that it is too late for policing interventions. In these circumstances, residents feel unsafe and move out of the area and the only viable option for improvement is large-scale neighbourhood renewal and demolition of part or all of the area.

The most significant programme of designing out crime and environmental re-design began in 1997 with the election of the Labour government that drew on the ideas of Coleman and Jacobs and the Left Realist theoretical criminological approach (see Chapter 2) to tackle what Prime Minister Tony Blair termed "crime and the causes of crime" (Blair, 1993) and, to that end, centred policy on civil renewal and urban regeneration. As Lees (2014: 924) puts it, "in New Labour's urban renaissance the council estate played a symbolic and ideological role as a signifier of a spatially concentrated, dysfunctional underclass." Blair himself contended that

> Over the last two decades the gap between these worst estates and the rest of the country has grown ... It shames us as a nation, it wastes lives and we all have to pay the costs of dependency and social division
>
> (Blair, 1998)

Many inner-city estates were demolished and rebuilt by private developers for urban regeneration to create a more sociable environment with a "mixed economy" of housing alongside canals and riverside bars, green spaces, traffic restrictions and pedestrianisation.

CPTED requires the police to take an active role in crime and disorder reduction solutions and work with non-criminal justice agencies or sectors, which might not traditionally be known for their interest in crime. However, Criminology as a specific academic field of study is a growing discipline and attracts interest from those who might not have previously been interested in knowing or finding out about crime and other disorderly behaviours. Hence, CPTED requires the police to work proactively with such specialists as geographers, urban planners, and urban designers, who can influence the development of the urban environment.

Neighbourhood renewal demands that substantial resources be spent in time and money, but research by Alonso et al. (2019) has found that such programmes can be "substantially important" (p. 61) in addressing violence and property crime in deprived areas with substantial reductions in burglary, robbery, vehicle crime, and violent crime in the areas studied in their research. Hence, CPTED can be effective in crime reduction, but the more deprived an area is, the more resources need to be allocated. Alonso et al. (2019) also found a "diffusion of benefits" (Felson and Clarke, 1998) whereby the crime reduction benefits seen in the deprived areas used in the research "diffused" into the more affluent neighbouring areas.

In addition to urban re-design, neighbourhood renewal must also address other key "criminogenic" sociological factors, such as unemployment, family breakdown, and educational opportunity. Whilst Jones (1998) warns against assuming a causal relationship between high unemployment and high crime rates, many criminological studies have been undertaken to explore this link.

Unemployment, Crime, and "Strain"

Social and economic disadvantage increases the possibility of what American sociologist Robert Merton (1938) categorises as "strain". Merton argues that Strain is a consequence of the lack of a structured and legitimate means for some people to attain their goals (usually wealth, a home, a job, and a desired standard of living) which can lead to the exploration of alternative means of acquiring material wealth. For some, the opportunity to attain material wealth through legitimate means diminishes more rapidly than others during periods of recession – a time when we are also often warned of the likelihood of an increase in personal and property crime.

Merton argues that those who are unable to meet the cultural goal of success can experience one of the five following reactions under the "strain" of anomie:

- Conformity, whereby people accept the goal of success and accept legitimate means of achieving it
- Ritualism, whereby people lower their expectations of success and continue to accept legitimate means of achieving it
- Retreatism, whereby people reject the goal of success and legitimate means of achieving it (so, in other words they just give up and accept the consequences)
- Innovation, whereby people accept the goal of success but reject legitimate means of achieving it (so may turn to crime)
- Rebellion, whereby people reject the goal of success and, together as a group, reject legitimate means of achieving it. In these circumstances, individuals and groups may rebel against whoever is perceived to have put that goal in place (so, they may form subcultures and engage and in collective offending behaviour) (Merton, 1938).

Hence, the reactions that ought to concern the police the most are Innovation and Rebellion as both may manifest in the onset of criminal behaviour, albeit in different ways. Criminal behaviour caused by "Innovation" would usually be conducted by sole perpetrators, whereas the Rebellion reaction is most likely to be observed as group offending because those who "rebel" as a means of protest usually do so in groups rather than individually. An Innovative reaction does not need group or peer influence and encompasses property and theft offences to compensate for economic losses caused by lack of success due to low paid employment or unemployment or poor educational attainment leading to a lack of economic opportunity. Crime committed as a result of the Rebellious reaction is more likely to emerge from protests against a social issue, such as gender, race (as in protests by the Extremist Right), or economic capitalism (as in protests by the Far Left). The police have a number of tools at their disposal in order to keep the peace and facilitate peaceful protest to reduce the risk of "rebellious" reaction. Strategies such as Community Mediation (College of Policing, 2018) involve working with individuals or groups before a protest event to reduce the risk of conflict during it. Policing becomes more difficult and potentially more dangerous when peaceful protest turns to riot and violent conduct where strategies need to change from mediation to order maintenance (see College of Policing, 2018 for a more detailed discussion of public order policing and tactics). Hence, it is a much more effective, efficient, and lawfully compliant approach to focus upon mediation and negotiation with protest groups. Violent public order offences are often group- or peer influenced or what we refer to in criminological study as "subcultures."

Subcultures and "Moral Panics"

Subcultures are sometimes known as "counter-cultures" because the attitudes and values held by those engaged in a specific subculture are seen to be in opposition to those held by what we may term "mainstream" society. Contemporary British criminology emerged in the 1960s and 1970s alongside a range of more specific youth culture movements (such as Mods, Rockers, Skinheads, and Fascists) formed largely out of shared identity or cultural values. Some of these groups engaged in violence between each other facilitated by, primarily, identity-based conflict. Images and experiences of crime and disorder cause the public to feel unsafe and are often perceived as a threat to public safety and social order. Yet Stanley Cohen argues that in some circumstances, reactions by the public, state agencies, and media to behaviour that is perceived to threaten society's values create "folk devils" of those pursuing the behaviour, and "moral panic" across society. According to Cohen (1973: 1):

> Societies appear to be subject, every now and again, to periods of moral panic. A condition, episode, person or group of persons emerges to become defined as a threat to societal values and interests. In situations of moral panics, the police must act to satisfy the public that they are doing their job properly.

Cohen argued that the media portrayal of deviancy is a leading element in both the public's identification of "folk devils" and the propensity for the actions of a particular group of people to promote a "moral panic." In Cohen's study of conflict between Mods and Rockers in Clacton on Easter Sunday 1964, two groups engaged in violent confrontation leading to some beach huts being vandalised and windows being broken. The police subsequently arrested 97 people.

Cohen found the press to be guilty of exaggerated and distorted reporting of the events, thereby amplifying the deviant image of Mods and Rockers and initiating inevitable calls from the public for more effective policing to control them. According to Cohen, "a crucial dimension for understanding the reaction to deviance of the public and agents of social control is the nature of the information received about the behaviour in question" (Cohen, 1973: 7). This media amplification process has the effect of producing further deviance and criminality to which the police then need to respond due to public demand for a crackdown on perceived deviant groups. It is at this point that Cohen's ideas bring together the subcultural theories that draw on the work of Durkheim and Merton with labelling theories that originally developed in the work of Howard Becker and Edwin Lemert. It is to these labelling theorists that we now turn.

Labelling

Labelling theorists argue that no behaviour is inherently deviant or criminal, but comes only to be considered so when others confer this label upon the act.

The most well-known labelling theorist, Howard Becker, argues that societies create deviance by making the rules, which, when broken, constitute deviance and subsequently cause society to label those who break these rules as deviants or outsiders (Becker, 1963). He elaborates (1963: 4):

> Social groups create deviance by making the rules whose infraction constitutes deviance and by applying those rules to particular people and labelling them as outsiders. From this point of view, deviance is not a quality of the act the person commits, but rather a consequence of the application by others of rules and sanctions to an offender.

Edwin Lemert (1951) developed this idea by considering two aspects of labelling: how the deviant behaviour originates (which Lemert refers to as primary deviance) and how the labelling of a person as deviant might impact upon their future behaviour (which he referred to as secondary deviance). Lemert made a distinction between primary and secondary deviation, whereby the former is concerned with why and how an act is labelled as deviant by an institution or authority (such as the courts which label a person as criminal or a school that might label a missing child as a truant) and the latter is concerned with the impact on the individual accepting the deviant label and subsequently identifying themselves as deviant. In this latter context, the impact of labelling can be to potentially amplify or enhance future deviance and criminality. This final point has significant implications for the impact of policing policy upon young populations. Indeed, labelling theorists would argue that police intervention with young people have the potential to amplify rather than reduce deviance and disorder and this theoretical perspective is supported by a number of empirical studies which we will highlight in the next section.

Policing Young People

Contemporary recognition of youth as a period of vulnerability has led to a number of recent innovations in how police respond to crime, deviance, and disorder associated with young people. Young adults, defined as individuals aged 18–25, represent around 10% of the UK population but account for 30–40% of cases involving police time each year (The Police Foundation, 2018: 2). According to the Association of Chief Police Officers (ACPO), contact between the police and young people is inevitable, and police should acknowledge that the commission of low-level criminal behaviour or disorder is part of the journey from childhood to early adulthood (ACPO, 2012) and give appropriate consideration to the various social, psychological and neurological maturation of young people.

The All Party Parliamentary Group for Children (APPGC) found a lack of trust in, and fear of, the police among many children and young people with some children suggesting the police used poor and unconstructive communication and a lack of mutual respect (All Party Parliamentary Group for Children, 2014). ACPO also found that young people were met with suspicion in reporting victimisation and, hence, felt labelled and criminalised (ACPO, 2012). This suggests that the police should give consideration of the Victims Code (see Chapter 2) and a "citizen-focused policing" approach in dealing with young people. Citizen-Focused Policing was a strand of the Community-Orientated Policing approach established under the Police Reform Act 2002 but has since lost some prominence as a policing focus. Children living in care, who do not always receive the welfare support they require and those with vulnerabilities or special needs who have language or communication difficulty, or mental health needs, should be afforded special attention. The APPGC also suggested that young peoples' views of the police are shaped by their first encounters with them (All Party Parliamentary Group for Children, 2014). So, outreach work in early years' education may help address this, and the APPGC cites some good examples of positive engagement between the police and young people including children and young people getting involved in police initiatives through their schools and communities, such as Safer School Partnerships or Voluntary Police Cadets.

Mistrust is particularly evident in stop and search encounters. While young people understand why the police need to use stop and search, they feel they are stopped too often and for insufficient reason, that they are not treated with respect, and that the police do not explain the process or reason for the stop (All Party Parliamentary Group for Children, 2014). Much of this problem can be addressed through the correct use of stop and search procedures and justifiable reasonable suspicion. The Police Foundation suggests that the future direction in policing young people should include an increased awareness of effective police interactions with young adults, enhanced knowledge of how effective responses can be put in place, improved perceptions of fairness among young adults, increased options for responding to low-level young adult offending at point of arrest, and higher victim satisfaction with policing responses to young adults (The Police Foundation, 2018: 15).

Practical Task

To what extent do you believe that crime patterns and policing responses are a product of social structures?

Identify a recent crime problem that you are aware of and conduct some preliminary research on how a range of different media have reported this crime.

To what extent do you think that these media portrayals construct a realistic picture of these crimes?

Where else could you look for sources of information that might challenge the media portrayal of criminality?

Psychological Criminology

The final body of theory to turn to is psychological (mental) disorder and policing. Hence, this final section of the chapter provides an exploration of psychological disciplinary theory to aid an understanding of the concept of psychological disorder before moving on to look at the impacts on policing. Psychological Criminology emerged in the early 1900s with roots in psychiatric study and the works of Sigmund Freud (an Austrian Neurologist) and John Bowlby (a British Psychologist). The premise of psychological criminology is that crime is caused by an underlying psychological or cognitive problem with interventions focused on attempts to correct problems and disorders through (primarily) Cognitive Behavioural Treatment (CBT). The involvement of the police with suspects who may be suffering from a psychological disorder begins long before any intervention work is considered and is recognised as a core component of everyday frontline policing (Paterson and Pollock, 2016). Police are also involved in managing mental ill health through inter-agency approaches that involve the management and supervision of offenders under a Risk Management strategy.

The Mental Health Act 2007 defines mental disorder as "any disorder or disability of the mind," but the most authoritative guide to mental disorder, the Diagnostic Manual of Mental Disorder (DSM), defines it as:

> A clinically significant behavioural or psychological syndrome or pattern that occurs in an individual, is associated with present distress (e.g., a painful symptom) or disability (i.e., impairment in one or more essential areas of functioning) or with a significantly increased risk of suffering death, pain, disability, or an important loss of freedom.

The DSM categorises the range of disorders as:

Psychosis – a loss of contact with reality, usually including false beliefs about what is taking place (delusions) or seeing or hearing things that are not there (hallucinations).

Organic illnesses – these can be present from birth or caused by illness or accident (e.g. heart attack, brain haemorrhage, or brain injury) or a developmental illness (e.g. amnesia or Alzheimer's).

Personality disorders – these range from treatable disorders, such as severe conditions controllable with medication and close supervision (such as psychopathy).

Schizophrenic illnesses – there are three main types of schizophrenic conditions:

- Catatonic (characterised by an absence of response to stimulus)
- Paranoid (assuming a different identity, usually due to hearing voices in the head)
- Anxious (obsessive compulsions)

Neurosis – a type of anxiety disorder whereby people respond to particular objects or situations with fear and dread, as well as with physical signs of anxiety or nervousness, such as a rapid heartbeat and sweating. A person is unable to control the response, or the anxiety interferes with normal functioning. Anxiety disorders include generalised anxiety disorder, post-traumatic stress disorder (PTSD), obsessive-compulsive disorder (OCD), panic disorder, social anxiety disorder, and specific phobias.

Mental Health and Crime

Despite being perceived as a group of society's "folk devils" and the occasional media-driven moral panic surrounding the link between mental disorder and crime, it is estimated that individuals diagnosed with a mental disorder are responsible for only 5% of all violent and criminal offences (Halle et al., 2020). The group that appear the most likely associated with violent crime are those with severe mental disorders such as schizophrenia (Fazel et al., 2009). Those who suffer from mental health problems are, in fact, much more likely to be victims of crime than offenders (Varshney et al., 2016), suggesting that the police are far more likely to come across people with mental health problems as victims than offenders. In fact, it is possible that much of the demand for police intervention with people with mental health needs does not relate to criminal behaviour at all but to deal with cases relating to complex welfare, public safety and vulnerability needs (HMICFRS, 2017).

Furthermore, many mentally disordered offenders are likely to suffer "comorbidity" where their mental health is combined with other risk factors known to influence offending behaviour (such as substance misuse, unemployment, experience of historical sexual abuse), hence increasing their likelihood of engaging in offending behaviour. As Halle et al. (2020) suggest, only a small percentage of crimes committed by individuals with mental illness can be directly related to their psychiatric symptoms. Strategies aimed at reducing criminal behaviour by those with mental illness ought to focus, at least in part, on reducing the other risk factors mentioned above. Findings by Fazel et al. (2009) suggest that those with a schizophrenic disorder are more likely to commit violent crime if they are substance abusers too. Several studies have been conducted into the relationship between mental health and crime with one of the most comprehensive studies from a UK context (by Halle et al., 2020) finding that the arrest and conviction rates of those with mental health disorders did not differ significantly in comparison to those without a mental health disorder. This finding suggests there is not a significant link between being diagnosed with a mental health disorder and becoming involved in crime. Halle et al.'s study also found no significant link between mental illness and the commission of any particular crime type but other studies, particularly those conducted outside of the UK have found this link.

Policing Mental Ill Health

Debates about whether mental health should be core policing business have been ongoing for many decades and the police are often the first service called to deal with mental health emergencies. Despite finding that the "police approach to people with mental health problems is generally supportive, considerate and compassionate", HMICFRS have significant concerns about the degree to which police should be involved in responding to mental health problems given the skills needed to provide the necessary level of professional support (HMICFRS, 2018: 3). It also appears that the public may not see that dealing with people with mental health problems should be a role and function for the police. Research findings by HMICFRS on the views of the public of the police's responsibility in dealing with people with mental ill health reported that only 2% of those surveyed felt it was the police's responsibility to respond to mental health-related calls and 70% felt it was the main responsibility of the health services.

Nevertheless, the police have an important role in protecting society from dangerous individuals and individuals from endangering themselves when there is an imminent life-threatening risk (Paterson and Pollock, 2016). The College of Policing has detailed and extensive authorised professional practice guidance on dealing with suspects with mental health needs (College of Policing, 2016), and police officers receive training to manage mental health patients. The College of Policing estimates that anywhere between 2% and 20% of incidents dealt with by the police have a mental health link (College of Policing, 2015). Under Section 136 of the Mental Health Act 2003, the police have a legal duty to deal with people suspected of having a mental health problem whom they believe may harm, or are threatening to harm, themselves or someone else regardless of whether it is suspected that a crime has been committed. First, under Section 136, a police officer may take a person, whom they believe may harm, or are threatening to harm, themselves or someone else to an approved suite for a full mental health assessment by a psychiatrist (King's Fund, 2019; Riley et al., 2011). It is unlawful to use a police station as a place of safety in all but "exceptional" circumstances and never for anyone under the age of 18 (Department of Health, 2017). Hence, the place of safety should be a hospital or local authority residential accommodation suitable for those with mental health needs.

To reduce the number of patients detained under Section 136, all police forces but one in England and Wales operate a triage system whereby the police are supported by specialists agencies at the scene of an incident, in a control room, or on a telephone to support police officers in deciding whether a suspect may need to undergo a mental health assessment at a place of safety (HMICFRS, 2018). The use of the triage scheme has led to a reduction of approximately 21% in the use of detention under Section 136 of the Mental

Health Act (Reveruzzi and Pilling, 2016: 32). The HMICFS (2018) suggests that the need for triage services indicates there is not enough emphasis on early intervention and primary care to prevent the need for a crisis response by the police and too many aspects of the broader mental health system are broken leaving the police to pick up the pieces (Morgan and Paterson, 2019).

Conclusion

In this chapter, we have provided an overview of the dominant theoretical narratives that have influenced criminological thinking in the United Kingdom as well as other similar western democracies. It is important to note that this chapter provides only an introduction to dominant sets of ideas, and there is further literature for you to investigate which interrogates these theoretical traditions in more detail. Importantly, the chapter draws together changes in politics and criminal justice policy alongside the theoretical traditions that influence the political and policy narratives. Criminal justice and policing policy is driven by the political ideas of any historical period which leads to a mixture of consistency in policing policy (the public want to see their police officers on the street) as well as dissonance and innovation as new ideas become popular and then fade as new forms of thinking replace them. In Chapter 4, we will bring this discussion up to date with the application of criminological theory to the changing shape of policing strategy, policy, and practice.

References

All Party Parliamentary Group for Children (2014) *"It's All About Trust": Building Good Relationships Between Children and the Police.* Available at: www.familylaw.co.uk/docs/pdf-files/appgc_children_and_police_report_-_final.pdf

Alonso, J., Andrews, R. and Jorda, V. (2019) Do neighbourhood renewal programs reduce crime rates? Evidence from England? *Journal of Urban Economics.* 110: 51–69. Available at: www.sciencedirect.com/science/article/pii/S0094119019300130

Association of Chief Police Officers (2012) *Guidance on the Safer Detention and Handling of Persons in Police Custody (2nd Edition).* London: National Policing Improvement Agency.

Becker, H. (1963) *Outsiders: Studies in the Sociology of Deviance.* New York: Glencoe Free Press.

Bennett, T. (2000) *Drugs and Crime: The Results of the Second Developmental Stage of the NEW-ADAM Programme.* London: Home Office.

Benton, D. (2007) The impact of diet on anti-social, violent and criminal behaviour. *Neuroscience and Biobehavioural Reviews.* 31: 752–744.

Blair, T. (1993) On the Record Tony Blair Interview [Broadcast Transcript]. *On The Record, BBC 7 July 93.* Available at: www.bbc.co.uk/otr/intext92-93/Blair4.7.93.html

Blair, T. (1998) "The Will to Win." Speech at the Aylesbury Estate, 2 June.

Brunner, H., Nelen, M., Breakefield, X., Ropers, H. and van Oost, B. (1993) Abnormal behaviour associated with a point mutation in the structural gene for Monoamine Oxidase A. *Science.* 262(5133): 578–580.

Cohen, S. (1973) *Folk Devils and Moral Panics.* London: Routledge.

Coleman, A. (1985) *Utopia on Trial: Vision and Reality in Planned Housing.* London: Hilary Shipman.

College of Policing (2015) *College of Policing Analysis: Estimating Demand on the Police Service.* Available at: https://paas-s3-broker-prod-lon-6453d964-1d1a-432a-9260-5e0ba7d2fc51.s3.eu-west-2.amazonaws.com/s3fs-public/2021-03/demand-on-policing-report.pdf

College of Policing (2016) *Mental Health.* Available at: www.app.college.police.uk/app-content/mental-health/

College of Policing (2018) *Public Order: Tactical Options.* Available at: Tactical options (college.police.uk).

Council of Europe (2004) *Drugs and Alcohol: Violence and Insecurity?* Strasbourg: Council of Europe. Available at: https://rm.coe.int/16807460f0

Crime Survey for England and Wales (2017) *Data on Alcohol Related Incidents, Years Ending March 2011 to March 2017.* Crime Survey for England and Wales. Available at: www.ons.gov.uk/peoplepopulationandcommunity/crimeandjustice/adhocs/0093 72dataonalcoholrelatedincidentsyearsendingmarch2011tomarch2017crimesurveyf orenglandandwales

Dean, J. and Hastings, A. (2000) *Challenging Images: Housing Estates, Stigma and Regeneration.* Bristol: Policy Press. Available at: file:///C:/Users/dsep/Downloads/jr089-housing-estates-regeneration.pdf

Deehan, A., Marshall, E. and Saville, E. (2002) *Drunks and Disorder: Processing Intoxicated Arrestees in Two City Centre Custody Suites.* Police Research Series Paper 150. London: Home Office.

Department of Health (2017) *Guidance for the Implementation of Changes to Police Powers and Places of Safety Provisions in the Mental Health Act 1983.* Available at: https://assets.publishing.service.gov.uk/government/uploads/system/uploads/attachment_data/file/656025/Guidance_on_Police_Powers.PDF

Drugwise (2017) *How Much Crime Is Drug Related?* Available at: www.drugwise.org.uk/how-much-crime-is-drug-related/#:~:text=Cost%20of%20drug%2Drelated%20crime&text=That%20is%20a%20lot%20of,2%2D2.5%20billion%20each%20year

Durkheim, E. (1893) *The Division of Labour in Society.* New York: Glencoe Free Press.

Fazel, S., Gulati, G., Linsell, L., Geddes, J. R. and Grann, M. (2009) Schizophrenia and violence: Systematic review and meta-analysis. *PLoS Medicine.* 6(8): e1000120.

Felson, M. and Clarke, R. (1998) *Opportunity Makes the Thief. Practical Theory for Crime Prevention.* London: Home Office.

Goldstein, P. (1985) The drugs/violence nexus: A tripartite conceptual framework. *Journal of Drug Issues.* 15: 493–506.

Halle, C., Tzani-Pepelasi, C., Roumpini, N. and Fumagalli, A. (2020) The link between mental health, crime and violence. New Ideas in Psychology. 58: 1–8. Available at: https://reader.elsevier.com/reader/sd/pii/S0732118X18302551?token=0C7454E 3724238F79420831A18881253BA97A4F8C39A6952884F5D1650E3FB9051FD1 D6F3F94415C98E63C455F990C20&originRegion=eu-west-1&originCreation= 20210419074952

Her Majesty's Inspectorate of Constabulary and Fire & Rescue Services (2018) *Policing and Mental Health: Picking Up the Pieces.* Available at: www.justiceinspectorates. gov.uk/hmicfrs/wp-content/uploads/policing-and-mental-health-picking-up-the-pieces.pdf

Institute of Alcohol Studies (2017) Crime and Social Impacts of Alcohol. London: Institute of Alcohol Studies. Available at: www.google.co.uk/url?sa=t&rct=j&q= &esrc=s&source=web&cd=&cad=rja&uact=8&ved=2ahUKEwi9lsyw2InwAh XQbsAKHf-WBmcQFjARegQIGRAD&url=http%3A%2F%2Fwww.ias.org.uk% 2Fuploads%2Fpdf%2Ffactsheets%2FFS%2520crime%2520022017.pdf&usg= AOvVaw2y2Ksf2PkNdLHAu-eyf3ZQ

Institute of Economic Affairs (2015) *Alcohol and the Public Purse: Do Drinkers Pay Their Way?* Available at: www.evidence.nhs.uk/document?id=1628852&returnUrl= Search%3Fps%3D40%26q%3DTemperance%26s%3DDate&q=Temperance

Jacobs, J. (1961) The Death and Life of Great American Cities. New York: Vintage Books.

Jones, S. (1998) *Criminology.* London: Butterworths.

Jorgensen, C., Anderson, N. E. and Barnes, J. C. (2016) Bad brains: Crime and drug abuse from a neurocriminological perspective. *American Journal of Criminal Justice:* 41: 47–69. Available at: Bad Brains: Crime and Drug Abuse from a Neurocriminological Perspective | SpringerLink

King's Fund (2019, 1 October). *On the Front Line: Policing and Mental Health [Video file].* Available at: www.kingsfund.org.uk/audio-video/podcast/policing-mental-health

Lees, L. (2014) The urban injustices of New Labour's "New Urban Renewal": The case of the Aylesbury Estate in London. *Antipode.* 46(4): 921–947.

Lemert, E. (1951) *Social Pathology.* New York: McGraw-Hill.

Lister, S., Seddon, T., Wincup, E. Barret, S. and Traynor, P. (2008) *Street Policing of Drug Users.* Leeds: Joseph Rowntree Trust.

Lombroso, C. (1876) *The Criminal Man.* London: Duke University Press.

Merton, R. (1938) Social structure and anomie. *American Sociological Review.* 3(5): 672–682.

Morgan, M. and Paterson, C. (2019) It's mental health, not mental police. *Policing: A Journal of Policy and Practice.* 13(2): 123–133.

Newman, O. (1972) *Defensible Space.* Basingstoke: MacMillan.

Park, R. and Burgess, E. (1925) *The City: Suggestions for Investigation of Human Behaviour in the Urban Environment.* Chicago: Chicago University Press.

Paterson, C. and Pollock, E. (2016) Global shifts in the policing of mental health. *Policing: A Journal of Policy and Practice.* 10(2): 91–94.

Pearce, N. (2005) *Housing Will Crumble on Shaky Foundations.* Institute for Public Policy Research. Available at: www.ippr.org.uk/articles/archive.asp?id=1267& fID=55.

Reveruzzi, B. and Pilling, S. (2016) *Street Triage Report on the Evaluation of Nine Pilot Schemes in England.* Available at: www.ucl.ac.uk/pals/sites/pals/files/street_triage_evaluation_final_report.pdf

Riley, G., Freeman, E., Laidlaw, J. and Pugh, D. (2011) 'A frightening experience': Detainees' and carers' experiences of being detained under Section 136 of the Mental Health Act. *Medicine, Science and the Law.* 51(3): 164–169.

Sampson, R. and Byron Groves, W. (1989) Community structure and crime: Testing social disorganisation theory. *American Journal of Sociology.* 94(4): 774–802.

Seddon, T. (2006) Drugs, crime and social exclusion: Social context and social theory in British drugs–crime research. *British Journal of Criminology.* 46: 680–703.

Squeglia, L., Jacobus, J. and Tapert, S. (2014) The effect of alcohol use on human adolescent brain structures and systems. *Handbook of Clinical Neurology.* 125(Chapter 28): 501–510.

The Police Foundation (2018) *Policing and Young Adults: Developing a Tailored Approach*, July 2018. Available at: www.police-foundation.org.uk/2017/wp-content/uploads/2018/07/policing_and_young_adults_final_report_2018.pdf

Topiwala, A., Allan, C. L., Valkanova, V., Zsoldos, V., Eniko, F., Sexton, N., Mahmood, C., Fooks, A., Singh Manoux, P., Mackay, C. E., Kivimaki, M. and Ebmeier, K. (2017) Moderate alcohol consumption as risk factor for adverse brain outcomes and cognitive decline: Longitudinal cohort study. *British Medical Journal.* 357: 1–20. Available at: www.bmj.com/content/bmj/357/bmj.j2353.full.pdf

Varshney, M., Mahapatra, A., Krishnan, V., Gupta, R. and Deb, K. S. (2016). Violence and mental illness: What is the true story? *Journal of Epidemiology and Community Health.* 70(3): 223–225.

Williams, W. H., Chitsabesan, P., Fazel, S., McMillan, T., Hughes, N., Parsonage, M. mand Tonks, J. (2018) Traumatic brain injury: A potential cause of violent crime? *The Lancet: Psychiatry.* 5(10): 836–844.

Chapter 4

Policing Strategies

Introduction

This chapter draws on the discussion of Left and Right Realism in Chapter 2 and applies these opposing theoretical perspectives to key contemporary policing strategies. The chapter draws on key criminological academic and policy research to critique the different situations in which policing strategies may be used in practice as well as the effectiveness of the strategies. The chapter discusses the Right Realist informed strategies of stop and search and risk management and Left Realist informed community-orientated policing along with a discussion of hot spot Policing. The chapter moves on to discuss theories that explain how these interventions work, concluding with an introduction to administrative criminology and the widespread influence of rational choice theory and Situational Crime Prevention that emerged in the late twentieth century in England and Wales.

Situational crime prevention moves responsibility for crime reduction and prevention from the state to wider agencies, particularly public citizens, and this observation leads into a discussion of social citizenship and responsibilisation strategies. The final part of the chapter provides a brief outline of the responsibilities of the police in managing offenders under Multi-Agency Public Protection Arrangements (MAPPA) and the Sex Offender Register. This provides an introduction and context to the next chapter which focuses on changing perspectives on the role of police and policing and the growth in policy emphasis upon vulnerability, victimisation, and protection from harm.

Realism and Policing strategy

As discussed in Chapter 2, criminological explanations of policing and criminal justice interventions can be split into the opposing strategies of "hard" (order maintenance, risk management and public protection) and "soft" (crime prevention and community-orientated policing) which are respectively underpinned by the opposing criminological theoretical perspectives of

DOI: 10.4324/9781003081012-4

"Right" and "Left" Realism. As a reminder, Left Realists believe that it is not possible to deal with crime effectively if interventions are not informed by crime causes and Right Realists attach little importance to causation and, instead, focus on punitive interventions and the certainty and severity of punishment. Policing strategy can be broadly understood to be informed by these perspectives with Right Realism emphasising order maintenance and Left Realism emphasising strategies that encourage community orientation and engagement. This chapter begins with a discussion of "Right Realist" policing strategy.

Right Realist perspectives on policing incorporate any approach that seeks to incapacitate a suspect or where their liberty is restricted. This might include policing tools such as stop and search where a suspects' liberty or movement is restricted (through the use of handcuffs if appropriate) or arrest and detention where a suspect is deprived of free movement or liberty for a short period of time (up to 72 hours in the case of being detained and questioned). The incapacitative nature of Right Realist approaches can lead to criticism of the incompatibility of specific policing strategies with civil liberties and human rights. The most visible manifestation of these tensions emerges in examples such as the policing of public order protests, but the most publicly contentious area in terms of the tensions between liberty and security is police stop and search.

Stop and Search

Despite regular controversy, stop and search is understood by the police and Right Realists to be an important and fundamental tool for effective deterrence-driven policing. Yet, the use of stop and search is contentious in two respects. First is in its questionable impact upon crime reduction. Second is in its impact on trust and confidence in the police and police–community relations. Stop and search is often understood as the source of tensions between the police and young people from black and minority communities. There is a large body of literature on the challenges presented when using stop and search as a policing strategy, and we will explore these issues more in the next chapter. For the moment, it is just important to note that stop and search strategies are constantly subject to heated political debate and despite there being extensive research and reporting on this issue for over half a century the debate still incorporates very different perspectives from different communities.

The first significant piece of criminological research on this subject was undertaken by Stuart Hall and his colleagues on the policing of "mugging" in the Brixton area of London, an area with a high black and minority ethnic population, in the late 1970s (Hall et al., 1978). The public moral panic caused by high-profile media reports of widespread "mugging" and their association in news stories with a physical threat from young black males simultaneously generated increased public expectations of the police to manage this problem and tension in black communities that suddenly became subject to seemingly indiscriminate stop and search strategies. The perception that the stop and search strategy was less about crime control than racial prejudice of the police resulted in serious public disorder in various UK cities, most significantly in Brixton and generated significant community- and political-level questions about the use of long established "sus" laws in London (Fitzgerald et al., 2002; Waddington et al., 2004).

The government-ordered inquiry into the disturbance, by Lord Scarman, published in 1981, attributed the causes to deep-rooted social and economic problems affecting Britain's inner cities, including racial disadvantage and a loss of confidence and mistrust in the police by ethnic minority communities due to the arbitrary manner in which the police discharged their discretionary stop and search powers. Scarman recommended a return to a more community-oriented policing approach to facilitate improvements in relations between the police and ethnic minority communities. The findings of the Scarman Inquiry led to the enactment of the Police and Criminal Evidence Act 1984 (PACE) to better govern stop and search processes.

Section 1 of the Police and Criminal Evidence Act 1984 states:

a constable may detain in order to search any person, any vehicle or anything that is in a vehicle, in any place to which the public have access if they have reasonable grounds to suspect that stolen or prohibited articles, bladed or sharply pointed articles or prohibited fireworks will be found.

As there is significant public emphasis upon how stop and search powers are used, we will look at each aspect of this legal definition. There are some key points to make regarding the above definition regarding vehicles. Any vehicle refers to vehicles that are powered (such as a motor vehicle) or unpowered (such as a trailer or horse box but not a bicycle), attended or unattended, and anything inside or on (such as roof box) a vehicle. Stolen or prohibited articles refer to anything stolen under the Theft Act 1968 and include the proceeds of stolen goods (such as money gained from selling the goods).

Other legislation governing stop and search includes:

- Section 23 of the Misuse of Drugs Act 1971 (stopping and searching for controlled substances)
- Section 47 of the Firearms Act 1968 (stopping and searching for firearms)
- Section 60 of the Criminal Justice and Public Order Act 1994 (stopping and searching to prevent acts of serious violence)
- Section 43 of the Terrorism Act 2000 allows for the stop and search of a person that is reasonably believed to be a terrorist to discover whether the person has in their possession anything that constitutes evidence that they are a terrorist (maps, substance, photographs on a mobile phone, etc. ...)

- Section 43A allows for stopping and searching a vehicle, the driver, a passenger, or anything in the vehicle or being carried by the driver that is reasonably suspected is being used for the purpose of terrorism

What constitutes "Reasonable grounds for suspicion," as cited in PACE is loosely defined in law and thus presents potentially problematic situations for the police in their justification for conducting stop and search. To alleviate this challenge, the "SHACKS" mnemonic is used to help police officers to identify what may constitute sufficient *reasonable grounds for suspicion*:

- **S**een refers to things a police officer or a member of the public may have seen and reported to the police, including actions or behaviours of the suspect or those in the vicinity.
- **H**eard refers to things a police officer or a member of the public may have heard and reported to the police such as shouting, conversations, breaking glass, or a car or house alarm.
- **A**ctions refer to anything a potential suspect may be doing, such as running from a scene or seeking to hide or dispose of an object.
- **C**onversations refer to things a suspect or someone in the vicinity may have said to a police officer or something overheard that has been said to someone else.
- **K**nowledge refers to any known intelligence about a potential suspect gained through (for example) speaking to a suspect or a Police National Computer checks.
- **S**mell refers to any smells that give rise to suspicion, usually where a smell may be connected with any offence that may have taken place (as it is inappropriate to conduct a stop and search based only on smell even if the smell may lead to suspicion).

(Metropolitan Police, 2012)

Hence, the SHACKS mnemonic is designed to help a police officer build a picture of a situation to then decide whether there are reasonable grounds for a search. And it is the case that police officers use an array of categorical, physical, and behavioural signals to form suspicions (Quinton, 2011). Paul Quinton (2011) found the most likely factors that caused police officers to form suspicions about a potential suspect that lead to a stop and search were seeing someone known to the police, age, clothing or appearance (particularly clothing that could be used to hide things), race, and other indicating factors such as swaying, sweating, or where the appearance of someone's eyes may indicate evidence of drug use.

Miller et al. (2000) suggest that stop and search strategies can contribute to policing and crime reduction in the following ways:

- **Incapacitation** whereby an officer makes an arrest following a search, meaning a suspect is unable to commit further offences whilst in police custody.
- **Disruption** whereby a successful stop and search leads to the confiscation of a stolen or prohibited article and so the opportunity for a crime to take place is disrupted.
- **Deterrence** whereby a potential offender (individual deterrence) or other potential offenders (general deterrence) makes the rational choice (see below) not to commit further offences because the perceived risk of being stopped and searched is higher than the rewards of committing an offence.

Achieving these aims depends on there being a police presence in a particular location to undertake stop and search. For example, crime will only be disrupted if a police officer makes a confiscation and potential offenders will only be deterred from carrying stolen or prohibited articles if they think they are likely to be stopped and searched. It is difficult to identify what the fundamental characteristics of effective stop and search are because its use is context-specific, but, according to Tiratelli et al. (2018: 19),

> understanding what it is about stop and search that reduces crime should enable its use to be more targeted and could give officers a wider range of options when dealing with a situation.

Despite inconclusive evidence about the overall effectiveness of stop and search, effective use can reduce crime due to its disruptive (removing stolen or prohibited items from a suspect) and deterrent effect, and it is generally supported by the public due to its visible deterrent impact that can also generate a reduced fear of crime in communities. Stop and search, when used incorrectly, has the potential to significantly undermine public confidence and trust in the police and to inhibit public engagement, making other policing strategies such as intelligence-led policing and problem-oriented policing more difficult to achieve.

The impact of stop and search on crime rates remains inconclusive, but research by Tiratelli et al. (2018: 4) has found that higher rates of stop and search were occasionally followed by very slightly lower rates of crime with a 10% increase in stop and search leading to a reduction in crime of less than 1% in some instances. Although there was evidence of some reduction in drugs crime and burglary, there was little or no impact on theft, vehicle crime, criminal damage, and violent crime, which are arguably amongst some of the crime types the public fear the most. Miller et al. (2000) also suggest searches appear to have a minor role in detecting offenders. Tiratelli et al. (2018: 4) state, there would need to be extremely large increases in stop and search, of a scale likely to be unacceptable to some communities, in order to deliver only modest reductions in crime. The benefits derived from such increases would also need to be offset against the associated costs and weighed against their likely unequal impact on different communities.

Stop and search can cause resentment amongst young people, minority groups, and those from disadvantaged neighbourhoods who are disproportionately targeted by this strategy, and accusations of discriminatory policing in stop and search can feed into the negative aspects of cop culture that we will discuss in the next chapter as both the police and targeted communities identify each other with suspicion and mistrust which, as discussed above, can cause significant long-term damage to public trust in the police. And accusations that the over-representation of minority ethnic young people in stop and search is due to discriminatory policing are often cited and reported. Fitzgerald and Hough et al. (2002) reported that being black was a good predictor for being stopped and searched along with being under 30 years old and male. Hence, age and sex may also be a predictor of overuse of stop and search. Waddington et al. (2014) suggested that, rather than discriminatory policing, the reason for the disproportionality in stop and search experienced by young men and those from a minority ethnic background may lie in their more frequent use of public spaces in high crime areas than other groups. Hence, their more frequent use of the streets renders them "available" to the police for a stop and search.

Stop and search can be employed as either a reactive response policing strategy whereby police respond to individual calls from the public after a crime has taken place, or it can be used in a pro-active and community-oriented manner in response to demands from the community. Tiratelli et al. (2018) suggest stop and search may be particularly effective as part of a hot spot strategy where policing resources and activities are targeted to those places where crime is most concentrated (College of Policing, 2017). Preventing crime in these hot spot areas can have a significant impact on overall crime rates (see below). Stop and search can be effective as a short-term "order maintenance" strategy – a perspective described by Right Realists as Zero Tolerance, but it needs to be accompanied by an alternative long-term strategy and clear communication with communities to avoid the threat of community conflict and public disorder, as described above in Brixton and which highlights the dangers of this approach.

Zero-tolerance policing (ZTP) is a misunderstood concept in its application to policing practices tending only to be associated with what may be termed "hard" policing approaches (relating to reactive and order maintenance policing). Actually, with its theoretical base in the Broken Windows theory (see later in the chapter), Zero Tolerance is more aligned with "softer" approaches that seek to promote early intervention to prevent the escalation or growth of crime problems. While Zero Tolerance is often associated with tough policing, it also theoretically demands problem-solving strategies aimed at improving the social environment. Hence, the objectives of zero tolerance overlap with the softer policing approaches that focus upon community orientation and engagement, social interaction, problem-solving, and policing by consent. Along with Broken Windows research (see below), the softer side of Zero Tolerance provides us with a theoretical focus for the move from Right Realist and order maintenance policing to Left Realist community-oriented policing, which emerges in policy terms with the "Third Way" policing and crime reduction agenda that emerged in 1997. The election of a Labour government in 1997 after nearly 20 years of Conservative government led to a shift away from Right Realist strategy towards a Left Realist community-oriented policing philosophy which has continued through successive governments.

The election of what was branded "New Labour" in 1997 had at its heart a law and order strategy focused on dealing with "crime and the causes of crime" (Blair, 1993). This strategy underlined that the Right Realist, order maintenance, and reactive approach to reducing crime and disorder advocated by the previous Conservative governments of the 1980s and 1990s had achieved little impact in terms of reducing crime or fear of crime. Increasingly, from the mid-1990s, references were made to the Third Way, denoting a new political philosophy aimed at achieving a national consensus on the basis of non-ideological politics and de-polarisation of established political positions of Left and Right Wing ideologies. Labour's law and order policies were also manifested in a hybrid of some of the features of Positivism and Left and Right Realism, acknowledging the failure of Positivist attempts to reduce crime through changing the offender or their environment as well as the limitations of Right Realist approaches to crime reduction through broken windows policing and imprisonment of offenders.

Broken Windows

The first research study that underpins "Third Way" policing and crime reduction is the "broken windows" thesis by James Wilson and George Kelling published in 1982. According to Wilson and Kelling, if "broken windows" are not repaired in a neighbourhood, then others will soon be broken. These signs of disorder, or "signal crimes," must be dealt with swiftly; otherwise, more crime will inevitably follow. The priority for public order or community "beat" policing in these contexts is to foster community pride through informal and local forms of social control that improve the quality of life in an area and restore a sense of order. Wilson and Kelling proposed that the police should increase their presence on the streets and increase their levels of intervention with non-criminal behaviour. This includes moving along groups of children, monitoring derelict properties, and stopping people dropping litter or making excessive amounts of noise.

In an earlier piece of work, "Crime and Human Nature" (1975), Wilson, alongside Herrnstein this time, identified what he believed to be the underlying causes of crime that led to the collapse of moral and social authority in these neighbourhoods. According to Wilson and Herrnstein, crime rates were affected by:

- Shifts in the age structure of the population (namely, more young men)
- Changes in the benefits offered by crime
- Broad social and cultural changes affecting individual or collective social control

Therefore, the aim of the criminal justice system should be to target these three factors in an effort to reduce the harm caused by widespread offending behaviour. The emphasis placed upon young people and informal social controls represented the beginning of the focus upon anti-social behaviour and the criminalisation of uncivil or socially unacceptable behaviour. Wilson and Kelling believed that anti-social behaviour laid the conditions for future criminality and that the only way to stop crime was through making early interventions with these individuals and communities. High levels of crime were to be blamed upon the weakened authority of key social institutions such as the family, schools, the police, the criminal justice system, and organised religion which needed to be restored. Symbolic crime control measures, such as tough policing and punitive sentencing policies, were needed to re-assert the values of the law-abiding majority.

The fundamental premise of Wilson and Kelling's Broken Windows argument is that disorder and crime are usually inextricably linked, in a developmental sequence whereby low-level "disorder," if left unchecked, can generate further disorder and criminal behaviour. Their argument follows that if the window is broken and left unrepaired, other windows will also be broken. When there are no more windows to break, different forms of criminal behaviour occur (such as graffiti or arson) and continue until the area looks neglected and at risk of dereliction as inhabitants move out.

Hence, the aim of policing "broken windows" is to identify and deal with crime and disorder or "criminogenic problems" at as early a stage as possible to prevent their escalation. This approach is consistent with the objective of community-oriented policing strategies such as neighbourhood, reassurance, and problem-oriented approaches (see later in this chapter), which reflect the findings of Wilson and Kelling's research in three main ways:

- **Reduced fear of crime**

The increase in foot patrols in New Jersey where Wilson and Kelling's Broken Windows research took place, resulted in no significant reduction in crime, but residents felt safer and believed that foot patrol had had an impact on crime rates. However, residents also took fewer precautions to protect themselves; a potentially negative outcome if people are manipulated into thinking crime levels are lower than they are.

- **Increased public confidence in policing**

Citizens in the foot patrol areas also had a more favourable opinion of the police than those living elsewhere. This proved beneficial to beat officers, who "held higher morale, greater job satisfaction, and a more favourable attitude toward citizens in their neighbourhoods than did officers assigned to patrol cars" (Wilson and Kelling, 1982).

- **Preventing disorder**

Broken windows policing was an effective means of preventing disorderly and deviant behaviours, which, whilst not illegal or subject to police intervention or arrest, serve to impact negatively upon the quality of life of communities. Wilson and Kelling (1982: 1) observed:

> Many citizens, of course, are primarily frightened by crime, especially crime involving a sudden, violent attack by a stranger. This risk is genuine in many large cities. However, we tend to overlook or forget another source of fear -- the fear of being bothered by disorderly people. Not violent people, nor, necessarily, criminals, but disreputable or obstreperous or unpredictable people: panhandlers, drunks, addicts, rowdy teenagers, prostitutes, loiterers and the mentally disturbed.

Community-Oriented Policing

Although a vague concept, community policing incorporates various strategies aimed at improving and maintaining engagement, co-operation, interaction, and trust between the police and the public to reduce crime and disorder and improve the quality of life of local people. It is based on an evidence-based problem-solving approach to understanding and rectifying the underlying causes of crime. It supports three critical elements of Third Way ideology: a belief in the value of *community*, and an emphasis on *responsibility* and *accountability* in two ways. First, by improving engagement between the police and community, thereby promoting visibility, public confidence in the police, and legitimacy and accountability of the police with the public. Second, this approach promotes "active citizenship" and personal responsibility by encouraging the community to engage with the police and take responsibility for reporting and providing evidence of crime and disorder problems to the police.

The community policing philosophy has manifested in two essential and complementary community policing strategies: Reassurance Policing and

Neighbourhood Policing that seek, respectively, to address fear of crime and to identify community problems and propose neighbourhood-level solutions. Community policing therefore incorporates localised pro-active policing strategies with local accountability resting at its heart. Community-orientated policing is now more a way of doing (or a philosophy of) policing rather than a policing strategy as implied in Morash and Ford's definition that:

> Community policing is the delivery of police services through a customer-focused approach, utilising partnerships to maximise community resources in a problem-solving format to prevent crime, reduce fear of crime, apprehend those involved in criminal activity and improve a community's quality of life.

Hence, community policing is designed to meet the aims of what we would traditionally think of as the purpose of policing with, maybe, an improved focus on the public as a customer. Community policing is a pro-active strategy that aims to engage with the community to identify problems and work with the community and other agencies to reduce local crime and disorder problems. The concept of community policing was first devised in the late 1970s by John Alderson, Chief Constable of Devon and Cornwall Police Constabulary, as a means of providing an alternative and more effective method of policing (Alderson, 1979). Alderson (1979) argued that traditional authoritarian policing was proving inappropriate for liberal societies experiencing increasing levels of crime and argued for a new style of policing in the UK that should:

- *contribute to liberty and equality*
- *help reconcile freedom with security and to uphold the law*
- *help protect human rights*
- *dispel criminogenic social conditions*
- *create trust in communities*
- *strengthen feelings of security*
- *investigate, detect and prosecute crimes*
- *curb public disorder*
- *facilitate free movement.*

The change in focus of policing from authoritarian to libertarian that Alderson argued for should be understood within the social context of that period. The end of the Second World War (1945) to the late 1950s in Britain is often termed the golden age of policing. Communities were cohesive with high levels of "Mechanical Solidarity" (Durkheim, 1897/1993) and a sense that policing by consent had been achieved in Britain to "the maximal degree ever attainable" (Reiner, 2001: 49). From the late 1950s, the "mechanical" ethos of society changed with the rise of the youth "counter-culture" and from the 1980s with the breakdown in social consensus, outbreaks of public disorder, community conflict and accusations of racism towards the police.

Most police reforms during the 1980s, aside from implementation of the Police and Criminal Evidence Act 1984, were aimed at strengthening law enforcement and upholding social order rather than strengthening police–community relations. Any focus on a community-oriented approach was, at best, loosely implemented and designed to encourage the police to become more of a supportive service rather than a repressive force and consolidate a more amicable relationship with the community (Paterson and Pollock, 2011). The Labour government elected in the General Election of 1997 put a community-oriented policing philosophy at the heart of its policing policy with the implementation of the partnership focused Crime and Disorder Act 1998 and then the Police Reform Act 2002. One of the key developments under this latter piece of legislation was the creation of Police Community Support Officers (PCSOs) to take on responsibility for foot patrol and "beat policing" in communities as well as a wider range of policing roles undertaken by civilians and commercial organisations that would engage communities and support the Neighbourhood and Intelligence-Led Policing functions.

All police forces now have Neighbourhood Policing Teams (also referred to as Safer Neighbourhood Teams) and their responsibilities are diverse and heavily dependent on the needs of a local area. The implementation of Neighbourhood Policing should be highly localised to reflect the highly localised nature of crime and disorder problems. Every neighbourhood is different – and so are the crime and disorder problems faced by those who live there. However, the broad aims of Neighbourhood Policing can be described as follows:

- Reduce crime and anti-social behaviour
- Ensure policing is accessible to the community through accountable and named police officers and PCSOs
- Ensure police officers are familiar with their community and the community familiar with them
- Ensure police officers are visible in communities
- Ensure two-way communication between the police and communities
- Empower communities by involving the community in deciding policing priorities and solutions to local crime and disorder problems.
- Improve public perception and the image of the police
- Help build partnerships to contribute to crime and disorder reduction

Neighbourhood Policing is the routine day-to-day policing of and with the community, but other policing roles also contribute to community policing. For example, deploying public order police at peaceful protests to protect protestors from threats of violence from opposing groups or reassure the community that there is a policing presence in the event of violent disturbance.

Similarly, armed response officers may be deployed into the community when, for example, a terrorist threat is heightened, or a serious violent offence has been committed.

Most foot patrols in neighbourhoods are conducted by PCSOs and Special Constables, who work in a specific targeted patrol area and are familiar with local people and local crime problems. As most of their time is spent on foot patrol at the heart of the community, PCSOs are central to the first phase (Scanning) of any Problem-Orientated Policing strategy (see Chapter 6) through their role in providing high visibility patrols that simultaneously reassure the public, maintain public order and provide vital local intelligence.

There is very little research conducted into the impact of PCSOs on crime and anti-social behaviour reduction. However, the Home Office conducted the first evaluation of the role, function, and effectiveness of PCSOs in 2006 and found that 85% of police forces considered that providing a visible presence on the streets was an essential role of PCSOs. Interacting with the community and dealing with anti-social behaviour and low-level crime were considered the next most essential functions (Cooper et al., 2006). However, some forces were not using PCSOs to provide a visible presence at all but to support police officers in day-to-day tasks. PCSOs do seem to have taken over community patrol duties from uniformed police officers with most PCSOs spending a minimum of 50% of their time on the beat in their local areas compared to uniformed police officers who spent a maximum of 37% on the beat. However, neighbourhood police officers did spend most of their time dealing with neighbourhood "incidents."

Cooper et al. (2006) also found that police officers and PCSOs recognised the importance of each of these functions in addition to the importance of approachability, which they found was vital to members of the community for passing on information to them and for building relations with the public. Many PCSOs are also encouraged to take pro-active steps to build community relations by visiting local places such as shops and schools. Some police officers also suggested that the public perceived that PCSOs were less busy than police officers and so had more time to listen to their concerns; again, this is vital to members of the public who wish to pass on information and police forces who need up to date local intelligence.

PCSOs are seen as an excellent resource for gathering intelligence and information about potential suspects and often knowing more than the police about offenders, emerging problems and emerging trends (such as where anti-social young people are currently congregating or the location of drug dens). Police officers also acknowledged that PCSOs are their "eyes and ears" (Cooper et al., 2006).

According to figures from the Institute of Government (2019), government spending on the police has reduced by 16% between 2009/2010 and

2018/2019 with the number of PCSOs also declining by 44%. The Institute of Government also suggests that if crime rates continue to rise as quickly as in recent years, the government may need to spend an extra £3.5 billion in recruiting more police officers on top of what is currently planned. Undoubtedly, some of the recruitment of police officers will be to address the current rise in complex crimes, but the 3% rise in recorded offences for 2019/2020 includes offences where visible or patrol policing by police officers or PCSOs may be particularly useful such as offences involving knives or sharp instruments, theft from the person, and violent crime (Office for National Statistics, 2020). Although PCSOs attract criticism due to their focus on "soft" or Left Realist styles of policing, their deployment can reduce crime and disorder. Experimental evidence of patrol policing by PCSOs in a "hot spot" crime area of Peterborough over a 12-month period shows that victim-generated crimes were reduced by 39% by PCSO patrols, compared to control conditions (Ariel et al., 2016). Patrol policing using PCSOs can be particularly useful in a hot spot strategy due to the concentration on small geographical areas for patrol work.

Hot Spots Policing

Crime is not spread evenly across communities and neighbourhoods. Rather, there is significant clustering of crime in "hot spots" concentrated in much smaller locations such as addresses, street blocks, or small clusters thereof (Braga et al., 2012; Weisburd and Telep, 2014). Moreover, crime problems may also be concentrated on specific facilities within these cluster areas with bars, churches, and apartment buildings having been found to affect crime rates in their immediate environment (Eck and Weisburd, 1995). Crime and disorder problems in hot spots vary with various research studies focusing upon different high volume crime such as drug use, violence, prostitution, burglary and anti-social behaviour.

Significantly, "hot spot" locations account for about 50% of all crime events. Hence, focusing interventions such as patrol policing in these areas could make a significant contribution to crime reduction. Hot spots policing is largely considered an effective tool in tackling geographical or "place-based" crime problems, and there are a multitude of initiatives and approaches used within hot spots policing that have proven to be successful in reducing crime and disorder (Weisburd and Telep, 2014). Braga et al. (2012) also report positive results in their research into policing interventions at hot spot crime sites.

Much hot spots policing research has focused on situational crime prevention techniques (see later in this chapter) and increased directed policing patrols. Questions persist as to whether increasing patrol policing has a deterrent effect where increased certainty of arrest deters potential offenders and research on this is, according to Kleck and Barnes (2014), decidedly mixed.

The obvious "common sense" cry is that more patrolling police officers would prevent crimes such as burglary where a policing presence may act as a deterrent, and help increase detection rates (Sutton and Hodgson, 2013). However, Clarke and Hough (1984) claim that:

> ...a patrolling policeman in London could expect to pass within 100 yards of a burglary in progress, roughly once every eight years but not necessarily catch the burglar or even realise that the crime was taking place.

Sutton and Hodgson (2013), meanwhile, suggest this principle is based on three questionable premises and, therefore, question its use as evidence of ineffectiveness of routine police foot patrol. Kleck and Barnes' (2014) research indicates that police manpower levels do not affect crime rates by affecting perceptions of the risk of arrest and punishment. However, alterations in what police do and how they do it, rather than how many officers there are to do it, may affect perceptions of arrest risk (Kleck and Barnes, 2014: 735). As noted above, hot spot policing grew out of the shift from thinking about the causes of crime and criminality to focusing on crime prevention. In the next section, we look at what is often called Administrative Criminology in a bit more detail.

Administrative Criminology and Situational Crime Prevention

From the late 1970s, the work of Ron Clarke and Derek Cornish in the United Kingdom and Lawrence Cohen and Marcus Felson in the United States argued, in contrast to Positivist theories of earlier decades, that, regardless of psychological disposition or sociological influences, offenders engage in crime in order to advantage themselves in some way. Viewed from this perspective, crime is a consequence of an active decision-making process, whether this is the decision to commit crime at all, or specific choices made in terms of the place, time and target of a crime. This return to classical theoretical thinking with its central emphasis on individual voluntarism and free will led to a renewed focus on psychologically and economically grounded theoretical thinking such as rational choice theory and routine activity theory.

Administrative criminology originally emerged during the early 1980s in Britain as a critique of positivist, state-led attempts to find the scientific causes of crime. It supports Garland's (1996) notion of "responsibilisation" in that it situates responsibility for crime with the offender (through rational choice theory) and responsibility for its control with the public (through situational crime prevention).

Administrative criminologists and rational choice theorists view crime as being driven by opportunity. From this perspective, motivation is a secondary or background factor. Cohen and Felson's (1979) routine activity approach encourages a triangular understanding of crime causation that comprises the

· A motivated offender

· A potential victim/target

· The absence of a capable guardian

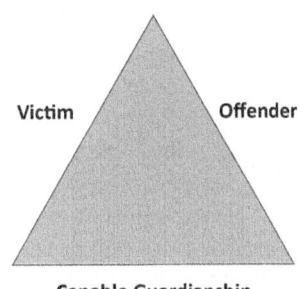

Figure 4.1 The Crime Triangle: A Motivated Offender; A Potential Victim/Target; The Absence of a Capable Guardian.

three key factors that lead to a criminal act taking place. Therefore, when all three of these factors exist simultaneously a crime event is likely to occur.

The three factors thus determine the where, when, and how of criminal action (and often ignore the why). By separating the three areas, it is possible to isolate factors that can be controlled in order to stop a crime event from occurring. For example, these theories emphasise the importance of the police as capable guardians.

From a crime prevention perspective, this means that if we disrupt one of the critical elements, particularly the *absence of a capable guardian* then a crime is unlikely to occur. One of the most appropriate methods of increasing guardianship is to modify the environment through situational crime prevention; an approach to crime prevention that revolves around reducing opportunities for crime and targeting volume crimes that can achieve the maximum impact (Pease, 1998). It comprises measures directed at highly specific forms of crime that involve the management, design, or manipulation of the immediate environment in as systematic and permanent way as possible to reduce the opportunities for crime by the following ways (see Cornish and Clarke, 2003):

- Increasing the perceived effort of committing the crime
- Increasing the risks of committing the crime
- Reducing the rewards from committing the crime
- Reducing provocations for facilitating crime
- Removing excuses for committing the crime

As with all situational crime prevention approaches, none of these five approaches to reducing opportunities for crime seek to address the causes of crime. Instead, attempting to block crime in practical and simple ways at a low social and economic cost. Administrative criminologists see two other advantages of situational crime prevention. First, the emphasis on "prevention" suggests that, if successful, Situational Crime Prevention will stop or reduce significantly the occurrence of crime and, second, responsibility for crime prevention rests with the individual rather than the state.

Although the aim of situational crime prevention is to remove responsibility for managing crime from the state and "responsibilise" (see below) the community, the role of the police is key to effective situational crime prevention in some respects. For example, effective neighbourhood watch requires engagement between the community and local policing, target hardening may entail the police providing crime prevention advice, and formal surveillance through police patrols will, obviously, require local policing.

One of the most commonly stated disadvantages of situational crime prevention has been crime displacement, of which five types have been recognised:

- Geographical – crime moves from one location to another
- Temporal – crime moves from one time to another
- Target – crime is directed away from one target to another
- Tactical – one method of crime is substituted for another
- Crime type – one kind of crime is substituted for another

Research suggests that reducing opportunities for crimes to take place does not necessarily displace crime (Clarke and Felson, 1998) as long as individual interventions are developed as part of a crime prevention strategy that addresses these issues. It is therefore essential for crime prevention strategies to factor potential displacement issues into their planning to avoid any unforeseen environmental impact. Ron Clarke suggests displacement may occur for some very rare crimes, such as arson, but not for the "great majority" of crimes (Clarke, 2009: 270). In their studies of hot spots policing, Weisburd and Telep (2014) found some evidence that hot spots policing activity led to "method displacement" whereby prostitutes and drug dealers moved their criminal activities indoors in response to an increased police presence on the streets (Weisburd and Telep, 2014: 203). Braga et al. (2012) found that when displacement was measured, it was very limited and, moreover, the unintended consequences of hot spots policing approaches were more likely to be "diffusion of benefits." A wider diffusion of benefits has also been recognised in other evaluation studies and is a factor that must be built into any research study to fully understand the impact upon crime and community.

Responsibilisation

One of the other key political drivers that emerged in the wake of Situational Crime Prevention was what Garland (1996) describes as the responsiblisation of other policing and criminal justice actors. David Garland (1996) argues that high crime rates have become a normal social fact across wealthy western societies, including the UK. Garland's viewpoint appears reminiscent of that of Durkheim, expressed over a century ago, that crime is a normal feature of society and a society without crime is a utopian fantasy (Jones, 1998). Garland argues that crime must be managed through "responsibilisation." In other words, the focus of crime management must be upon crime prevention by responsible citizens (rather than by the state) in order to reduce opportunities for criminal behaviour. This is, of course, a contentious viewpoint because it implies that responsibility for crime control is being passed to the private citizen rather than being the sole responsibility of state agencies (such as the police and other criminal justice agencies). However, Garland rejects this and argues that a "responsibilisation" strategy involves the state retaining its traditional penal function (through police, courts, prisons) while at the same time engaging non-state agencies and organisations in the reduction and prevention of crime and disorder.

Politically, responsibilisation provided a key focus of the agenda of the Coalition government in the UK between 2010 and 2015. This contemporary form of Mechanical Solidarity (see Chapter 2) and Communitarianism focused on enhancing informal social controls and communal bonds and anticipated a future landscape of policing in which conscientious citizens play an active role in policing social order. This policy vision aligned with the financial restrictions on government spending in the wake of the 2008 financial crisis and encouraged a further shift in thinking about the policing of societies that re-interprets the role of the Police Service from being monopoly providers to being just one service provider amongst a multitude of others from the statutory, voluntary, and commercial sectors.

Furthermore, in many ways, this recent development represents an ideological shift back in thinking to pre-modern (or neo-feudal) societies in which systems of informal social control dominated at the local level prior to the establishment of a professional police force. This shift in discourse about the police and policing encourages us to think about what the potential future shape of policing will look like under globalised conditions where crimes often take place across international jurisdictions and as part of the digital revolution in ungoverned or policed virtual places.

Prior to the rise of the digital revolution, Gordon Hughes (1998) identified three possible futures for crime control in societies that are experiencing this shift to active citizenship (Faulks, 1998) at the same time as an increase in demand for policing resources amongst an anxious and uncertain populace due to fear presented by "risk societies" (Beck, 1992). The following section uses Hughes's crime control vision as a model to identify potential future trajectories for policing. The section adapts and updates two of the three futures of policing put forward by Hughes (1998) – the Active Community and Authoritarian Policing.

The Active Community

The policing future that was advocated by the UK government in the Police Reform and Social Responsibility Act 2011 invoked a vision of a multitude of different community partnerships that would work alongside the Police Service and the newly established Police and Crime Commissioners. This developing vision of policing beyond just the police was also embedded in the 2017 Police and Crime Act that further reformed policing and added fire and rescue services to the governing remit of Police and Crime Commissioners. A future vision of public safety professional is now emerging with much more explicit linkages and ultimately budget savings generated by collaborations between these historically discrete services. This further responsibilisation of agencies with policing functions may re-surface in the light of potential future cuts to the police budget and re-emergence of community solidarity following the Coronavirus pandemic.

The concept of the active community emphasises the democratic potential of these partnership approaches, particularly in terms of building pressure to address crime problems through radical political, social, and economic strategies that empower citizens and encourage their involvement in policing including greater emphasis on the volunteer agencies, charities, local community groups and their collaborative contributions to policing in its widest conceptualisation.

The ongoing emphasis of the Police Service as a local, community-oriented and engaged service is exemplified by the police embrace of localised political reform, as exemplified in the establishment of Police and Crime Commissioners. As is the case elsewhere in the criminal justice system, the twin drivers here are a desire to increase community confidence in the police coupled with an acknowledgement of the state's limited capacity to manage problems of crime and disorder by itself (or to afford to pay for them!). An increased emphasis on voluntary contributors, police diversion to local agencies and localised forms of restorative policing may further shift responsibility for crime reduction from state agents to these active and responsibilised communities.

The Active Community Supported by Authoritarian Policing

Despite all of this radical reform, it is important to not overstate the extent to which the role of the public police has diminished. The Police Service remains distinct from other policing providers because of it's legal powers to use coercive force. In affluent democracies with a large public sector such as the UK, this ensures that the Police Service has retained a central cultural and symbolic function in the maintenance of social order that separates it from policing agencies from the voluntary and commercial sectors. Both Beck (1992) and Giddens (1990) argue that late modern society is characterised by risk, an absence of trust and ontological insecurity (see below) which presents a challenge to the idea of responsibilised agencies and active citizens as it points to the detachment of individuals from their community and the breakdown of social ties. Therefore, instead of an active community with strong informal social controls, post-modernists such as Beck and Giddens help us to imagine a potential future where responsibilised communities are supported by a strong authoritarian state. From this perspective, the collective values of active and responsibilised communities are reinforced by authoritarian policing which aims to restore order in fractured communities where the informal social controls and traditional social ties that are central to the active community are missing.

Instead of the active community, we may have "high trust authoritarian communitarian societies" (Hughes, 1998); strong moral communities supported by a strong authoritarian state. This perspective is tied theoretically to Wilson and Kelling's (1982) "Broken Windows" thesis discussed earlier as it foresees the police retaining a central and symbolic role in the maintenance of social order, much as they have done for the past 200 years, but in support of a multitude of other policing providers. From this perspective, the police act as a symbolic authoritarian body that re-asserts the hierarchical and disciplinary nature of society, enforcing social norms where they are perceived to have broken down. Furthermore, the police become key players in neo-conservative moralising whereby individuals and groups deemed to be at-risk are targeted by high-profile policing strategies supported by extensive media coverage and "populist punitive" messages from state officials that aim to rebuild a sense of security amongst the wider citizenry. Hence, responsibilisation encourages us to look beyond policing agencies and the offenders they seek to control to understand contemporary debates about the role and function of the police and policing.

The policing strategy for England and Wales, Policing Vision 2025, helps us understand this contradiction as it unveils a vision of a future police force that is less reliant upon people and increasingly facilitated by the better use of technology. Better use of technology requires further engagement with the private sector and a responsibilisation of individuals and agencies with the appropriate expertise in other professions to support the delivery of the 2025 vision. Policing is thus delivered through a hybrid public-private model that is overseen by the state but has, as its engine room, a pluralised network of individuals and agencies. The increased complexity presented by challenges such as cybercrime, cross-border crime, and globally facilitated serious and organised crime means that this responsibilisation and pluralisation will continue to accelerate.

Contemporary community-based policing and crime reduction requires the police to take an active role in multi-agency working with statutory agencies, communities, and the private sector. The necessity of this multi-agency partnership approach was formally recognised in the 1998 Crime and Disorder Act which provided the legal requirement for statutory agencies to work together to address the problem of crime, and it has been reinforced in several further pieces of legislation that we have introduced in this chapter. Another key area of policing strategy, and the final one to be discussed in this chapter, risk management, is included as a key strategic priority in Policing Vision 2025.

Risk Management Policing

Risk management, as a key policing responsibility, emerged in 1997 with the enactment of the Sex Offenders Act 1997 and Criminal Justice Act 2003, which demanded a change of focus in the role and function of the police – from policing the public to managing offenders. Grounded in Post Modern Criminology, criminological interest in risk reduction has its roots in scholarly work by Anthony Giddens and Ulrich Beck on the risks of modernity and development of modern society. Beck defines a Risk Society as "a systematic way of dealing with hazards and insecurities induced and introduced by modernity" (Beck, 1992: 21). Writing in Germany in the early 1990s, Beck's work coincided with a heightened fear of anti-social behaviour amongst young people and sexual offences against children in the UK following the murder of two-year old James Bulger by two ten-year-old boys in 1993. Along with sharply rising crime rates, the incident was, in the imagination of the public, indicative of a society with declining morals and values, where crime was out of control, criminal justice interventions too soft and policing powers too weak.

As discussed earlier in this chapter, the election of what was branded "New Labour" in 1997 had at its heart a law and order strategy focused on dealing with "crime and the causes of crime" (Blair, 1993) but also special measures introduced for violent, sexual, and prolific offenders that have endured into the present day. Most contemporary academic research (published post-1997) into risk management and policing focuses upon sexual crime and domestic violence and, as argued in Chapter 2, research into prolific offenders emerged slightly before this as part of the developing body of research on repeat victimisation. Significant policy developments implemented by the new Labour government during this period included the Sex Offender Act 1997, which established the Sex Offender Register, and the Criminal Justice Act 2003, which established the MAPPA and Integrated Offender Management.

MAPPA is a mechanism requiring various "Responsible Authorities" (police, prison, and Probation Service) with specific expertise and responsibilities to co-operate and co-ordinate in managing serious sexual and violent offenders. The Responsible Authority is the primary agency for MAPPA. The designated Responsible Authority has a duty to ensure that the risks posed by specified sexual and violent offenders are assessed and managed appropriately. As a Responsible Authority, the police have a key role in the monitoring and management as the Lead Agency for most of those under MAPPA supervision who are not subject to probation supervision either immediately after sentence or once the statutory supervision period of sentence ends (MAPPA Guidance, 2012). The police also have significant responsibility for running the sex offender register, which anyone convicted, cautioned, or released from prison for a sexual offence against a child must sign. Individuals are required to register within 72 hours of their release into the community and then check in with and update the police on a regular basis, notifying them of changes to any living conditions and personal circumstances (Sex Offender Act 1997). The police's role in multi-agency policing and risk management is also evident in "Integrated Offender Management" which sees a range of partners including police, probation, prisons, local authorities, and voluntary partners working together to tackle the offenders who cause most harm in their communities.

Conclusion

In conclusion, this chapter has drawn on the key disciplinary perspectives of Left and Right Realism and applied their theoretical insights to key contemporary policing strategies, using relevant criminological academic and policy research to provide a critique of the effectiveness of policy and practice. The chapter has focused primarily on strategies aimed at policing communities such as stop and search, community-oriented policing, and hot spot policing and has argued that a focus on risk reduction requires extra responsibility for the police in relation to risk management. The chapter then discussed the criminological focus on responsibilisation, advocating that the state moves away from its exclusive responsibility for policing and crime reduction with the introduction of administrative criminological approaches that brings a range of agencies and communities into the delivery of policing services through the widespread influence of rational choice theory, situational crime prevention, and social citizenship. The final discussion of managing offenders under MAPPA and the Sex Offender Register provides an introduction to some of the content we will discuss in the next chapter which focuses on vulnerability, victimisation, and the changing cultures of policing and police organisations.

References

Alderson, J. (1979) *Policing Freedom*. Plymouth: MacDonald and Evans.

Ariel, B., Weinborn, C. and Sherman, L. (2016) 'Soft' policing at hot spots—Do police community support officers work? A randomized controlled trial. *Journal of Experimental Criminology*. 12(3): 277–317.

Beck, U. (1992) *Risk Society*. London: Sage.

Blair, T. (1993) *On the Record Tony Blair Interview [Broadcast Transcript]*. On The Record, BBC (7 July 1993). Available at: www.bbc.co.uk/otr/intext92-93/Blair4.7.93.html

Braga, A., Papachristos, A. and Hureau, D. (2012) Hot spots policing effects on crime. *Campbell Systematic Reviews*. 8(1): 1–96. Oslo: The Campbell Collaboration.

Clarke, R. V. and Hough, M. (1984) *Crime and Police Effectiveness, Home Office Research Study No 79*. London: HMSO. Available at: https://archive.org/stream/op1276605-1001/op1276605-1001_djvu.txt

Clarke, R. V. and Felson, M. (1998) *Opportunity Makes the Thief: Practical Theory for Crime Prevention. Police Research Series Paper 98*. London: Home Office.

Clarke, R. V. (2009) Situational crime prevention: Theoretical background and current practice. In M. Krohn, A. Lizotte, G. Penly Hall (eds.) *Handbook on Crime and Deviance*, 259–276. Cham, Switzerland: Springer.

Cohen, L. and Felson, M. (1979) Social inequality and predatory criminal victimization: An exposition and test of a formal theory. *American Sociological Review*. 44(4): 588–608.

Cooper, C., Anscombe, J., Avenell, J., Mclean, F. and Morris, J. (2006) *A National Evaluation of Community Support Officers. Home Office Research Study 297*. London: Home Office Research, Development and Statistics Directorate.

Cornish, D. and Clarke, R. (2003) Opportunities, precipitators and criminal decisions. *Crime Prevention Studies*. 16: 41–96.

Durkheim, E. (1897/1993) *Suicide: A Study in Sociology*. London: Routledge.

Eck, J. and Weisburd, D. (1995). Crime places in crime theory. In J. Eck and D. Weisburd (eds.) *Crime and Place*, 1–34. New York: Criminal Justice Press.

Faulks, K. (1998) *Citizenship in Modern Britain*. Edinburgh: Edinburgh University Press.

Fitzgerald, M., Hough, M., Joseph, I. and Qureshi, T. (2002) *Policing for London*. Cullompton: Willan.

Garland, D. (1996) The limits of the sovereign state. *British Journal of Criminology*. 36(4): 445–471.

Giddens, A. (1990) *The Consequences of Modernity*. Cambridge: Polity.

Hall, S., Roberts, B., Clarke, J., Jefferson, T. and Critcher, C. (1978) *Policing the Crisis: Mugging, the State and Law and Order*. Basingstoke: MacMillan.

Hughes, G. (1998) *Understanding Crime Prevention*. Maidenhead: Open University Press.

Institute of Government (2019) *Performance Tracker: Police*. Available at: www.instituteforgovernment.org.uk/publication/performance-tracker-2019/police

Jones, S. (1998) *Criminology*. London: Butterworths.

Kleck, G. and Barnes, J. (2014) Do more police lead to more crime deterrence? *Crime & Delinquency*. 60(5): 716–738.

MAPPA Guidance (2012) Available at: www.gov.uk/government/publications/multi-agency-public-protection-arrangements-mappa-guidance

Metropolitan Police (2012) Search Powers Prior to Arrest. Available at: https://www.met.police.uk/SysSiteAssets/foi-media/metropolitan-police/policies/stop-and-account-search-powers-prior-to-arrest-standard-operating-procedure-sop

Miller, P., Bland, N. and Quinton, P. (2000) *The Impact of Stops and Searches on Crime and the Community Police. Research Series 127*. London: Home Office.

National Police Chiefs Council (2019) *Policing Vision 2025*. Available at: www.npcc.police.uk/documents/Policing%20Vision.pdf

Office for National Statistics (2020) *Crime in England and Wales: Year Ending March 2020*. Available at: Crime in England and Wales – Office for National Statistics (ons.gov.uk).

Paterson, C. and Pollock, E. (2011) *Policing and Criminology.* London: Learning Matters, Sage.

Pease, K. (1998) *Repeat Victimisation: Taking Stock. Crime Detection and Prevention Series Paper 90.* Police Research Group. London: Home Office.

Quinton, P. (2011) The formation of suspicions: Police stop and search practices in England and Wales. *Policing and Society.* 21(4): 357–368.

Reiner, R. (2001) *The Politics of the Police: Third Edition.* Oxford: Oxford University Press.

Sutton, M. and Hodgson, P. (2013) The problem of zombie cops in voodoo criminology: Arresting the police patrol 100 yard myth. Internet Journal of Criminology. Available at: http://docs.wixstatic.com/ugd/b93dd4_1e07a756cb2e42c4a12d55788a9e81e9.pdf

Tiratelli, M., Quinton, P. and Bradford, B. (2017) *Does More Stop and Search Mean Less Crime? Analysis of Metropolitan Police Service Panel Data, 2004–2014.* London: College of Policing. Available at: file:///C:/Users/dsep/Downloads/Quintonetal2017Doesmorestopandsearchmeanlesscrime.pdf

Waddington, P. A. J., Stenson, K. and Don, D. (2004) In proportion: Race, and police and stop and search. *British Journal of Criminology.* 44: 889–914.

Weisburd, D. and Telep, C. (2014) Hot spots policing: What we know and what we need to know. *Journal of Contemporary Criminal Justice.* 30(2): 200–220.

Wilson, J. and Kelling, G. (1982) Fixing broken windows. *The Atlantic Monthly.* 249(3): 29–38.

Wilson, J. and Herrnstein, R. (1985) *Crime and Human Nature.* New York: Simon and Schuster.

Chapter 5

From Police Culture to Policing Vulnerability

Introduction

This chapter examines recent criminological shifts in focus from an emphasis upon police culture towards a more intersectional approach that seeks to understand individual and community vulnerabilities and their intersections with policing policy, strategies, and tactics. There has been an undoubted policy shift towards incorporating victim and survivor voices plus a better understanding of vulnerabilities and associated support mechanisms into policing strategies and tactics across international jurisdictions (Bartkowiak-Theron and Asquith, 2012; Paterson and Best, 2016). The expanding sub-discipline of victimology has had a significant influence upon criminal justice discourse and has led to paradigmatic policy changes upon the policing of crimes such as domestic abuse, hate crime, child exploitation, and sexual violence. The initial influence of feminist and critical race theorists over the emergence of victimology has been supplemented by the growth of intersectional perspectives which have influenced policing policy through a discourse that surrounds the concept of vulnerability.

Victim-focused discourse has been a core component of the political and managerial language of police chiefs and their political overseers for at least three decades, but few leaders have tried to take on the structural challenge of developing victim-oriented policing within an offender-oriented criminal justice system. As a consequence of this implementation challenge, victim-oriented support has often ended up being attached to existing community policing approaches rather than as a fundamental challenge to the prevailing police mission of law enforcement, order maintenance, and crime prevention. The language of police chiefs and politicians thus frequently speaks about the centrality of victims to policing policy, yet there is a challenge in translating this discourse into operational reality in a system that has two hundred years of history that has been built around offenders and is highly dependent upon the prevailing cultures of local police teams and partner agencies.

DOI: 10.4324/9781003081012-5

This chapter reviews the slow and elongated shift that has brought vulnerability to the heart of policing. First, we review the theoretical literature on police culture which has provided a central focus for criminological inquiry about police reform. Second, we review key empirical findings that have led to a broadening and lengthening of the analytical lens beyond police culture to a more nuanced appreciation of the policing of complex and dynamic social problems through collaborative structures. Following on from this, we review key policy changes and potential future policy trajectories.

Victimology, Vulnerability, and Policing

Although much progress has been made in engaging communities with policing across jurisdictions, there is a general consensus that the rights and needs of victims are yet to become a core element of day-to-day policing which remains offender-oriented and process-driven. Some of the most influential contributions to this discussion have been made by the Norwegian abolitionist, Nils Christie (1986), and more recently the victimologists, Sandra Walklate (2011) and G. S. Bajpai (2013), who critique the state ownership of crime that emerged from the formalisation of modern criminal justice systems in the nineteenth century and the subsequent marginalisation of victims of crime from criminal justice processes. Because of this, community policing is not, in its essence, driven by communities and the limitations of community policing endeavours arise because models of policing were not fundamentally reconfigured to deliver new aspirations. A policing approach that has citizens and victims at its core requires much more radical thinking.

One potential driver for a more community and victim-oriented policing philosophy is a focus on primary and secondary victimisation with a much more focused objective to reduce the effects of victimisation in communities using more radical forms of governance (Clark, 2005; Patten, 1999; Vitale, 2017). A community-oriented approach thus requires organisations tasked with the delivery of policing to form collaborations that include those communities who are most at-risk of harm and to think about how they collectively conceptualise policing needs (Paterson and Best, 2016).

The nineteenth century process of industrial modernisation encouraged policing to evolve from being a victim-driven commercial enterprise delivered through informal plural networks into a state-run and offender-oriented process (Foucault, 1991) that marginalised victims and the harms caused to individuals and communities (Bajpai, 2013; Kirchengast, 2006). Viewed through the long lens of history, community policing philosophies and strategies constitute endeavours to address this gap between what state police did and what communities wanted and needed. It is therefore no surprise that community policing endeavours across the globe have only offered slow and piecemeal reform compared to the demands of those who suffer from the most serious victimisation and harm. The aspirations of problem-oriented policing to move away from the management of single crime incidents to a more holistic response to crime problems and the harms they cause has been driven by similar factors. The following section introduces criminological analyses of police reform that were initially seen as the intellectual mechanisms for driving police reform and provides some theoretical critique of these endeavours before moving on to discussions about contemporary vulnerability-oriented reforms.

Police Culture and Legitimacy

Academic criminology had a significant influence over criminal justice policy during the 1970s and 1980s through the Marxist critique of the decline in police legitimacy associated with the persistent over-policing of young black males (Hall et al., 1978) and the feminist critique of the under-policing of gender violence (Cain, 1990; Stanko, 2008). The criticisms faced by the police during this period included questions about the use of police powers, discretion, and status and drove growth in a new wave of police cultural criminological literature.

The terminology of police or, "cop," culture was first used in the United States as a shorthand reference to the organisational culture of police agencies and what Skolnick described as the working personality of the police officer (Skolnick, 1966). Schein developed this idea in more general terms, referring to culture as the "deeper level of basic assumptions and beliefs that are shared by members of an organisation" (Schein, 1985: 6) or "the way we do things round here." Robert Reiner (1985) developed this concept within a British context, describing police subculture as categorised by the following key elements:

- A sense of mission
- Suspicion
- Isolation/solidarity
- Conservatism
- Machismo
- Pragmatism
- Racial prejudice

Reiner's analysis of police culture during the crisis of legitimacy presented an out-of-date image of a patriarchal and, as MacPherson (1999) described, institutionally racist institution that prioritised the action-oriented side of policing by securing swift resolutions to crime problems from easily identifiable group of offenders. This initial description of a single, monolithic police culture quickly developed into something more nuanced with recognition of the differences between street cops and management cops (Reuss-Ianni, 1982): officers working in different departments (Innes, 2003), male and female officers (Silvestri, 2003), and rural and urban forces (Garland and Chakraborti, 2007).

Culture as the Problem and Solution?

While early empirical analyses of police culture focused upon questions about whether the police could provide a fair and equitable service to all members of the public and the extent to which the service provided was delivered in a discriminatory manner across ages, ethnicities, genders, religions, disabilities, sexualities, and economic status or class, empirical research consistently demonstrates that newly recruited police officers join with a strong sense of public service and do not have authoritarian personalities as assumed in the earlier studies by people like Skolnick (1966) and Reiner (1985). Fielding (1988) and, a decade later, Waddington (1999) took this literature a step further with the observation that police officers demonstrate, in alignment with the public, "common values, beliefs and attitudes *(but)* within a police context" (Waddington, 1999: 293). Therefore, the focus of this cultural literature moved on to the transition stage of members of the public starting work as a police officer and attempts to understand how police officers learned how to do their job, to interact with the public, and the type of police officer they developed into.

In the United States study, "Styles of Patrol in a Community Policing Context" (2002), Mastrofski, Willis, and Snipes identified four officer typologies:

- **Professionals** – who demonstrate knowledge and awareness of strategic priorities and are community focused, with good communication skills
- **Reactors** – enforcement-focused police officers who engage in mainly reactive activities and are selective about who they will help
- **Tough Cops** – cynical and authoritarian law enforcers
- **Avoiders** – officers who keep a low profile and engage with crime only when it is essential

In this typology, the professionals provide the most supportive mechanism for the delivery of community-focused policing as they align their work with managerial aims and are also the officers who are most likely to be promoted. Unfortunately, Mastrofski's study found that these professionals only constituted 20% of the police workforce with 40% of officers fitting in the other categories. There is no similar research that has been produced in England and Wales, but the aim here is just to raise some of the challenges you should be aware of from discussions about the future of community policing strategies.

Beyond Police Culture as Theorisation

Although the previous section identified types and typologies of police cultures, its practical utility is limited as these cultural analyses do not differentiate between police talk and action. The perspective that is presented in the early work of Reiner (1985) follows these simplistic principles:

- The accepted practices and principles identified in police culture are applied by frontline police officers in their day-to-day work.
- Police officers focus their attention on individuals and communities deemed to be "police property" and prioritise crime fighting ahead of other police functions.

The sociological error with this analysis arises from the limitations placed on research who see "back stage" (Goffman, 1959/1990) police talk rather than "front stage" unsupervised routine police work, and this can lead criminological research to place too much attention on police "talk" rather than police "action." The question for researchers is thus to what extent do theories of police culture accurately describe police practice? This is where researchers need to undertake empirical studies by collecting quantitative and qualitative data on what the police do to ascertain whether there is any truth in the assumptions outlined in the theory. For example, the Marxist argument that the police act in an authoritarian manner is contested by the high degree of support and confidence the public have in the police, even during times of crisis (Bradford et al., 2009; HMICFRS, 2019; Loader and Mulcahy, 2003). Conversely, public support in policing rarely rises above 75%, so there are questions about what the experiences of policing for the unsupportive 25% of the public might look like.

Usefully, Waddington (1999) describes the discourse of police culture as providing a mechanism for police officers to act out their idealised vision of policing. Like everyone else, police officers will share stories that they find interesting, and these are understandably much more likely to emphasise action-oriented crime-fighting ahead of paper work. Consequently, Waddington provides us with an analytical perspective that presents police culture as a mode of expressive rhetoric and a defensive mechanism that retains the integrity of the police world and mission. Consider the following quote from Waddington:

> The police routinely come into conflict with the most marginal groups in society, and like antagonists generally, they demean their opponents... If the police can persuade themselves that those against whom coercive authority is exercised are contemptible, no moral dilemmas are experienced – the policed section of the population 'deserve it'.
>
> (Waddington, 1999: 301)

Reflective Task

How might police culture limit the impact of legislative reform upon police practice?

The literature on police culture helps us to understand how a police organisation thinks about crime, and it is also a cultural tool for police officers to assert their interpretations of their role, in particular the conflict and personal threats faced in frontline roles. "War stories" provide a sense of dignity and logic to what can be morally problematic work. Janet Chan (1996) argues that there are creative aspects to this culture which emerge "from the interaction between the socio-political context of police work and various dimensions of police organisational knowledge" (1996: 110). Hence, multiple dynamic police cultures exist across police forces, departments, stations, and shifts (horizontally) as well as at different points in the police hierarchy (vertically). In the next section, we will apply these models of police culture to some contemporary challenges.

Racialised Policing

Concerns about police discrimination against different minority groups exist in all democratic countries and can be traced back to fears about revolutionary working class Chartists at the point of the advent of Peel's police in the nineteenth century. Criminological interest in the subject of discrimination is most commonly focused upon the relationship between police and young men from minority groups who, it is argued, are both over-policed and under-protected as a consequence of the toxic mix of authoritarian governmental legislation, media-generated moral panics, and discriminatory policing (Hall et al., 1978). The impact of this process is most evident in stop and search statistics.

While the number of stop and searches has reduced dramatically since the previous decade, from 25 people per 1,000 to 11 people per 1,000, there continue to be significant disparities in who gets stopped and where. In 2020, 54 black people out of 1,000 were stopped and searched compared to 6 white people per 1,000 population (Home Office, 2021). As police officers act as the gateway to the criminal justice system, the experience for black people, in particular, continues to be one of discriminatory treatment all the way through the prosecution, courts and sentencing process.

The extent to which disproportionality in outcomes such as stop and search or deaths in custody is due to police discriminatory behaviour remains an area of fierce debate within criminology (Waddington et al., 2004). Black and Asian populations are younger and, in aggregate statistical terms, from poorer socio-economic areas than the white population and are subsequently more likely to come into contact with the police (Webster, 2003). Furthermore, 80% of the black people stopped and searched in the year ending March 2020 were stopped in the London Metropolitan area which skews nationwide figures and should encourage you to avoid simplistic regional data comparisons. The 1982 Scarman Report, the 1999 MacPherson Report, and the 2017 Lammy Report have all interrogated the problem of over-representation of minority group contact with the police and justice system, but little has improved in terms of statistical outcomes.

Reflective Task

What does this description from American criminologist, James Q Wilson (Wilson, 1968: 39–40), tell you about the way police officers decide which individuals are most likely to commit offences?

Can any of the criminological theories we have introduced in this book help you explain Wilson's statement?

The teenager hanging out on a street corner late at night, especially one dressed in an eccentric manner, a Negro wearing a "conk rag" (a piece of cloth tied around the head to hold flat hair being "processed"--that is, straightened), girls in short skirts and boys in long hair parked in a flashy car talking loudly to friends on the curb, or interracial couples--all of these are seen by many police officers as persons displaying unconventional and improper behaviour.

Discrimination is not just focused upon individual viewpoints. Lord MacPherson's Report into the failed investigation into the death of Stephen Lawrence described racism as an institutionalised problem,

the collective failure of an organisation to provide an appropriate and professional service to people because of their colour, culture or ethnic origin, which can be seen or detected in processes, attitudes, and behaviour, which amount to discrimination through unwitting prejudice, ignorance, thoughtlessness, and racist stereotyping, which disadvantages minority ethnic people.

(MacPherson 1999: para 6.34)

Reflective Task

Review and reflect upon Macpherson's contentious definition of "institutional racism."

Have you had an experience of institutional racism or discrimination in the workplace, at university, in school, or socially?

The complexity of the discussion about race, ethnicity, and policing is further complicated by the distinct although associated problem of Islamophobia in British society. Islamophobia describes a form of racism that you would expect to be expressed in religious terms, but it is often reported in official statistics as racism and evidence in terms of racialised policing only emerges in the data at the broad level of the Asian population. The same arguments emerge about under-protection and over-policing although with a level of complexity that renders simplistic conclusions difficult (Hargreaves, 2018; Zempi, 2020).

Gendered Policing

There are similar prevailing concerns about the failure of police and wider society to provide adequate protection for those at risk of serious and repeat offences such as sexual and gendered violence. The historical argument has been that a male-dominated force did not prioritise these offences, and the influence of police culture marginalised the attention given to offences that primarily impacted women and children, particularly in private places. Furthermore, female police officers only achieved formal equal recognition in policing in 1975 with the introduction of the Sex Discrimination Act and Equal Pay Act. The Police Service as a whole was thus historically skewed in terms of restrictions on the number of female police officers until the latter part of the twentieth century.

The proportion of female police officers has grown during the twenty-first century, and most police forces see relative parity in the numbers of male and female officers entering the organisation. Yet, there continue to be disparities at the top of policing hierarchies, and the growth in number of female officers entering the force is not proportionate with those progressing through the rank structure (Silvestri and Tong, 2020). This under-representation has had a secondary impact on the experiences of victims of crime, for example, a poor understanding of the impact of domestic abuse upon female victims, which has subsequently become an area of intensive research and policy activity.

The feminist movement in criminology has, over the past 80 years, sought to address the absence of interest in women as offenders and victims in criminological scholarship and the problems generated where "the construction, production and dissemination of criminological knowledge have been dominated by men and men's discourse" (Gelsthorpe, 2003: 8). Womens' issues were thus largely ignored in the context of crime victimisation and the impact of criminal justice processes. Several different perspectives on feminist criminology have emerged to enhance criminological thinking around achieving gender equality (Liberal Feminism), ending perceived male supremacy in key social, economic, and political spheres (Radical Feminism), ending women's financial dependency on men (Socialist Feminism) and ending the capitalist system that is perceived as biased in favour of the economic interests of men. Not only have the ideas of feminist movements been influential in academic and disciplinary development but also in developing policies and practices in the policing of domestic abuse such as better police training, better processes for the collection of statistics, and better arrest and prosecution practices (Stanko, 2008).

In the later 1990s, efforts to reduce repeat victimisation in England and Wales started to incorporate gender violence. In part, this was due to public concerns about violent crimes, but, more significantly, it was due to the enhanced public profile given to the vulnerability of victims of gender violence by non-governmental organisations and feminist scholars (Hanmer et al., 1989). One of the key drivers of change was recognition that individuals who experience domestic abuse in early life have an increased likelihood of further future harm, both as offenders and victims (Stanko, 2008). Added to this, there is now an understanding that repeat victimisation can also mean an incremental or sudden escalation in harm, with one in three murders across England and Wales following on from previous abuse (Stanko, 2008). In England and Wales, a plethora of legal and policy tools have been made available to police agencies to support and protect repeat victims, which include inter-agency working with databases that detail patterns of contact across a range of agencies and have the potential to better understand the needs of vulnerable people to support the appropriate deployment of resources.

It should also be acknowledged that these inter-agency collaborative approaches have sought to minimise some of the structural challenges presented by police-led responses where the symbolic emphasis upon the use of force has, to varying degrees, marginalised female officers from some police roles (Westmarland, 2001) and highlighted the structural inequalities faced by women in policing. Prokos and Padavic adopt more of a Marxist feminist stance, when they argue that structural disadvantages for women are built into police culture in the United States. Commenting on the experience of training at the police academy, they note that (2002: 446, 454),

> The explicit curriculum and the hidden curriculum at the police academy stood in stark contrast to one another. The explicit curriculum was gender neutral; the hidden curriculum was riddled with gender lessons... hegemonic masculinity continually reappeared in the hidden curriculum, inserted by male instructors and staff via their treatment of each other and of women... Male students learned that it is acceptable to exclude women, that women are naturally very different from men and thus can be treated differently, that denigrating and objectifying women is commonplace and expected, and that they can disregard women in authority.

Whether marginalisation is produced by institutionalised structures or the role of individuals remains a complex issue, it can be concluded that the literature finds enduring challenges for female victims of crime as well as equity of experience for female police officers.

Discriminatory Policing

The challenge of how to avoid discriminatory policing has also been raised by activists in the lesbian, gay, bisexual and transgender (LGBT+) communities. Scholarship has pointed towards the over-policing of sexual behaviour between men (Williams and Robinson, 2004) and the under protection of some aspects of LGBT+ communities, although significant progress in attempts to address hate crime (Pickles, 2019). The experience of LGBT+ communities, both within the police and subject to policing, was generally absent from police research until recently. In part, this was due to the comparatively invisible nature of LGBT+ communities when compared to visible minority ethnic groups or female officers but also the failure of the Police Service to keep statistical data on LGBT+ data across forces and ranks. Like other minority groups, there is anecdotal evidence of LGBT+ officers over-emphasising their relationship with the dominant police culture in order to embed themselves alongside their colleagues.

The historical proscription of homosexuality as a criminal act has generated further tensions related to the perceived deviance of the homo-sexual lifestyle. This has resulted in an under-policing of the LGBT+ community and an unwillingness to report homophobic incidents to the police. Specific concerns have also been noted about the poor policing of domestic violence cases amongst the LGBT+ community (Williams and Robinson, 2004). The Police Service have responded to these concerns with an intensi-fication of efforts to promote the work of LGBT+ officers and highlight areas of concern related to victimisation and policing in the broader LGBT+ community.

Practical Task

The Gay Police Association (GPA) was founded in 1990 as The Lesbian and Gay Police Association and became the Gay Police Association in 2001 and latterly the Police LGBT+ Network. The organisation aims to promote better relations between the Police Service and LGBT+ people whilst also working towards equality of opportunity in the Police Service.

Visit the Police LGBT+ Network website to evaluate their aims and objectives.

https://lgbt.police.uk/

Intersectionalities of Vulnerability

Empirical evidence has consistently demonstrated that each of the demo-graphic characteristics we have reviewed in this chapter should not be looked at in isolation but, instead from an intersectional perspective that allows us to understand how multiple individual or group characteristics overlap and impact upon the vulnerability of an individual. One good example to look at here is young people who are often the focus of public concerns about crime that are difficult to distinguish from media-driven moral panics and which frequently mask vulnerability to victimisation. There is a large body of literature that documents relations between young people and the police (Anderson et al., 1994; Jamieson et al., 1999; McAra and McVie, 2005) and the increased likelihood of contact with the criminal justice system as a young person that has further disproportionalities for young black and Asian men (Webster, 2003).

High visibility in publicly accessible spaces coupled with frequent media reporting about the problem of youth increases the likelihood of young people being treated as "police property." Research has demonstrated that police interpretations of suspicious behaviour often revolve around class and socio-economic status and their related cultural manifestations such as dress, language, and demeanour. There has been subsequent concern about the extent to which police discretion exerts a form of moral, or social discipline (Choongh, 1998) over multiple strands of diversity such as age, class, gender, and race to create a permanent sub-group of police suspects. Recognition of this challenge has led to growth in different forms of police-led diversionary strategies and tools that include restorative cautioning and community justice panels amongst a range of other options to divert a larger number of young people away from the gateway to the criminal justice system (Clamp and Paterson, 2017).

Reflective Task

How might labelling and subcultural theories help us to understand the negative impact and implications of police contact with young people?

From Culture to Vulnerability

A critical enduring question for democratic police organisations across the globe is where do the police fit into the future of community-oriented policing strategies, particularly in social and political situations that are characterised by enduring historical tensions or where communities feel victimised by the state and police. Peter Manning (2010) provides an excellent overview of the literature on the under-policing and under-protection of specific types of victims of crime. Similarly, Wisler and Onwudiwe (2007) review the implications of the over-policing of social groups and the associated victimisation that subsequently remains undetected or invisible when communities disengage with police, resulting in a justice and security deficit (Mastrofski et al., 2002). This latter issue gained global attention in the United States, thanks to the advocacy of the Black Lives Matter movement, and similar analysis could also be provided of unjust policing of minority groups in a multitude of other democratic countries.

In democratic societies, policing requires trust between citizens and institutions to function justly and effectively. There is a strong international evidence base available that demonstrates that trust, confidence, and legitimacy are enhanced when there are co-operative arrangements which support the interests of all stakeholders (Tyler, 1990). Citizens in a democracy have a right to equal justice and public agencies are required to support this. Thus, any activity that furthers inequality, such as the over-policing of vulnerable communities, should be avoided, and policing strategies and tactics should be promoted where they are of greatest benefit to the least advantaged members of society. Rawls refers to this understanding of justice as *the difference principle* (Rawls, 1971, 1993) which Manning (2010) identifies as a key potential measure of policing success.

Viewed in this way, policing strategies should adopt a distributive approach that recognises existing social, material, and political inequalities and seeks to address the vulnerabilities in these communities. This critique raises questions about the continued viability of strategies such as hotspot policing that have a tendency to focus the most coercive policing strategies towards the most disadvantaged and vulnerable citizens and thus further entrench inequality (Kapoor, 2013; Manning, 2010; Vitale, 2017).

Influenced by feminist, critical race, and intersectional critiques, policy trajectories across criminal justice agencies have attempted to situate victims' interests and a more nuanced appreciation of vulnerability into policing. This shift in thinking asserts the importance of the psychological and democratic benefits of situating victims at the heart of any police response (Ibarra and Erez, 2005; Taylor, 2012) in attempts to increase public confidence in policing and to deliver more efficient and effective policing services. The potential implications for police legitimacy, effectiveness, and efficiency are significant.

Recognition that repeat victims generate disproportionate demands on police organisations makes a focus on victims' needs a strategy which can generate efficiencies in service delivery through better crime prevention (Farrell, 2001; Stanko, 2008). Responding directly to repeat victimisation expands the crime prevention function to multiple agencies with access to more sophisticated intelligence and data and more effective proactive policing. Much of the initial repeat victimisation work in England and Wales from the 1990s focused upon property crimes, in particular burglary, where simple target-hardening prevention activities had a significant impact upon rates of repeat victimisation (Farrell, 2001). Police forces in England and Wales developed their own individualised responses to repeat victimisation with burglaries, and this led to dramatic reductions in crime rates, although often without a sophisticated appreciation of which preventive measures had worked most effectively and why (Farrell, 2001).

This focus upon repeat victimisation through community engagement provides us with further links to the theoretical literature on *collective efficacy* which has a direct lineage through environmental criminology and back to the work of the Chicago school in the 1920s and 1930s. Sampson and Groves argue that a focus upon social disorganisation in communities helps to identify enduring solutions to crime problems by focusing interventions at the relationship between communities and crime (Sampson and Groves, 1989). This approach focuses less on the distinctions between victims and offenders and instead the collective harms, vulnerabilities, and social justice issues that offenders, victims, and communities face (Christie, 1986).

One of the key mechanisms for victim-oriented reforms has been an increased focus upon understanding the impact of policing through the lens of vulnerability. The language of vulnerability draws upon academic discourse in the fields of ethics and human rights law as part of its attempt to re-orient police thinking around the vulnerability that is encountered by police officers and other agencies. Bartkowiak-Théron and Asquith (2017) describe this approach to policing as requiring a universal precautions model that recognises all forms of vulnerability and requires policing actors to identify and respond to the individual, social, and institutional contexts of vulnerability that they encounter.

The universal precautions model draws on the longstanding recognition that encountering vulnerability has always been a core element of the policing experience (Banton, 1964; Bittner, 1967; Skolnick, 1966; Westley, 1970). Collectively, these authors created the sociology of policing through their identification and analysis of policing being primarily concerned with the management of social welfare and order rather than that of crime. Despite this empirical reality, contemporary debates about policing often still revolves around misguided assumptions that police officers just need to learn the law and how to administer this. The new police curriculum gives much more emphasis to risk management and the recognition of vulnerability and the rights of those who are subject to policing strategies and tactics. The universal precautions model recognises the leadership role that police officers provide in communities as both sources of protection but also as gatekeepers to the criminal justice process.

This perspective on policing recognises that there are specific forms of vulnerability that police officers and other agencies need to identify such as age, ethnicity, gender, poor mental or physical health, and previous victimisation. It therefore becomes essential for police officers to have the requisite skills to identify and respond to these vulnerabilities in diverse sets of circumstances, to intervene with legal tools where appropriate, and to explore options for support from external agencies at other times. This evidence-based approach is underpinned by the criminological insights from Tom Tyler (1990, 2017) on the importance of procedural justice (i.e. the way justice is done) in maintaining social order in a sustainable manner.

In practical terms, the above analysis simply acknowledges that the police have always delivered a combination of legal and social welfare functions but that the welfare function is often under-stated in public discussion as well as in police recruitment, training, and culture. Recognition that social challenges such as supporting the homeless, child safeguarding, and mental health crises are core police functions and are valued is long overdue. Similar recognition and skills development is required of the need for effective collaboration to address these issues and to put the vulnerable person (whether they are an offender, victim, or witness) at the heart of the policing response. Bartkowiak-Théron and Asquith (2012) note that these policing responses require multi-agency governing bodies that can address the multiple layering of complex social needs in individuals and communities and to minimise the most extensive harms that emerge. This wider definition of policing inevitably leads to a re-conceptualisation in thinking about what police responses to these problems should look like and the need for collaborative, multi-disciplinary action that incorporates shared policies, data access, knowledge exchange and a growth in expertise in the critical social problems that blight specific communities.

Adverse Childhood Experiences (ACEs) and Trauma-Informed Policing

One example of where the empirical findings of new research has had a significant impact upon policing policy is in the area of childhood trauma and the impact upon long-term mental health. Research by Barnardos (2014) has demonstrated that children who have what is described as adverse childhood experiences (ACEs) have significant long-term impacts with 60% having significant speech, language, or communication difficulties and between 24% and 30% having a learning disability. Furthermore, there are significant impacts upon mental ill-health with 18% of this group suffering from depression, 10% from anxiety disorders, and 5% from psychotic-like symptoms (Barnardos, 2014).

Improving the policing of young people has been a focus of police leaders since 2010, when the Association of Chief Police Officers launched the Children and Young Peoples Strategy (ACPO, 2010). The driver behind this change in strategy in the policing of young people involved attempts to appreciate and understand childhood victimisation in its social context as a consequence of a series of high-profile policing failures related to the exploitation of children (see Jay, 2014, for one example). It was clear that in some instances, police officers and organisations, as well as a range of community partners, had misinterpreted childhood vulnerability as deviance and that this had led to inappropriate responses that put children and young adults at risk. Contemporary examples of this problem can be found in modern slavery, sex trafficking, and prostitution cases as well as in so-called county lines trafficking routes where children are systematically exploited in the pursuit of profit for organised crime groups and would have historically been understood as offenders rather than victims.

This recognition that ACEs can have an impact on individual development and behaviour in later life that influences life chances and continued susceptibility to exploitation reframes our understanding of the police cultural literature. From the Chicago school onwards, assumptions were often made about young people and their relationship with crime which now need to be re-assessed and a change process is in place across policing services which seeks to situate vulnerability at the heart of the policing response.

Life course studies across several countries have recognised the link between ACEs, offending, and anti-social behaviour (Craig et al., 2017; Farrington, 2003; Fox et al., 2015). Within the literature, there are usually ten factors identified which explain how ACEs have an impact on future life experience and health outcomes (Felitti et al., 1998). These are:

Abuse:

- Physical – experiencing physical punishments in the home
- Sexual – experiencing sexual abuse in the home
- Verbal experiencing verbal abuse such as insults, belittling language, and name-calling in the home

Neglect:

- Emotional – lack of appropriate emotional support and reassurance for the child
- Physical – absence of essential needs such as food, clothes, heating

Household factors:

- Alcohol and drug use of parents
- Mental health issues in the immediate family
- Domestic violence and abuse towards another adult in the child's home
- Parents in prison
- Parental separation (emotions and instability that accompany parental separation)

Essentially, the more of these factors a child experiences in their childhood, the more likely it becomes, in statistical terms, that they will begin offending in the future. The offending/victimisation relationship is complex, and this perspective should not be interpreted as meaning that adverse childhood experiences make a person an offender or a victim. Instead, the experiences represent risk factors that help us to understand how best to assess and respond to a set of circumstances in an appropriate manner.

The policing of ACEs is now embedded into community-orientated approaches to crime reduction where the police are required to understand the causes of a problem as well as how to deal with anti-social and criminal behaviour in an approach that aligns with the left-realist model which we introduced earlier in the book. Increased understanding of vulnerability involves an awareness of how trauma impacts upon children and adults as well as the novel development of trauma-informed policing (Bateson et al., 2019) which has become increasingly critical to policing. In Wales, the programme, which has been backed by more than £6.5m of Home Office funding, has led to more than 5,000 front-line officers and police staff being trained to respond to crimes involving children to enable them to recognise whether they may be experiencing ACEs.

It may seem strange from a twenty-first century perspective, but the term child abuse is still quite new and realisation of the importance of the state taking action to protect children from physical abuse only emerged in the 1970s and started to have an impact in the policy arena in the 1980s. Similar protections in relation to sexual abuse followed in the 1980s with the establishment of Childline by the television presenter Esther Rantzen and what became known as the Cleveland Affair in 1987 where two paediatricians identified over 100 children who had been sexually abused whilst living in care (Campbell, 1988). The public enquiry that followed, led by the High Court judge Dame Elizabeth Butler-Sloss, made several recommendations related to multi-agency working particularly, between the police and social workers. Multi-agency working has since become an integral part of policing and crime reduction. Anyone pursuing a career in criminal justice will quickly become familiar with a range of multi-agency structures and acronyms such as the Multi-Agency Safeguarding Hub (MASH) which brings together professionals to make decisions about the most effective ways to protect children and young people or the Multi-Agency Risk Assessment Conference (MARAC) for people at high risk of domestic abuse or sexual violence where police, probation, health and education come together to find a response that can best support the victim and try to reduce future victimisation.

The 2014 Care Act set out the statutory responsibility to integrate support, including from police, for adults at risk of abuse or neglect and established Safeguarding Adults Boards. Similarly, Sections 80–83 of the Policing and Crime Act 2017 amended Section 135 and 136 of the Mental Health Act 1983 to provide a new statutory responsibility for police officers to work in partnership with a medical practitioner, registered nurse, or approved mental health professional, before removing a person to a place of safety. Increasingly, policing is delivered through networks of public safety professionals who build a myriad of collaborations and partnerships that cross previously discrete professional and disciplinary boundaries (Crawford and L'Hoiry, 2017).

Empirical data demonstrate that these networked approaches are flourishing although our understanding of their effectiveness is still incomplete.

Conclusion

This chapter brings the first part of the book to a close. In Chapter 6, we will start to apply the theoretical tools that have been introduced so far to help us solve practical problems, before moving on to look at how we use and generate research to support better policing. The first half of this chapter provided a light touch overview of issues of vulnerability and contributions from the literature on police culture to contextualise the latter focus on harm and risk which brings our review of the criminological landscape and its alignment with the police education qualifications framework to its natural end point.

References

Anderson, S., Kinsey, R., Loader, I. and Smith, S. (1994) *Cautionary Tales: Young People, Crime and Policing in Edinburgh*. Aldershot: Avebury.

Association of Chief Police Officers (2010) *Children's and Young Peoples Strategy 2010–2013*. Available at: www.pc.rhul.ac.uk/sites/child_police/wp-content/uploads/2013/11/ACPO-Children-and-young-people-document.pdf

Bajpai, G. (2013) Locating the crime victim in criminal procedure ideologies. *SSRN*. Available at: https://doi.org/10.2139/ssrn.2332566

Banton, M. (1964) *The Policeman in the Community*. London: Tavistock.

Barnardos (2014) *Living with Adversity: A Qualitative Study of Families with Multiple and Complex Needs*. London: Barnardos. Available at: www.barnardos.org.uk/sites/default/files/uploads/Living%20with%20adversity%20%20A%20qualitative%20study%20of%20families%20with%20multiple%20and%20complex%20needs%20-%20Full%20report%202014.pdf

Bartkowiak-Theron, I. and Asquith, N. (2012) *Policing Vulnerability*. London: Federation Press.

Bartkowiak-Théron, I. and Asquith, N. (2017). Conceptual divides and practice synergies in law enforcement and public health: Some lessons from policing vulnerability in Australia. *Policing and Society*, 27(3), 276–288.

Bateson, K., McManus, M. and Johnson, G. (2019) Understanding the use and misuse of adverse childhood experiences in trauma-informed policing. *Police Journal*. 93(3): 131–145.

Bittner, E. (1967) The police on skid row: A study of peacekeeping. *American Sociological Review*. 32(5): 699–715.

Bradford, B., Jackson, J. and Stanko, E. (2009) Contact and confidence: Re-visiting the impact of public encounters with the police. *Policing and Society*. 19(1): 20–46.

Cain, M. (1990) Towards transgression: New directions in feminist criminology. *International Journal of the Sociology of Law*. 18(1): 1–18.

Campbell, B. (1988) *Unofficial Secrets: The Cleveland Case*. London: Virago.

Chan, J. (1996) Changing police culture. *British Journal of Criminology*. 36(1): 109–134.

Choongh, S. (1998) Policing the Dross: A social disciplinary model of policing. *British Journal of Criminology*. 38(4): 623–634.

Christie, N. (1986) The ideal victim. In E. A. Fattah (ed.) *From Crime Policy to Victim Policy*, 17–30. London: Tavistock Publications.

Clamp, K. and Paterson, C. (2017) *Restorative Policing*. London: Routledge.

Clark, M. (2005). The importance of a new philosophy to the post-modern policing environment. *Policing: An International Journal of Police Strategies and Management*. 28(4): 642–653.

Craig, J., Piquero, A., Farrington, D. and Ttofi, M. (2017) A little early risk goes a long bad way: Adverse childhood experiences and life course offending in the Cambridge study. *Journal of Criminal Justice*. 53: 34–45.

Crawford, A. and L'Hoiry, X. (2017) Boundary crossing: Networked policing and emergent 'communities of practice' in safeguarding children. *Policing and Society*. 27(6): 636–654.

Farrell, G. (2001) How victim-oriented is policing? In A. Gaudreault and I. Waller (eds.) *Tenth International Symposium on Victimology: Selected Symposium Proceedings*. Available at: How victim-oriented is policing? (lboro.ac.uk)

Farrington, D. (2003) Developmental and life course criminology: Key theoretical and empirical issues. *Criminology*. 41(2): 221–225.

Felitti, V., Anda, R., Nordenberg, D., Williamson, D., Spitz, A., Edwards, V. and Marks, J. (1998) Relationship of childhood abuse and household dysfunction to many of the leading causes of death in adults: The adverse childhood experiences study. *American Journal of Preventive Medicine*. 14(4): 245–258.

Fielding, N. (1988) *Joining Forces: Police Training, Socialisation and Occupational Competence*. London: Routledge.

Foucault, M. (1991) Governmentality. In G. Burchell, C. Gordon and P. Miller (eds.) *The Foucault Effect: Studies in Governmentality*, 87–104. Chicago: University of Chicago Press.

Fox, B., Perez, N., Cass, E., Baglivio, M. and Epps, N. (2015) Trauma changes everything: Examining the relationship between adverse childhood experiences and serious, violent and chronic juvenile offenders. *Child Abuse and Neglect*. 46: 163–173.

Garland, J. and Chakraborti, N. (2007) Protean times: Exploring the relationships between policing, community and race in rural England. *Criminology and Criminal Justice*. 7(4): 347–365.

Gelsthorpe, L. (2003) Feminist perspectives on gender and crime: Making women count. *Criminal Justice Matters*. 53(1): 8–9.

Goffman, E. (1959/1990) *The Presentation of Self in Everyday Life*. London: Penguin.

Hall, S., Critcher, C., Jefferson, T., Clarke, J. and Roberts, B. (1978) *Policing the Crisis: Mugging, the State and Law and Order*. London: MacMillan.

Hanmer, J., Radford, J. and Stanko, E. (1989). *Women, Policing, and Male Violence*. London: Routledge.

Hargreaves, J. (2018) Police stop and search within British Muslim communities: Evidence from the British Crime Survey 2006–2011. *British Journal of Criminology*. 58(6): 1281–1302.

Her Majesty's Inspectorate of Constabulary and Fire and Rescue Services (2019) *Public Perceptions of Policing in England and Wales in 2018*. Available at: www.bmgresearch.co.uk/hmicfrs-publishes-public-perceptions-of-policing-in-england-and-wales-2018-report/

Home Office (2021) *Stop and Search Statistics*. Available at: www.ethnicity-facts-fig-ures.service.gov.uk/crime-justice-and-the-law/policing/stop-and-search/latest

Ibarra, P. and Erez, E. (2005). Victim-centric diversion? The electronic monitoring of domestic violence cases. *Behavioral Sciences and the Law.* 23(2): 259–276.

Innes, M. (2003) *Investigating Murder: Detective Work and the Police Response to Criminal Homicide*. Oxford: Oxford University Press.

Jamieson, J., McIvor, G. and Murray, C. (1999) *Understanding Offending Among Young People*. Edinburgh: HMSO.

Jay, A. (2014) *Independent Inquiry into Child Exploitation in Rotherham (1997–2013)*. Available at: www.rotherham.gov.uk/downloads/download/31/independent-inquiry-into-child-sexual-exploitation-in-rotherham-1997---2013

Kapoor, V. (2013) *Access to Justice as the Pariah of the Development Rhetoric: Critical Evaluation of Governance and Policing Through the Human-Rights Based Approach to Development*. The 5th Annual Conference of the Asian Criminological Society. Tata Institute for the Social Sciences, Mumbai.

Kirchengast, T. (2006) *The Victim in Criminal Law and Justice*. London: Palgrave Macmillan.

Loader, I. and Mulcahy, A. (2003) *Policing and the Condition of England*. Oxford: Clarendon Press.

MacPherson, L. (1999) *The Stephen Lawrence Inquiry*. London: Home Office.

Manning, P. (2010) *Democratic Policing in a Changing World*. London: Routledge.

Mastrofski, S., Willis, J. and Snipes, J. (2002) Styles of patrol in a community policing context. In M. Morash and J. Ford (eds.) *The Move to Community Policing: Making Change Happen*. Thousand Oaks, CA: Sage.

McAra, L. and McVie, S. (2005) The usual suspects? Street-life, young people and the police. *Criminology and Criminal Justice.* 5(1): 5–35.

Paterson, C. and Best, D. (2016) Policing vulnerability through building community connections. *Policing: A Journal of Policy and Practice.* 10(2): 150–157.

Patten, C. (1999). *A New Beginning: The Report of the Independent Commission on Policing for Northern Ireland*. London: UK Government. https://cain.ulster.ac.uk/issues/police/patten/patten99.pdf

Pickles, J. (2020) Policing hate and bridging communities: A qualitative evaluation of relationships between LGBT+ people and the police in the North East of England. Policing and Society. 30(4): 741–759.

Rawls, J. (1971). *A Theory of Justice*. Cambridge, MA: Harvard University Press.

Rawls, J. (1993). *Political Liberalism*. New York: Columbia University Press.

Reiner, R. (1985) *The Politics of the Police (First Edition)*. Brighton: Wheatsheaf Books.

Reuss-Ianni, E. (1982) *Two Cultures of Policing: Street Cops and Management Cops*. New Brunswick, NJ: Transaction Publishers.

Sampson, R. and Groves, B. (1989). Community structure and crime: Testing social-disorganization theory. *American Journal of Sociology.* 94(4): 774–802.

Scarman, L. G. (1982) *The Scarman Report: The Brixton Disorders 10–12 April 1981*. London: Home Office.

Schein, E. (1985) *Organisational Culture and Leadership*. San Francisco, CA: John Wiley.

Silvestri, M. (2003) *Women in Charge: Policing, Gender and Leadership*. London: Willan.

Silvestri, M. and Tong, S. (2020) Women police leaders in Europe. *European Journal of Criminology*. Available at: https://repository.canterbury.ac.uk/item/8v377/women-police-leaders-in-europe-a-tale-of-prejudice-and-patronage

Skolnick, J. (1966) *Justice without Trial: Law Enforcement in a Democratic Society*. New York: Wiley.

Stanko, E. (2008) Managing performance in the policing of domestic violence. *Policing: A Journal of Policy and Practice*. 2(3): 294–302.

Taylor, C. (2012) *Policing Just Outcomes*. Perth: Edith Cowan University.

Tyler T. (1990) *Why People Obey the Law*. Princeton, NJ: Princeton University Press.

Tyler, T. (2017) Procedural justice and policing: A rush to judgement? *Annual Review of Law and Social Science*. 13: 29–53.

Vitale, A. (2017) *The End of Policing*. New York: Verso.

Waddington, P. A. J. (1999) Police (canteen) sub-culture: An appreciation. *British Journal of Criminology*. 39(2): 287–309.

Waddington, P. A. J., Stenson, K. and Don, D. (2004) In proportion: Race, and police stop and search. *British Journal of Criminology*. 44(6): 889–914.

Walklate, S. (2011) Reframing criminal victimisation: Finding a place for vulnerability and resilience. *Theoretical Criminology*. 15(2): 179–194.

Webster, C. (2003) Race, space and fear: Imagined geographies of racism, crime and violence and disorder in Northern England. *Capital and Class*. 27(2): 95–122.

Westley, W. (1970) *Violence and the Police: A Sociological Study of Law, Custom and Morality*. Cambridge, MA: MIT Press.

Westmarland, L. (2001) *Gender and Policing: Sex, Power and Police Culture*. Cullompton: Willan.

Williams, M. and Robinson, A. (2004) Problems and prospects with policing the lesbian, gay and bisexual community in Wales. *Policing and Society*. 14(3): 213–232.

Wilson, J. Q. (1968) *Varieties of Police Behaviour*. Cambridge, MA: Harvard University Press.

Wisler, D. and Onwudiwe, I. (2007). *Community Policing: A Comparative View*. International Police Executive Symposium, Geneva Centre for the Democratic Control of Armed Forces. Available at: www.dcaf.ch/sites/default/files/publications/documents/WPS_No6_new.pdf

Zempi, I. (2020) Veiled Muslim womens' responses to experiences of gendered Islamophobia in the UK. *International Review of Victimology*. 26(1): 96–111.

Chapter 6

Problem-Solving for Police Officers

Introduction

When we ask the question, what is the point of criminology for police officers, one of the obvious answers that emerges is problem-solving. The ability to understand and use research and data alongside your professional police knowledge will improve your problem-solving skills. This problem-solving approach also encourages independent assessments of effectiveness, impact, and evaluation of your own and others' practice. The complexity and dynamic nature of twenty-first century societies and the crime problems they produce makes problem-solving skills an essential element of contemporary policing.

This chapter introduces the concept of problem-solving and its preventive aims alongside a number of different problem-solving models. The chapter seeks to encourage you to use a range of different sources of evidence to help you with the problem-solving process, particularly where you are witnessing regular recurrences of the same types of crime. The National Decision Model (NDM) will be introduced to illustrate mechanisms for embedding research into practice, improving defensible decision-making, addressing risks, and minimising potential harms and associated financial costs in an evidence-based way. The SARA and ATLAS models will be introduced in this chapter and linked to relevant theory (rational choice theory, routine activities theory, and social crime prevention) and practice (crime prevention, policing models and strategies, community engagement and procedural justice; vulnerability and exploitation).

A case study approach will be prominent in this chapter with an introduction to different types of problem-focused evidence reviews that are reviewed and assessed with the purpose of developing innovations that help improve the delivery of policing services. This includes short introductions to problem profiles, rapid evidence assessments (REAs), and systematic reviews of readily available documentation. The combination of case studies and access to different research resources allows us to appreciate how an understanding of local crime problems combined with access to research evidence can improve policing at the local, national, and global levels. There will be links provided

DOI: 10.4324/9781003081012-6

to videos and webpages that will help bring these case studies to life and will encourage you to think about what you might have done had you been in the same position as the police officers involved in the cases.

Making Sense of Crime Problems

Practical Task

Before you read on any further, have a think about what the main crime problems are in your area. Now have a look at your local crime and policing website (www.police.uk/pu/your-area/).

Are the crime problems that the statistics highlight the same as the ones you imagined?

Most new students of policing and new police officers are initially surprised by the breadth of activities that the police undertake. Day-to-day police work integrates crime-focused activity with engagement with individuals and communities, preventive activity around low-level social problems, mental health support, and other forms of social risk management, plus a range of bureaucratic activities. Many of these duties are undertaken alongside local partners who, since the introduction of the 1998 Crime and Disorder Act, also have a statutory duty to contribute to the prevention of crime and disorder in their area. Police officers thus need to have skills in collaborative working as the solutions to the problems they face often extend beyond the remit and responsibility of police agencies.

It is therefore important at this stage to re-assert the important conceptual distinction between the terms "policing" and "the police." A broad range of social control mechanisms can be captured within the term "policing." These might include, for example, the role of families, religious institutions, schools, and other local statutory or non-governmental agencies. Policing is thus what the police do, but the police are not the only agency responsible for policing. "Policing" as a process, or a mode of social control, must be separated from "the police" as an institution who are responsible for specific policing activities. This conceptualisation of our problem in broad terms is critical. If we decide to conceptualise our problems in solely police terms, then we will only have police-oriented solutions. Yet, if we broaden our configuration of a problem to wider policing processes, then we will automatically engage other non-police agencies who are involved in those policing processes in the proposed solution.

It is worth making a couple of historical points here before we move on to the first case study. Policing as a mode of social control pre-dates the existence of the police institution in England and Wales. The professional police institution that we recognise today was established in 1829 as the London Metropolitan Police and then supplemented throughout the early and middle part of the nineteenth century as regional police forces throughout the country during an extended period that saw our current modern systems of local government and justice formed. From the early part of the nineteenth century onwards, there was a fundamental shift from loose and informal policing arrangements in which a multitude of often private policing agencies competed for work to a professional police force paid for by central and local government that retained strong constabulary independence. During this period, the police institution was separated from most other policing agencies, for example, private security, through the acquisition of the state-sanctioned legal powers with which it's personnel were provided. The most significant of these powers are the power to remove liberty and the power to use physical force (Bittner, 1970), which separate the police from other institutions or processes that have policing functions.

This discussion might initially seem quite abstract, but it has critical importance when you are making decisions about how a problem might be resolved. Have a think about how you might respond to the following set of circumstances.

Case Study

You arrive at the scene of some conflict between a group of young males. Three young men are shouting abuse at a younger man who has lashed out at the others with a knife. On arrival at the scene, everyone seems to calm down, and the three young men leave. The younger person is still clearly agitated, so you try to calm him and seek to collection some information about his identity. The young man's details appear to correspond with a 15-year-old male who has been reported as missing from home and absent from school who is considered at risk due to his age and link to gangs.

What do you do next?
Who do you need to speak to?
Which problems need policing in this case study?

You perform a search and find a six-inch kitchen knife and 30 individually wrapped items of illegal drugs and take the young person to custody. In custody, he is found to have significant burns to his body. The young person will not disclose further details.

What is the problem that you are policing?
Who else needs to be involved in this policing process?
What is your desired outcome?

While it may be quite clear what path a police officer would need to pursue in these circumstances to address any criminal behaviour, it is much more challenging to address the wider policing issues that are raised by the context in which these actions and behaviour have taken place. While, in simple terms, police work is fundamentally about the administration of the law, it is not possible to avoid the complexity that is unearthed by engagement with the social problems that ultimately produce behaviour that ends up being regulated by the law of the land.

It is therefore essential that police officers have the skills to make appropriate decisions that simultaneously recognise the legal issues presented in a set of circumstances and the social, moral, and ethical issues that are engaged as soon as police are involved in incidents. It is this breadth of the police role that we are thinking about when we refer to the term "problem-solving" as rather than just resolving an individual incident (or crime event) you are trying to prevent future crimes from taking place (i.e. addressing the source of an ongoing sequence of crime events). The next section provides a short historical account of the emergence of problem-solving strategies and the growing influence of social scientific and criminological thought and methodologies in the latter part of the twentieth century that has subsequently evolved into the concept of evidence-based policing which we will discuss in Chapter 7.

Problem-Oriented Policing

Most prominently, criminology introduces police officers to the role of social scientific data and the role of academic evidence in supporting and quality assuring problem-solving processes as well as the decision-making involved in developing strategic and tactical response to police problems. Although crime prevention has been cited as a primary goal of the police since the advent of the police institution, it is widely recognised that by the middle part of the twentieth century police institutions had become primarily response services. This response-driven service was not just unique to England and Wales, but it presided in other countries that had established locally administered professional state police models such as the United States, Canada, and Australia.

Consistent rises in crime rates and demands on police services led to frustration with the dominant responsive technocratic approach that was utilised by many police agencies to manage and co-ordinate responses to crime (i.e. how fast calls were responded to and considered to be resolved). In the United States, Hermann Goldstein (1977, 1979, 1990) and later John Eck and William Spelman (1987) developed the concept of problem-oriented policing as an alternative approach. Problem-oriented policing works by identifying the root causes of recurrent problems in a community and solving them by using preventive evidence-based strategies that seek to address longer term problems rather than individual crime incidents. Such an approach requires the police to be proactive rather than reactive as they look for and seek out crime and disorder problems, a process that can require considerable research capacity. This problem-solving strategy puts a significant focus upon the role of front-line neighbourhood police who act as the eyes and ears of the local community and feed their understanding of local problems into police intelligence systems. The process involves officers undertaking in-depth studies of discrete police problems and developing preventative strategies that reduce dependence upon the criminal justice system through engagement with other public sector agencies, community groups, and, where appropriate, the private sector (Goldstein, 2010). This approach requires police officers to make sense of data from multiple sources to understand what causes crime to take place and encourages police officers to engage with criminological theory as they attempt to explain why local crime problems are emerging. This way of thinking is sometimes called applied criminology as the disciplinary knowledge of criminology is being applied to real-life problems rather than being discussed in abstract or theoretical terms.

Problem-oriented policing calls for a precise specification of problems through an analysis of the "dynamics of offending" and deviates from the common misperception of the possibility of reducing "crime" to a single moment or event. In other words, "crime" must be analysed in the context of multiple variables which need to be subjected to rigorous evaluation. This includes: who (the offender); does what (offence); to whom (victim); when (time); where (place); why (reason); how (method); and to what effect (possible impact of the offending). Once problems are found, problem-oriented policing embraces an evidence-based approach to solving issues through an analytical model known as SARA: Scanning (clustering incidents together); Analysis (of the relevant offending dynamics); Response (action taken to address, reduce or prevent the crime or disorder problem); and Assessment (of the first three phases – particularly the response) that is used in different forms across the globe (Eck and Spelman, 1987: 2–3; Leigh et al., 1996).

The SARA model seeks to communicate the purpose of problem-oriented policing to all levels of policing agencies although it has been recognised that many attempts to implement problem-oriented policing, as initially imagined by Goldstein, have drifted towards beat officer problem-solving which, in practical terms, is more closely associated with community policing (Skogan and Hartnett, 1997). Addressing this challenge, Goldstein (1997) has distinguished problem-oriented policing from community policing by arguing that the latter is focused on engaging the community in its existing tasks, whereas the former is broader in that it seeks to solve problems and devise solutions by engaging the community in problem-solving where the solution requires it.[1]

The purpose of policing, as interpreted by police organisations and many policing scholars, is largely focused upon issues of crime control, public protection, and order maintenance carried out by uniformed officers, which means, in practice, there is a tendency to marginalise work on the causes of crime. This underlying philosophy of crime control is evident in countless analyses of police culture as well as approaches to recruitment, training, and development (Paterson, 2011). Thus, change is imagined in pursuit of problem-oriented policing but rarely enacted in the shape of that imagined vision (Goldstein, 2010). Organisational inertia can frustrate these change processes, largely because concepts of policing across the globe are infected with action-oriented notions of crime control, violence, and coercion which lead to the police being defined primarily by their capacity to use force (Bittner, 1970; Brodeur, 2010) rather than their potential to secure justice and address complex social problems.

Even where deliberate attempts are made at problem-solving, a particular limitation of this policing strategy is that its emphasis upon resolving the underlying causes of crime extends beyond the police and into areas such as the management of online spaces, the impact of unemployment or school exclusion, and other local community concerns related to anti-social behaviour. These are all areas over which the police often have limited influence and control. Critics also often question whether these are the problems that the police should really be tasked with, but as the police are one of the few response services that are contactable on a 24/7 basis, they are often drawn into issues beyond their crime control priorities and that relate to public anxiety and fear of crime or low-level incivilities and disputes in neighbourhoods which are not necessarily linked to crime. Thus, we return again to the earlier point that effective police officers and agencies need to involve other relevant stakeholders that are directly engaged in working with individuals as offenders or victims to understand the causes, consequences, and solutions to crime from the "bottom-up." As leadership figures in the community, police officers and police community support officers are ideally situated to perform this role.

We will now look at how the Police Service in England and Wales has responded to the development of problem-oriented policing with a focus upon some case studies and the potential use of different problem-solving models. But, before we move on, take a moment to think about some of the questions raised within this section about the boundaries of crime, deviance, and disorder and the police officer's role in responding to these problems.

Reflective Task

What do you think should be the main responsibilities of the police?
What are the functions that police most regularly perform?
Is it possible to put some formal boundaries around where definitions
of police work start and end?

Problem-Solving in Practice

Case Study 1

Operation Engage was a police-led operation set up in 2005 that focused on an area of Lancashire where there were a large number of missing children. The Operation Engage team worked with a total of 30 children, all girls, over a period of three years. The team built up ongoing, trusting, and supportive relationships with the young people, who over time disclosed a range of sexual and violent abuse. All of the children were in the care of local families or services and, in most cases, cared for in children's homes.

Your Role

You have been tasked with developing an evidence-based project as part of the local police's contribution to a broader partnership approach to tackling child sexual exploitation.

As part of this project, you will need to:

- Find, access, and use the College of Policing Crime Reduction Toolkit (College of Policing, 2021a) to inform your decision around which intervention might be most suitable for tackling this form of exploitation.
- Consider some of the challenges you might encounter in making a case for the selected intervention.
- Develop a strategy for reviewing the intervention.

Case Study Task

Which Initiatives Would You Suggest and Why?

Things to consider:

- What does the evidence state is the potential effect of the selected intervention?
- What would you need to consider when implementing your intervention (e.g. staff training, partnership working, project monitoring)?
- What impact does this information have on your decision to use this intervention in this situation?
- What are the financial and human resource requirements you will need to implement this intervention (e.g. costs, human resources, time needed to complete the project)?
- What is the time frame for completion of this intervention?
- When would you start to expect to see results?

The College of Policing Crime Reduction Toolkit will provide you with some of the answers to the questions above, but you may also need to extend your search beyond this resource.

Where else could you look for helpful information?

What Are Some of the Challenges You Might Come Across and Need to Overcome?

Part of the problem-solving process is to ask questions about existing practices (the A in ATLAS) and to scan for information (the S in SARA). It is normal to find this a challenging process and to only make partial progress towards your desired answer. It is worth giving some consideration to what some of the challenges might be when you are identifying a potential intervention:

- How do you decide what is the best option and when do you know that you have completed your review of available resources?
- What do I do if I cannot find a suitable intervention?
- How might I make a case for a novel intervention?
- How can I identify unpredictable or unintentional consequences of the intervention and mitigate against these risks?

Once you have reviewed these questions and prepared some answers, then have a look at the link below. There is an excellent summary of the problem-solving work done by the Operation Engage Team available here – https:// popcenter.asu.edu/sites/default/files/library/awards/tilley/2009/09-01(R).pdf

Putting Problem-Solving into Practice

The use of research evidence to solve problems has been a core focal point for critical decision-making and problem-solving in other professions for hundreds of years. Medicine, education, law, and the social professions (probation and social work) are just a few examples of this trend. There are different ways (models) of doing problem-solving, and these different professional approaches are widely documented and available for you to research. There is a body of literature that focuses upon implementation science which is a useful reference point when you start to familiarise yourself with the challenges of problem-solving in professional contexts. For the moment, we will stick with those models that are most prominent in the policing context.

In an earlier part of this chapter, we introduced the SARA model which was developed in the late 1980s and has been adapted for use as a problem-solving tool in various ways for police forces across the world. We will review SARA later in the chapter, but the College of Policing currently encourages police officers to use the ATLAS model which we outline below. To use the model, you should start in the top left corner with the Ask question and then complete each stage of the module by following a clockwise direction.

The key aim for anyone who is new to this area of work is to familiarise yourself with the different models and to use whichever model feels most intuitive and useful. The purpose of the models is to structure your approach to problem-solving in the same way that you might do with reflective practices. ATLAS encourages police officers to first, *Ask* questions about how they might improve a specific approach to a problem. This part of the process often involves people challenging existing practices and raising questions about how a problem might be addressed in a different manner. It is this determination to ask questions and to challenge existing practices that has resulted

What is EBP? Introducing "ATLAS"...

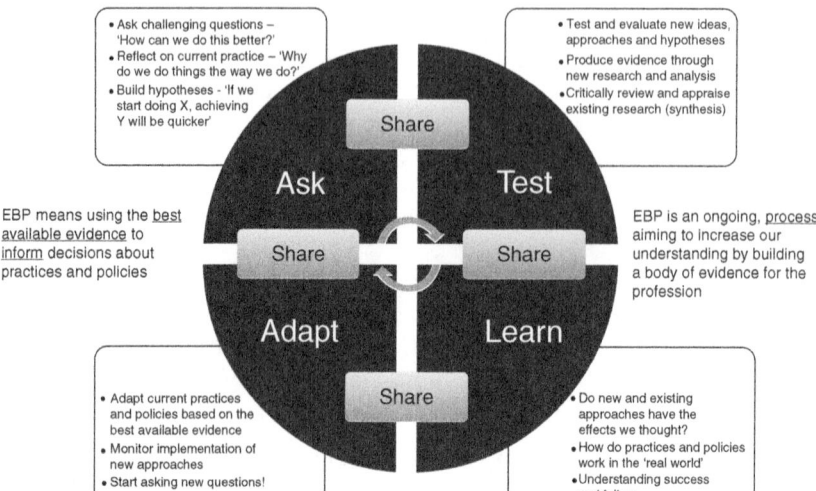

EBP means using the best available evidence to inform decisions about practices and policies

EBP is an ongoing, process aiming to increase our understanding by building a body of evidence for the profession

Figure 6.1 The Atlas Model.

in such a significant emphasis in the new policing degrees that focuses upon critical thinking skills (see, e.g., Bottomley et al., 2020). Once questions have been asked and new ideas or hypotheses have been developed, it is essential to *test* these new ideas in the field and within the context of existing research.

The College of Policing encourages a range of approaches to critically review existing research and to analyse the outcomes of this research. These approaches to research include reviewing evidence available in the College of Policing Crime Reduction Toolkit that we referred to earlier in this chapter as well as other College-based resources such as the Policing and Crime Reduction Research Map (College of Policing, 2021c) and the National Police Library (College of Policing, 2021b). Other potential research approaches include the development of problem profiles which help police forces develop a better understanding of an emerging crime profile, or pattern of incidents, or a subject profile which seeks to provide more information about a person or group of people. Research methodologies such as rapid evidence assessments allow police officers to quickly review available evidence and to synthesise findings. If a deeper understanding is required, additional resources can be put into developing a systematic review of literature which seeks to capture all available and relevant information. These testing and evaluation methodologies were developed initially in other professions, and they are now widely used in policing to generate evidence that others can access and use when they are looking for alternative approaches to policing problems.

The third stage of the ATLAS process is to *Learn*. Once new ideas have been developed and tested, we need to make sense of the findings of our research and evaluation to learn whether our interventions have had the impact that we hoped for. Challenges often emerge when we try to differentiate what should work in a specific context from what actually works in a specific context. Although a more scientific approach to policing is being encouraged, this science needs to be tested in the complex reality of people and society. Interventions that work in one local area may not work in a different area, and this is where the professional knowledge of police officers becomes critical in interpreting research findings and deciding where and how to implement them. The learning process is thus not just about using science uncritically but learning about how to develop and *adapt* ideas and interventions across different contexts.

Adaptation provides the fourth stage of the ATLAS process as new learning is implemented and monitored. The ATLAS process continues, so new questions should be asked about the effectiveness of new interventions, and the fifth stage of the process, *Share*, is mobilised as you share your learning and experiences with others to help embed this reflective processing of asking questions, testing ideas, learning about new ways to do policing, and adapting your approaches accordingly. Chapter 7 will introduce you to the detail and process of research, but, for the moment, we will continue to focus upon problem-solving by moving onto consideration of how your decision-making is supported during the problem-solving process. You can find information about the ATLAS model here as it will be useful to refer back to this when you are addressing specific problems – https://whatworks.college.police.uk/About/News/Documents/ATLAS.pdf

Making Decisions

The College of Policing has already embedded problem-solving processes and structures into its systems, and it has provided numerous tools to support you work. The next step in your approach to problem-solving is to find ways to support your decision-making. The College of Policing's NDM is a risk assessment and decision-making process designed to help you make decisions in a range of different circumstances. You can find more information about it here – www.app.college.polihce.uk/app-content/national-decision-model/the-national-decision-model/

The NDM can be used in unpredictable as well as planned situations and can be used by individuals as well as teams. The model can be used retrospectively to reflect upon and review decisions and actions in both simple and complex circumstances. As with the SARA and ATLAS models, the starting point is to break down the key elements of the models and to look at these in sequential order. As you can see below, there are five sequential elements of the NDM that are bound together by the code of ethics.

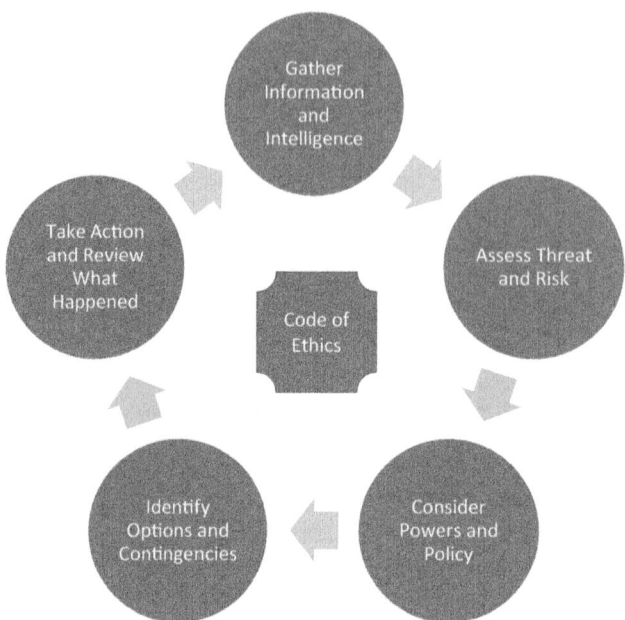

Figure 6.2 The National Decision Model.

The NDM aims to improve the delivery of policing in accordance with our democratic values and to enhance the flexible use of discretion and professional judgement. This purpose acknowledges the contested relationship between values at the policy level and values in practice once they have come into conflict with the "common-sense" organisational assumptions that condition the policing (and any other) environment. Within this context, a multitude of contested value systems emerge, both embracing and contesting official codes of standards, ethics, and behaviour. This helps to explain the resistance to police education that becomes apparent amongst some experienced police officers and allows us to envisage a growing cohort of police officers emerging from a reformed police education system who have a much more extensive education in the application of the democratic values intrinsic to community policing philosophies (Paterson, 2011).

Research on policing has consistently demonstrated that operational police work is rarely guided solely by legal precepts but also by the extensive discretion of police officers in how they enforce the law (Chan, 1997; Reiner, 2019). The impact of the values of individual police officers is therefore experienced by the general public at the street level where operational policing is practised. The term "values" implies the use of subjective judgements and attitudes towards others, while legal perspectives place an emphasis on "rules" which can be seen to impart restrictions on discretionary decision-making. This can create a perception that legal rules are in conflict with organisational values and individual perspectives.

Contemporary analyses of police culture emphasise the interpretive and creative aspects of police culture as well as the existence of a multitude of cultural layers which can help us to envisage processes of organisational change. Most usefully, Manning (1993) has suggested that there are three subcultures of policing – senior command, middle management, and the rank and file – which can be used to enable processes of police reform. Manning's conceptual separation of three subcultures of policing helps us to interpret the organisational emphasis that is placed upon values and ethics at different levels of the police hierarchy and explains police resistance to new initiatives that do not already exist within the framework of existing police (cultural) knowledge. Thus, rather than understanding police culture as static and monolithic, it is more helpful to emphasise the importance of the social, legal, and political sites in which policing takes place. Reforming police culture and providing a meaningful position for values within policing demands change from all three subcultures of policing (Chan, 1996).

Using the NDM, police officers and policing organisations can develop a cyclical process, guided by the code of ethics, to review policing strategies, tactics, and resourcing and to support reform processes. The rest of this section introduces and briefly discusses each of the six elements that make up the NDM.

The Code of Ethics

The Police Code of Ethics (2020) was established in 2014 and sits at the heart of the NDM as recognition of the need for all police decisions to be in alignment with the principles set out in the code (College of Policing, 2020). The Code of Ethics adds the principles of fairness and respect to the existing policing principles that were developed in tandem with the Principles of Public Life in 1995 (Nolan, 1995). The principles reflect the importance of individual and organisational accountability, honesty, integrity, openness, and selflessness as well as the aspirations of objectivity and leadership by example. These principles underpin the standards of professional behaviour that were consolidated in the Police (Conduct) Regulations 2012 and are often complemented by agreed values and principles for individual regional forces. These principles and standards of professional behaviour tie together the other five elements of the NDM and are captured in the mnemonic, CIAPOAR. Following on from the Code of Ethics, we will now briefly explore each of these five elements.

Information – Gather Information and Intelligence

This stage emphasises the importance of all police officers as critical decision-makers who define each situation based upon the information and intelligence that they gather.

Assessment – Assess Threat and Risk and Develop a Working Strategy

This is the analytical stage where the decision-maker assesses the situation, potential threats, and risks of harm before deciding what, if any, action needs to be taken. The assessment stage has multiple dynamic factors including questions about whether new information and intelligence is required, how manageable are visible risks, and what could potentially go right and wrong if a specific course of action is pursued. At this point, it is important for the individual to consider whether they can manage the situation alone or whether they need to bring in assistance.

Powers and Policy – Consider Powers and Policing Policy

This stage requires police officers to think about which tools they have available to use in terms of police powers, policing policy, and available legislation. While the first question might be about which powers are available to the police officer, the officer also needs to consider existing national and local policy as well as available research evidence to contextualise their decision-making. It is this contextualised decision-making that is critical for good decision-making to ensure that chosen courses of action are in alignment with any changes to legislation and policy guidance and the most up to date best practice evidence.

Options – Identify Options and Contingencies

Once a range of courses of action have been identified, the police officer needs to identify the route that offers the most positive outcome and the least risk of harm. Critical issues to consider at this point include whether the officer is confident that they have sufficient information available to make appropriate decisions, whether suitable resources and support are available as well as issues relating to the amount of time available to make a decision and the secondary impact of any decisions upon the circumstances and other members of the public. Police officers can ultimately be held to account for their decision-making in the courts and in any subsequent disciplinary proceedings and will be asked to demonstrate that the decisions they made were reasonable in the circumstances as well as proportionate, necessary, legitimate, and ethical.

Action and Review – Take Action and Review What Happened

The final stage incorporates two distinct steps as decision-makers act and implements decisions whilst also, where appropriate, keeping those decisions under review and beginning the process of reflecting upon action. Once decisions have been made, it is important to inform others of your actions and to record what you did and why to support recollection and reflection. A key component of reflective practice is to monitor what happened after you made a decision and to reflect upon whether the course of action that you followed produced the expected or desired outcomes.

The NDM provides an iterative process whereby the process can be continually implemented until an incident is considered complete and the formal review process begins. The iterative and reflective process should mean that a culture of questioning is embedded into your work as part of the cycle of reflection to consider the outcomes of a course of action and what might be done differently in future circumstances. In Chapter 7, we will look at the review and evaluation process in more detail as we look for independent evidence that supports specific policing decisions, strategies, tactics, and policies.

The NDM builds upon the influential work of Kolb (1984) and others in developing a model of reflective practice which encourages professionals to look at their future and previous actions with a critical eye, to seek help and support where needed, and to review and audit outcomes. A long history of reflective practice exists in other professions such as law, medicine, teaching, and social work, but a shift in this direction has until recently been met with resistance by police organisations (Christopher, 2015; Paterson, 2011). During the early part of the twenty-first century, the Police Service in England and Wales has witnessed renewed developments in this area with a greater educational focus on reasons, judgements, and values. This shift to a more reflective practice of policing reflects the sustained challenge faced by police organisations in delivering cultural change and operational police officers who take ownership of their decision-making and can adapt to the complex needs presented in twenty-first century communities (Paterson, 2011). Here is a case study example for you to look at. Have a go at applying the NDM.

Case Study – Problem-Solving with the NDM

We have been contacted by front-line officers facing what is being described as "a large scale anti-social behaviour problem" in a small seaside resort town. The police officers are seeking evidence of what works in order to assist in problem-solving the issue.

The specific problem consists of the following:

- Anti-social behaviour in multiple locations; the main issues concern fast food outlets

- Offenders identified of ages between 10 and 20 years old
- Various different offences have been identified and arrests have been made for:
  - Criminal Damage, Public Order, Possession of Offensive Weapons, Breaches of Section 35s, Drug offences.
- Anti-social cycling has made a large contribution to public anxiety and fear of crime:
  - Riding down the road the wrong way.
  - Riding in front of buses and causing them to brake suddenly with examples of injury to passengers.

Collectively, these individual problems have contributed to community fear of crime and a backlash on social media with local groups planning protests against persons involved in the ASB. Some of the blame is being directed at outsiders who come into the town, but it is believed that there are problems emerging out of the local population too.

Therefore, we are asking for information from other police officers or forces who have been faced with similar problems, or researchers who have looked at this type of issue:

- How did you resolve your issue locally – what worked?
- Do you have any evidence reviews conducted on this subject?
- Do you have any known interventions to solve this issue?
- Have you conducted any evaluations around those interventions?

1   What evidence could the officer use?
2   Where would the officer find this evidence?
3   How do we work out if the evidence is useful?

As you will have seen in this example, one of the key skills police officers possess is their informed and ethical decision-making and the knowledge of when and whom to engage to support a policing response. The final section of this chapter engages with partnership working and collaboration directly. All sciences are in a continuous cycle of development and the role of the social sciences, as an academic discipline, is to capture the best contemporary knowledge for sharing across the profession. This knowledge has been used for many years to improve police practice and this section extends that ambition to incorporate the wider body of agencies that support policing responses to social problems.

Collaborative Approaches to Problem-Solving

There has been a slow but sustained shift in thinking about how emergency responses should be best structured to reflect the needs of twenty-first century societies and to help resolve the increasingly complex challenges that societies face (Sienkiewicz-Malyjurek, 2019; Skinns, 2008). The scale of this task should not be underestimated with different institutional cultures and legal frameworks forming and reflecting different historical prioritisation of prevention, response, and investigation in the context of understanding policing and crime problems. For example, while fire services have had a preventive focus embedded through relevant legislation since their inception, the idea of preventive policing only emerged in the latter part of the twentieth century, as a discretionary component of policing, more than 150 years after the establishment of professional police (O'Malley and Hutchinson, 2007). Proactive policing and preventive demand reduction are now core aspects of police work, but it is important to recognise that these are only comparatively recent developments and many police forces across the world still prioritise responsive law enforcement. In contrast with health and fire, preventive measures continue to be comparatively underfunded in policing and, because of this, they do not always carry the institutional support that senior leaders, such as Police and Crime Commissioners (PCCs), would wish for.

The Policing and Crime Act 2017 re-affirmed the partnership emphasis of the Crime and Disorder Act 1998 and placed public safety reform firmly on the agenda of PCCs and emergency services through a statutory obligation to collaborate that has been taken up in different ways by PCCs across England and Wales. This is not just a British phenomenon. Societies across the world are looking anew at concepts such as public safety and citizen security to reflect upon the barriers that are sometimes generated by institutional separation and the mechanisms required to address siloed behaviour and practices.

In England and Wales, this change is captured most explicitly in the role of PCC offices, the extension of their reach to fire services, and the ambition to transition from joint-working in partnerships to collaboration through a more unified governance framework (Loveday, 2018). There are longstanding examples of such developments with high-profile critical incidents in cases of public health and terrorism, but the key challenge is to normalise collaboration in institutions that have had historically discrete identities, purposes and culture. A re-configuration of what policing means to collaborations and how it can be effectively and efficiently achieved is required.

Attempts to build partnerships and change the public safety environment are longstanding and often bedevilled by differences in institutional purpose, organisational cultures, and sometime inter-professional and budgetary rivalries (Skinns, 2008). It is important therefore to develop an open mindset that minimises the potential impact of these aforementioned obstacles and seeks out the benefits of partnership working. There are multiple examples of good practice which include partnerships between mental health and policing to improve responses to mental health crises as well as collaborations with non-governmental organisations to improve support for victims of crime after arrests have been made (Paterson and Pollock, 2016). At one level, collaboration means sharing buildings and resources to enhance agility and savings in terms of business delivery, but for individual police officers, the challenge is to develop collaborative purpose and cultures in partnerships to create shared goals and clarity about individual and organisational responsibilities (Crawford, 2005).

The international evidence tells us that people are of primary importance when undertaking localised public safety work (Sienkiewicz-Malyjurek, 2019). First, responders such as police officers must have a mindset that is aligned with community needs to enable them to build up confidence from the community and to work across a range of diverse activities. Successful partnership working emerges out of these relationships and should be supported by the creative use of technology to encourage agile working and the provision of data that enables officers to work and understand real-time challenges at a distance from the workplace.

Problem-Solving for Twenty-First Century Policing

Collaborative community policing models have become the model of choice for democratic police agencies seeking to enhance legitimacy and build public confidence although there remain significant critiques of the extent to which this has been successful (Skogan, 2008). There is recognition that much progress has been made in engaging communities with policing across jurisdictions, but there is a general consensus that the rights and needs of victims are yet to become a core element of day-to-day policing which remains offender-oriented and process driven. The limitations of community policing endeavours arise because models of policing were not fundamentally reconfigured to deliver new aspirations. As such, the historical purposes of policing that we highlighted at the start of the book prevail with their focus upon social control, law enforcement, crime prevention, and the protection of the interests of the state. Community policing is often subsumed into these ways of thinking about policing rather than presenting a challenge to existing ways of thinking about policing.

The focus upon problem-solving, reflective practice, evidence synthesis, and democratic policing seeks to take policing through this next century with a stronger scientific underpinning. There may be more radical changes to come as police find ways of addressing primary or secondary victimisation and reduce the effects of victimisation on the community and engage communities in the reform process through radical forms of governance. Twenty-first century policing requires police organisations to think about how they conceptualise policing and then, in more practical terms, assess how they should address issues of structure, governance, partnership, roles, functions, and problem-solving in line with this conceptualisation of policing. It is these issues of thinking about policing, the role of evidence, and what research can contribute to your understanding and conceptualisation of policing that we turn to next.

Note

1 Weitekamp et al. (2003: 310) have elaborated on this by suggesting that "All community-oriented police work includes problem-solving strategies, but not all problem-oriented police work is necessarily community oriented."

References

Bittner, E. (1970) *The Functions of the Police in Modern Society*. Washington, DC: National Institute of Justice.

Bottomley, J., Wright, M. and Pryjmachuk, S. (2020) *Critical Thinking Skills for Your Policing Degree*. St Albans: Critical Publishing.

Brodeur, J. (2010) *The Policing Web*. London: Routledge.

Chan, J. (1996) Changing Police Culture. *British Journal of Criminology*. 36(1): 109–134.

Chan, J. (1997) *Changing Police Culture: Policing in a Multicultural Society*. Cambridge: Cambridge University Press.

Christopher, S. (2015) The police service can be a critical reflective practice... if it wants. *Policing: A Journal of Policy and Practice*. 9(4): 326–339.

College of Policing (2014) *National Decision Model*. Available at: www.app.college.police.uk/app-content/national-decision-model/?s=

College of Policing (2020) *Code of Ethics*. Available at: www.college.police.uk/What-we-do/Ethics/Ethics-home/Pages/Code-of-Ethics.aspx

College of Policing (2021a) *Crime Reduction Toolkit*. Available at: https://whatworks.college.police.uk/toolkit/Pages/Welcome.aspx

College of Policing (2021b) *National Police Library*. Available at: www.college.police.uk/library

College of Policing (2021c) *Policing and Crime Reduction Research Map*. Available at: https://whatworks.college.police.uk/Research/Research-Map/Pages/Research-Map.aspx

Crawford, A. (2005) *Plural Policing: The Mixed Economy of Visible Patrols in England and Wales*. Bristol: Policy Press.

Eck, J. and Spelman, W. (1987) *Problem-Solving: Problem-Oriented Policing in Newport News*. Washington, DC: Police Executive Research Forum.

Goldstein, H. (1977) *Policing a Free Society*. Cambridge, MA: Ballinger.

Goldstein, H. (1979) Improving policing: A problem-oriented approach. *Crime & Delinquency*. 25(2): 236–258.

Goldstein, H. (1990) *Problem-Oriented Policing*. New York, NY: McGraw-Hill.

Goldstein, H. (1997) LEN interview: Herman Goldstein, the father of problem-oriented policing. *Law Enforcement News*. 23(461): 8–11.

Goldstein, H. (2010) On further developing problem-oriented policing: The most critical need, the major impediments, and a further proposal. In J. Knutsson (ed.) *Problem-Oriented Policing: From Innovation to Mainstream. Crime Prevention Studies Vol. 15*, 13–48. London: Lyne Rienner.

Kolb, D. (1984) *Experiential Learning: Experience as the Source of Learning and Development*. Englewood Cliffs: Prentice Hall.

Leigh, A., Read, T. and Tilley, N. (1996) *Brit POP II: Problem-Oriented Policing*. Police Research Group. Crime Detection and Prevention Series Paper 93. London: Home Office.

Loveday, B. (2018) Police and crime commissioners: Developing and sustaining a new model of police governance in England and Wales. *International Journal of Police Science and Management*. 20(1): 28–37.

Manning, P. (1993) Toward a theory of police organization: Polarities and change. Paper presented at the *International Conference on Social Change in Policing*. 3–5 August, Taipei.

Nolan, M. (1995) *Standards in Public Life: First Report of the Committee on Standards in Public Life*. Available at: https://assets.publishing.service.gov.uk/government/uploads/system/uploads/attachment_data/file/336919/1stInquiryReport.pdf

O'Malley, P. and Hutchinson, S. (2007) Reinventing prevention: Why did crime prevention develop so late? *British Journal of Criminology*. 47(3): 373–389.

Paterson, C. (2011) Adding value? A review of the international literature on the role of higher education in police training and education. *Police Practice and Research: An International Journal*. 12(4): 286–297.

Paterson, C. and Pollock, E. (2016) Global shifts in the policing of mental health. *Policing: A Journal of Policy and Practice*. 10(2): 91–94.

Reiner, R. (2019) *The Politics of the Police*. Oxford: Oxford University Press.

Sienkiewicz-Malyjurek, K. (2019) Relational behaviours and organisational capabilities in public safety networks. *Management Decision*. 58(2): 1067–1083.

Skinns, L. (2008) A prominent participant? The role of the state in police partnerships. *Policing and Society*. 18(3): 311–321.

Skogan, W. and Hartnett, S. (1997) *Community Policing, Chicago Style*. New York: Free Press.

Skogan, W. (2008) Why reforms fail. *Policing and Society*. 18(1): 23–34.

Weitekamp, E., Kerner, H. and Meier, U. (2003) Community and problem-oriented policing in the context of restorative justice. In E. Weitekamp and H. Kerner (eds.) *Restorative Justice in Context: International Practice and Directions*. Cullompton: Willan.

Chapter 7

The Evolution of Evidence-Based Policing

Introduction

Evidence-based policing (EBP) is the tool that the College of Policing wants police officers to use to understand what the best available evidence is to inform their day-to-day practice as well as new policy, strategies, and tactics. Evidence has always played a central role in policing through criminal investigations to the preparation of cases for presentation at court, but the global development of the EBP movement has made the links between police, policing, and criminology much more explicit. This is particularly evident with the introduction of a new police education qualifications framework (PEQF) that has embedded criminology and social scientific research into initial and continuing preparation of police officers for their role. EBP is not a peculiarly British concept but a new way of thinking about professional policing which is taking root across many parts of the globe. It is also a contested concept, and this chapter introduces different perspectives and definitions of EBP and links them to the different theoretical perspectives introduced in the first half of the book.

Prior to doing this, the chapter provides a short history of policing research to provide some context for the emergence of EBP as an institutionally focused applied research tool. This historical context is important as it demonstrates how different schools of thought about police and policing have emerged at different historical junctures and influenced the types of research that get undertaken. This context helps explain why different perspectives on EBP might exist. In England and Wales, EBP is a form of police-owned science, and an approach to research that is officially supported by the College of Policing via its inclusion in policing undergraduate degrees. Yet, there are many different critical perspectives that surround the role of policing research in different societies and lots of different forms of EBP that have emerged in different parts of the world. These critical discussions about policing research and EBP will be followed with a more in-depth investigation of research tools and skills in Chapter 8.

DOI: 10.4324/9781003081012-7

Researching the Police

Criminological research of police organisations in England and Wales was scarce and limited in its focus until after the Second World War although there is valuable historical data which allows us to research the role of the professional police since their establishment in 1829. Early Reithian histories of police organisations in England and Wales were named after Charles Reith whose prominent historical accounts of the idea of police and policing and the principles that underpinned their role and function in society shaped early scholarly investigations into how the police worked (Reith, 1938, 1956). Reith's over-arching narrative focused upon the civilising potential of police institutions in comparison to the historical reliance upon militarised responses to problems of social order (Reith, 1938). Reith tells a heartwarming story of enlightenment era progress delivered by benevolent and radical police reformers that was eventually challenged by the narratives of social conflict that became more prominent during the 1960s and 1970s onwards as a Marxist critique of the police institution emerged that challenged the Reithian vision of policing by consent and purely benevolent police role and function. Viewed from a distance, both the Reithian vision and the Marxist critique were inflected with ideological simplicity. The police were either on the side of the citizen and a consensus vision of shared progress or they were on the side of a malignant state whereby the police were a tool to be used by powerful elites to coerce and control wider society. It was not until the 1980s that police research took on a more managerial and explicitly applied role with the aim of improving police efficiency and effectiveness.

In the 1980s, police research took what has since been described in criminology as an administrative turn (Garland, 1996) as the increasing influence of the UK Home Office re-asserted the government's presence and influence over policing research. This administrative turn has a direct lineage through to EBP with its focus upon delivering evidence-based effectiveness at the street-level and evidence-based strategy to shape how policing adapts and evolves as an organisation. The successes of administrative criminology supported the development of what became known as the new police science and moulded policing scholarship into three divergent, although inter-linked, schools of social scientific and criminological study.

- Sociological analysis of police and policing
- Cultural and Marxist analysis of police and policing
- Administrative analysis of police and policing (the new police science)

The next section reviews each of these broadly defined areas in turn to set the context for the emergence of EBP in the early part of the twenty-first century.

Sociological Analysis of Police and Policing

Michael Banton's (1964) "The Policeman in the Community" is widely regarded as the first in-depth sociological study of the police in the United Kingdom. Banton critiqued the consensus narrative about police officers as the thin blue line between crime and deviance or social order and provided a more nuanced portrayal of the day-to-day role of police officers. Banton's work, like Egon Bittner and Jerome Skolnick who were undertaking similar work in the United States (Bittner, 1970; Skolnick, 1966), emphasised the importance of the police peacekeeping role and his immersive approach to undertaking this research encouraged others to undertake similar types of research studies.

Banton, Bittner, and Skolnick were undertaking research at a time when there was a growth in social conflict and allegations of police corruption and misconduct were gaining a higher public profile. Banton's study also emerged at the same time as the Police Act 1964 which produced the most significant reforms to policing in this historical period and which gave the insights about the peacekeeping function greater historical relevance. Concerns surrounding police inefficiency and the need for more effective forms of governance provided Banton with a prominent position as a sociologist documenting the real-life challenges of the role of the police officer in society. Banton's work highlighted the critical importance of the relationship between police officers and communities and the wide discretion that police officers had to interpret the law. Banton's analysis of the role of the police officers continued to depict a consensual vision of society, but his critical contribution, along with his American counterparts, was to situate our understanding of policing firmly within the relationships between police officers and wider society. These innovative ethnographic accounts of policing laid the methodological groundwork for a much more radical shift in policing scholarship that emerged in the 1970s.

Cultural Analysis of Police and Policing

The sociological focus upon relations between police officers and wider society soon developed into analysis of the cultural significance of police officers and police institutions in British society. If you think for a moment about the images that first appear in your brain when you think about the term "police" or "policing," then you will have a sense of what cultural analysis of policing looks like. The police are a cultural institution that portrays certain symbolic aspects of Britishness in the same way as images of Buckingham Palace, Oxford and Cambridge universities, or people eating fish and chips do. Police images can also be constructed in much more negative ways, and the historical period in which these cultural analyses emerged was often described as experiencing a crisis in police legitimacy (Hall et al., 1978). Inspired by Banton and others, researchers used ethnographic approaches to submerge themselves in the culture and experiences of front-line policing. A body of research emerged out of this historical period which focused upon police culture through the work of scholars such as Reiner (see Bowling et al., 2019, in its fifth edition), Holdaway (1984), and Fielding (1988). Building upon previous insights into the important role of police discretion, this literature highlighted the key function of "cop culture" in everyday police work and the ways in which public expectations and police officer interpretations of these expectations informed the way in which policing was delivered to the public and the wide diversity of experiences of policing by different social groups.

Building upon the earlier work of Banton and the associated work of scholars like Lipsky (1980) in the United States, these researchers analysed the impact of police culture upon the street-level administration of justice by police officers and their role as "street-level bureaucrats." These studies drew attention to the comparative invisibility of street-level policing and the distance between police officers accounts of policing and the accounts of sergeants and inspectors whose supervisory and managerial roles distanced them from the street. This police culture literature quickly differentiated between the experiences of "street cops" compared to managers (Reuss-Ianni and Reuss Ianni, 1983) and identified the importance of "canteen culture" and generalised conceptualisations of police officer characteristics in informing how street-level policing was delivered (Bowling et al., 2019; Waddington, 1999a).

The first phase of this cultural literature emphasised the negative aspects of police culture and the threat of unfair and inequitable policing to groups that were structurally minoritised according to age, ethnicity, gender, religion, sexuality, or class. This body of literature represented the times it was written in as police institutions experienced ongoing crises of legitimacy during times of significant social unrest and several high-profile police and political corruption scandals. Public trust in policing decreased and crime rates increased amidst social and economic turbulence. The tense relationship between the police and minority ethnic groups provided the most startling illustration of mistrust amongst the general public about the role of the state in civil society. Between 1980 and 1985, England experienced ongoing civil unrest with continued outbreaks of urban disorder (or riots) and increasingly political conflicts between marginalised poor communities, an increasingly diverse society, and unreformed police forces.

A second phase of academic work on police culture emerged in the 1990s which provided a more nuanced and appreciative interpretation of the impact of occupational cultures on street-level policing (Chan, 1996; Waddington, 1999b). These research studies again represented the times they were written in with increased social and economic prosperity reflected in lower levels of social conflict, decreasing crime rates and police reforms that increasingly re-defined police forces in the terminology that we use today of, the Police Service. Chan's work in Australia was delivered during a period of significant police reform and, slowly, England and Wales were moving in a similar vein with sustained reforms to the governance and management of the police that was increasingly captured in a growing body of administrative police analysis undertaken by universities, think tanks, and the UK government.

Administrative Analysis of Police and Policing

In response to the growth in critical accounts of policing, the UK government commenced a series of radical reforms and also developed its own prominent policing research body in the Home Office. The establishment of the Home Office Research Group and the growth in studies of policing that emerged during this period illustrated the emergence of a more administrative school of policing scholarship which was conceptually distinct from the more critical cultural and Marxist literature that preceded it and the sociological observations that emerged after the Second World War and continued, albeit with decreasing regularity due to more tightly focused research funding agendas.

Challenging the actions of the police is an essential function of democratic societies and the more critical schools of thought provide this function although often with little, if any, engagement with the police. The administrative school that emerged out of the UK Home Office had a more explicit aim to improve the quality of the relationship between the police and civic society and to deliver more efficient, effective, and equitable policing services and would develop into what is now referred to as crime science (Smith and Tilley, 2005) and the new police science (Weisburd and Neyroud, 2012). Policing in democratic societies takes place within dynamic contexts and the police need to represent wider values (Durkheim's collective conscience) in terms of agreed notions of social justice, inclusion, fairness, transparency, and international human rights standards. These requirements of democratic policing have increasingly come to the fore with the evolution of EBP which embraces research on police professionalism, accountability, legitimacy, and the efficiency of service delivery. The development of a strong, critical but applied knowledge-base to underpin policing policy developments identified the clear link between the professional use of discretion, understood as making appropriate street-level situational judgements, and the broader democratic issues of ensuring public accountability and police legitimacy. The accumulation of these insights made academic analysis of the police role from all of the perspectives above an essential component of the function of criminology. The concept of EBP, as defined by the College of Policing, retains a comparatively narrow and administrative focus (Williams and Cockcroft, 2018), but it does reflect the concerns and interests of sociological, cultural, and Marxist scholarship, albeit in a very different language to these academic disciplines and traditions. The impact of this work is clearly evidenced in the strategic shift to a Police Service and the continued emphases placed upon community engagement and the critical importance of police legitimacy and transparent forms of public accountability. Recent developments in police curricula include understandings of vulnerability, the need for inter-agency working, and the more complex skills sets required from police officers have all been influenced by international criminological insights.

Reflective Task

Which of these criminological research traditions do you think benefits wider society the most? The answer you provide to this question will provide some clues to the criminological theories and perspectives that you will favour throughout your studies.

From Criminological Research to Evidence-Based Policing?

EBP is a *new* and *contested* idea although the concept (concept is basically another word for an idea) of evidence-based practice is not new at all. Evidence-based practice underpins most professions and has a long history in professions associated with policing such as law, social work, and probation as well as other different sectors of work such as health and education. The health sector probably has the most rigorous scientific history when it comes to evidence-based practice and for the most obvious reasons. The example I hear cited most often is, *would you get on an operating table if you did not intrinsically trust the organisation and people who would be operating on you to have the appropriate expertise?* Similarly, why would we give people powers to arrest and deprive liberty unless we intrinsically trusted them, their professional judgements, and the evidence-base that was used to inform these judgements. In both these instances, we expect our professionals to devise strategy and operational practice based upon the best available evidence.

So, back to policing. Policing is almost unique amongst British criminal justice professions in not having historically required its employees to undertake a minimum of undergraduate level degree study where they learn about the evidence-base that underpins practice. Policing has historically been understood as a craft-based vocation where new police officers learn from older police officers about how to police their communities. This approach to learning about work empowers oral traditions, but it also has the potential to generate resistance to new ideas and change by embedding new recruits into a culture of "this is the way we do things around here" (Schein, 1992). This near 200-year-old interpretation of policing as a craft-based vocation is changing with the College of Policing in England and Wales pushing an agenda which seeks to see policing become an evidence-based profession supported by degree-level education.

So, going back to the opening statement, EBP is new but, because it is new, it remains slightly unclear what EBP is, or means (see Wood et al., 2017 for further discussion). It is an immature idea that, at the time of writing, is still finding its place in policing in England and Wales. For this reason, this chapter will refer to EBP as a contested concept, and the rest of this chapter will introduce you to some of these different and sometimes competing interpretations of the meaning and role of EBP. We will introduce you to different definitions of EBP and different applications of EBP using different methodologies. But for now, it is time to introduce, first, the relatively recent history of EBP and, second, the different and contested definitions of EBP.

As Chapter 6 acknowledged, EBP has evolved out of an idea that emerged in the 1980s called Problem-Oriented Policing (POP). POP starts off with the simple idea that if police officers and organisations are just reacting to calls from the public all the time, then they are not looking for the problems that underpin and cause these calls for service. This is a cyclical challenge for people as the underpinning problems that cause crime are constantly changing. It is at this point that criminological theory becomes useful as the theoretical tools that we have introduced in this book help us to understand what causes crime in the first place.

A good example of this cyclical challenge is the war on illegal drugs. Has anyone noticed drug problems disappear when someone is arrested for dealing drugs? Well, no. Because… that does not ever happen. In practice, many drug markets are so well established that as soon as someone is removed from the street after arrest, they are almost immediately replaced by someone else who is interested in the benefits of the lucrative but generally short career of the street-level drug dealer (Sweeney et al., 2008). As long as the demand for illegal drugs remains, then people will attempt to meet this demand with supply. Economic theory tells us that the removal of supply will drive up prices, yet it does not necessarily reduce demand and therefore does not stop the crime problem. A problem-oriented approach would look at both the demand and supply aspects of the drug problem and attempt to reduce the market for illegal drugs in a sustained manner by addressing the full range of criminal behaviours and harms associated with this market (see, e.g., Sutton, 2010).

In the above example, the law enforcement response to the crime problem is quite straightforward but the underpinning problem is dynamic (always changing) and often difficult to understand. Hence, a strong and up-to-date evidence-base is required to inform strategic- and operational-level decision-making across police organisations. In the 1990s, Larry Sherman took the ideas of evidence-based practice from other professions and started to apply them via a methodology he called EBP (Sherman, 1998). Sherman, and many others, argued strongly that policing strategies and tactics could be much more efficient and effective if they were based upon a rigorous and up-to-date evidence base.

A quick aside: academics love the word rigorous. In fact, so do a lot of professions because it means you have done a lot of work to come to a specific conclusion. Most importantly, a rigorous evidence-base is where you draw conclusions about something after reading and analysing multiple sources and case studies. It is important to understand that we do not draw our own conclusions on an issue by reading one source and then repeating it. We read one source and then test how reliable it is by reading another source. And then, if we find something different in that second source, we move on to a third source. And so on, and so on until we are confident that we have come to a clear conclusion based upon this rigorously interrogated evidence-base.

As this chapter notes, there are competing perspectives surrounding what the best way might be to generate evidence to support policing practice. Outside of Sherman's work on EBP, Ken Pease and other crime scientists have argued for the use of Bayesian statistics to help support POP and to determine what reduces crime levels. Drawing on Sparrow's (2016) critique of EBP as an academic invasion of policing territory, Pease and others argue for the benefits of a Bayesian approach in drawing upon police knowledge first and continually testing this professional knowledge-base with the use of academic evidence rather than adopting the Sherman EBP model where the academic evidence is the starting point (Roach and Pease, 2017).

Pease and Laycock (2018) argue thus,

- By and large, policing experience rather than research is what makes for credibility amongst police officers.
- The precepts of realism can be applied at the individual officer level as much as at the organisation level.
- The major advantage of applying realism at the individual level is that it feeds directly into experience.
- The primary obstacle to application at the individual level is a lack of time and limited access to what has gone before.
- Our vision is of a simple requirement upon officers explicitly to anticipate the results of their actions and adjust their predictions in the light of what happens, with a back office facility providing requested information about what has happened before, and conducting such sophisticated analyses as may be required.

Bayesian statistics involves the use of, first, prior probability, where you predict that something is likely to happen, second, evidence, where you test what happens and, third, using the accuracy of your findings to make future probabilistic decisions. This process continues as an iterative cycle to allow refinement of strategy and tactics (Harsanyi, 1983) and thus combines professional and academic knowledge and practices.

Anyway, back again to Larry Sherman and EBP. Sherman published his initial ideas about what EBP might be in a number of articles in the 1990s and 2000s (a couple of these articles are in the reference list at the end) and started what became a movement towards EBP in the United States. This shift towards policing strategies and tactics requiring an evidence-base now exists across many parts of the globe although there are lots of different interpretations of what EBP might mean to different people and what is seen to be "good" or rigorous evidence. There are lots of people who were inspired by Sherman but have subsequently gone off to develop ideas in their own way. That is how science and scientific progress works and in the next section we will look at some of these different perspectives on EBP.

The College of Policing (2020a) asserts "In an EBP approach, police officers and staff create, review and use the best available evidence to inform and challenge policies, practices and decisions."

Did that clear things up for you? I thought not. Some history might help.

Reflective Task

Here are some different definitions of EBP: list the key differences and similarities that you can see between these definitions. We will return to this task at the end of the chapter.

> Evidence-based policing is the use of the best available research on the outcomes of police work to implement guidelines and evaluate agencies, units and officers using the best research.
>
> (Sherman, 1998: 3)

> Evidence-based policing means that research, evaluation, analysis and scientific processes should have a seat at the table in law enforcement decision making about tactics, strategies and policing.
>
> (Lum and Koper, 2017: 3)

A Potted History of Research, Evidence, and Thinking About Policing

For most of the twentieth century, the prevailing mode of thought in western democracies had been that the police could solve crime and disorder challenges through a reactive approach. In the past two decades of the twentieth century, this perspective started to shift in England and Wales and other western democracies with a re-birth of community policing philosophies and an incremental shift to a more proactive strategic approach to crime problems that sought to intervene, where possible, prior to a crime taking place. This was not a new idea but a re-discovery of an old one, echoing the policing style proposed in "The Instructions and Police Orders for 1829–30," largely attributed to (albeit not without contest, see Lentz and Chares, 2007) Sir Robert Mayne, Sir Charles and Rowan and Sir Robert Peel, during the birth of the professional police in England and Wales:

> It should be understood at the outset, that the object to be attained is 'the prevention of crime'. To this end every effort of the police is to be directed. The security of persons and property, the preservation of the public tranquillity, and all the other objects of a police establishment, will thus be better effected than by the detection and punishment of the offender after he has succeeded in committing the crime.
>
> (Mayne and Rowan, 1829: 3)

The re-discovery of community policing and its evolution alongside POP during the late 1980s and 1990s signalled a return to Peelian thinking and offered the police an alternative to reactive and single incident-focused responses. The crisis of legitimacy (Hall et al., 1978) that characterised images of policing during the later 1970s and 1980s emerged during a period of significant social and political unrest. The backlash to the politicisation of the police during the 1984–1985 Miner's Strike and the urban disorders that characterised the early-mid-1980s led to a re-assessment of the police role in the community and, as community policing philosophies grew in popularity, an acknowledgement of the central role of the community in identifying and reporting crime and disorder to the police. Henceforth, this renewed recognition that the police are more likely to successfully tackle crime where policing strategies are based within and informed by community members themselves provided political support for the police to develop problem-oriented partnerships with other agencies (such as schools, colleges, local community agencies, and other statutory bodies that included local authorities, the Probation Service and social work) to identify and address the underlying causes of crime, deviance, and disorder. Thus, the crisis in police legitimacy and the political drive that it initiated in terms of partnership approaches generated momentum towards a growing influence from criminologically informed knowledge upon policing via the UK Home Office.

Some Additional Reading

You can learn more about the UK Home Office's influence over policing and crime prevention policy through the 1980s and 1990s by accessing the full set of reports they produced which are now held in the National Archives – https://discovery.nationalarchives.gov.uk/details/r/C13431866

In the twenty-first century, global changes in the governance and delivery of policing services led to new and innovative ways of thinking about and responding to crime, with a growing input from civil society organisation and the commercial sector, in particular through technological contributions (Bayley and Shearing, 2001). The dynamic nature of social changes along-side the impact of globalisation has seen policing shift slowly towards a more community-oriented and democratically inclusive style that aligns with other modes of liberal democratic politics. Examples of this include the establishment of Police and Crime Commissioners who, as elected officials, hold regional responsibility for the co-ordination and resourcing of responses to crime and disorder and have legal powers to remove Chief Constables from office.

Both community policing and POP remain partially complete endeavours, yet they are critical drivers for the evolution of EBP which provides the momentum and change necessary to embed Goldstein's problem-based approach into the day-to-day reality of the police profession. EBP, in its College of Policing form, thus has the potential to address some of the challenges that POP and evidence-based approaches have encountered in the shape of police organisational structures, culture, and leadership (Mastrofski et al., 2002; Skogan, 2008). As Sherman (2013) notes, EBP is both an organisational change tool and a means of embedding better use of data into policing.

Before we look specifically at EBP in England and Wales, it is worth reviewing similar developments in other English-speaking western democracies. Police in the United States and Australia have undergone similar reform efforts to England and Wales as part of an evolution of the prevailing model of crime control and enforcement towards a more evidence-informed approach that seeks to galvanise support amongst and local communities, and increase police legitimacy. Community policing and POP are international best practice models which encourage increased partnerships between the police and the community to improve understandings of local problems and potential triggers for disorderly or criminal behaviour that impact upon the quality of community life. The evidence-base which reviews these reforms remains subject to much debate amongst criminologists with critics suggesting that community-oriented discourse often remains distanced from operational realities which continue to be dominated by a law enforcement ethos (McCold and Wachtel, 1998; Skogan, 2008). These obstacles to the implementation of community and POP are common across geographical boundaries and indicative of enduring tensions concerning the purposes of policing and who is responsible for co-ordinating and resourcing responses to crime in twenty-first century democracies (Manning, 2010).

In different ways, community policing and POP are components of an enduring police reform movement. The drive to a more accountable, transparent, and democratic form of policing (Manning, 2010) has global-level similarities across the English-speaking western democracies but also distinct localised experiences in individual nation states and the various policing structures that exist within these states. These reform endeavours have met with significant resistance (see Skogan, 2008 for an overview) and are often felt by police officers and police organisations as having been imposed upon them by external forces. It is within this tension that we see the political economy of policing made visible as different perspectives on the overarching purpose of policing come into conflict. It becomes clear at this point that the visions of policing that exist in political communities, in think tanks and campaigning groups, amongst academics and with senior police leaders, managers, and police officers are very different. While EBP emerged as yet another reform endeavour that was being done to police, it also presents an opportunity for police organisations and police officers to drive reform from the bottom-up in a way that might align with the political ideas that underpin community policing endeavours.

While the concepts of community policing and POP seek to improve relationships between communities and police officers, they have often struggled to provide an effective change mechanism through which to realise their strategic ambitions (Goldstein, 2003; Sherman, 1998, 2013). The challenge of engagement with implementation science and organisational development has increasingly been recognised by police organisations and has led to enduring calls across international jurisdictions for a much more radical transformation of policing (Bazemore, 2000; Moore and Forsythe, 1995). The challenges that police organisations encounter across the globe may have many similarities but, at the local level, a detailed appreciation of police organisation's history, present, and future trajectory is required along-side an understanding of the relationship between policing and other forms of social and political development.

Canada (Council of Canadian Academies, 2014) and Ireland (Commission on the Future of Policing in Ireland, 2018) have recently undertaken funda-mental reviews of policing. However, the absence of a conceptual and philo-sophical understanding of policing as distinct from the institution of "the police" often results in tinkering around the edges of police reform (Vitale, 2017) rather than delivering on the calls for fundamental reform (Paterson and Williams, 2018). It can be argued that EBP should not just be understood as a continuation of the community policing and POP reform movement but that it is the mechanism for change that Goldstein (2003) and Moor et al. (2009) were both calling for (albeit in very different ways).

Viewed through a long-term lens of incremental change, EBP builds upon John Alderson's (1979: 199) vision of a new style of policing in England and Wales, which would, "dispel criminogenic social conditions, create trust in communities, strengthen feelings of security and curb public disorder." With the establishment of the College of Policing, these bold ambitions are now being supported by the evolution of a police-owned science that seeks to re-invigorate the Peelian principle of policing by consent as a part of a fun-damental re-assessment of what professional policing means. The growth of EBP in England and Wales cannot be separated from the development of policing undergraduate degrees, the establishment of the College of Policing, and this aim to align policing as a career route with other long-established degree entry routes in similar professions such as law, social work, and the Probation Service.

Contemporary policing thus requires new skills sets, attributes, and experiences to deliver scientifically supported proactive policing strategies, to use informed discretion in an appropriate and lawful manner, and to intervene with social problems before they evolve into more serious conflicts. The complexity of this contemporary police role is captured in the need for police officers to develop collaborative relationships with a range of statutory (local authorities, schools, health services, etc.) and non-statutory agencies (charities, community groups, campaign groups, etc.) as well as those communities who experience crime and policing. The twenty-first century police officer must therefore adopt a leadership position within the community to help keep the peace, negotiate conflict, and coordinate attempts to address social problems that they have little direct control over (Weitekamp et al., 2003). The argument has long been that such a community leadership role will generate a more positive response from communities and an appreciation of police officers as problem-solvers rather than authoritarian law enforcers (Bradford and Jackson, 2010; Wycoff and Skogan, 1994: 379).

The emergent industrialised modernism of the nineteenth century drove the police and criminal justice reforms that formed our current criminal justice process and these systems have survived for nearly 200 years. This nineteenth century legacy needs reimagining again within the twenty-first century context of globalisation, mass migration, and the digital information revolutions. Technology, government, and businesses are already radically re-shaping themselves within these conditions to reflect our changing communities of interest, decreasing co-location and enhanced virtual communication. There is little doubt that this current social realignment is analogous to the period leading up to the initiation of a series of police reforms in 1829.

Mastrofski et al. (2002) and Skogan (2008) have provided compelling accounts related to why reform endeavours from the community policing era have often met with short-term successes but longer-term failures. Amongst the many arguments, key issues include tensions between community-oriented and law enforcement purposes, cultural dispositions towards crime-fighting amongst both police officers and the structural command and control legacy of police hierarchies and their evolution out of the military structures that preceded the 1829 reforms. At the street level, empowered police officers with enhanced discretion equates to reduced control over police officers and anxious police managers (Skogan, 2008). These challenges are thus not just police problems but social challenges as societies move away from modernist forms of control in the workplace to more networked models of working at a distance.

The Rise of Evidence-Based Policing

EBP is a key facilitator of the strategic changes to policing envisaged in future decades. Policing, in its widest and not just "police" sense, is expected to be influenced by wider social, political, and cultural changes that include the growing influence of the digital cybersphere upon crime and policing responses, the evolving role of artificial intelligence, workforce automation, rising inequality, aging populations, and global population flows driven by climate changes and conflict (College of Policing, 2020b). As society changes, its policing needs to adapt too and EBP is a tool that seeks to ensure that policing policy, strategy, and tactics are based upon the most up-to-date assessments of problems and not out of date assumptions.

The National Police Chiefs' Council has added strategic urgency to these developments by stating that EBP needs to be embedded in everyday practice by 2025 (NPCC, 2020). The prominence of EBP as a facilitator of organisational behaviour and change has made the links between police, policing, and criminology (as well as other academic disciplines) more explicit, particularly through the introduction of a new PEQF that has embedded criminology into the initial training, education and preparation of police officers for their role.

The concept of EBP first emerged in a 1998 paper by Larry Sherman which he presented at the Police Foundation. In this paper, Sherman (1998: 1) noted that,

> The new paradigm of evidence-based medicine holds important implications for policing. It suggests that doing research is not enough and the proactive efforts are required to push accumulated research evidence into practice through national and community guidelines. These guidelines can then focus in-house evaluations of what works best across agencies, units, victims and officers.

Sherman's ideas about a clearer relationship between research evidence and police practice were not necessarily novel. Indeed, Sherman acknowledges the intellectual debt he owes to Berkeley Police Chief August Vollmer who partnered with his local university in the early twentieth century to promulgate the idea that there should be a closer relationship between science and policing. For over a decade, Sherman had positioned medicine as the profession that criminal justice and policing should learn from with its strong scientific evidence-base that informed practice alongside its advanced training in scientific methods. Sherman thus drew upon the work of Goldstein (1979, 1990) that we introduced in Chapter 6 to push a more proactive and methodologically rigorous approach to solving problems but also recognised that medicine had experienced many challenges in successfully implementing evidence-based practices.

EBP thus acknowledges that science presents a battleground between research and practice and that EBP is a strategy that seeks to resolve the tensions between the immediate street-level demands of police practice and lab-based research environments (with a multitude of police chiefs and managers in between). As Sherman (1998: 3) acknowledges,

> Just as policing has become more proactive at dealing with crime, researchers are becoming more proactive about dealing with practice.

The evolution of evidence-based practice and Sherman's work in the United States had parallels in the United Kingdom where the Home Office had been targeting crime prevention funding towards applied research that could inform more efficient and effective mechanisms to reduce volume crimes such as car theft and burglary (Tilley and Laycock, 2018). This preventive turn in thinking about how to control crime has been widely appraised in criminological literature as part of the shift of governmental thinking from inclusive welfarist models to hollowed-out neoliberal approaches that attempt to shift the costs of crime control on to communities, businesses, and individual citizens (Garland, 1996).

EBP thus shifts the onus for finding the most efficient and effective forms of policing on to individual police agencies rather than central government, with the College of Policing as the facilitator and supporter of this change. According to Sherman's (1998: 4) Police Foundation paper, EBP involves two types of research:

1   Basic research about what works best in controlled environments
2   Ongoing assessment and evaluation of how police organisations implement best practice evidence

The first type of research is that which has traditionally been generated by universities in partnership with professions, but the second type of research extends this remit to research either generated through collaborations or by police organisations themselves. It is this latter type of research that brings us up to date with recent UK developments via the College of Policing in England and Wales and the Scottish Institute for Policing Research as police practice has historically been shaped by local customs and culture that produce a form of craft-based rather than evidence-based knowledge. Thus, the development of EBP is not just about the integration of research and evidence into police practice but also the science of implementation and the generation of a cultural shift towards ongoing research, evaluation, and development.

While the term EBP is most closely associated with Sherman's work, the principles of collaborative research generation for the purposes of improving police practice has spread widely at the local, national, and international levels. The Harvard Police Executive Sessions and the International Police

Executive Symposium have both driven international police-academic collaborations from the United States, whereas the Cambridge University Police Executive Programme and Sherman's collaboration with the National Police Academy in Hyderabad had similar impacts in the United Kingdom and India. Sherman moved to Cambridge University as Wolfson Professor of Criminology in 2007 and helped to embed the idea of EBP into already ongoing changes to police organisations in England and Wales. The principles of evidence-based practice have since been embedded through the work of the Scottish Institute for Policing which was established in 2007 and the later establishment of the College of Policing in England and Wales in 2012 as well as numerous other smaller collaborations.

It is useful to undertake a brief comparative analysis of the evolution of the Scottish Institute for Policing and the College of Policing in England and Wales to illustrate how perspectives on policing research and EBP can differ. The Scottish Institute was established as a collaboration between Police Scotland, the Scottish Police Authority, and 14 Scottish universities (SIPR, 2020) with the purpose to "carry out high quality independent research and to make evidence-based contributions to policing policy and practice." Conversely, the College of Policing in England and Wales (2020a) is the "professional body for everyone who works for the police service in England and Wales." The College of Policing in England and Wales houses the What Works Centre for Crime Reduction and thus retains ownership, or at least final editorial sign off, of the evidence it publicises unlike the Scottish Institute which has a looser collaborative framework. These subtle structural differences are important as they influence how organisations translate research into practice and make evidence-based practice a policing reality.

The aim of the College of Policing in England and Wales is ultimately to gain Royal Charter status and to establish itself as the source of standardised best practice resources and as the professional guide for police officers to how to use these resources to improve practice. Yet, both the College of Policing and the shift to evidence-based practice remain new and the translation of EBP into everyday practice remains only partially complete. EBP tools such as ATLAS, SARA, and POP may have entered the lexicon of police discourse and language but their impact upon practice has been shaped in a highly uneven manner.

Re-thinking Evidence-Based Policing

Our thinking about EBP already needs some revision. As this chapter has highlighted, evidence-based policing was driven firstly by Sherman's harnessing of the concept of evidence-base practice, but, over the past decade, developments in EBP have been driven largely by commerce and politics with the governmental establishment of policing professional bodies and the policy transfer of EBP from the United States to the United Kingdom and other international jurisdictions. Going back to the beginning of this chapter and the different schools of policing research, it is easy to see how those with a conflict perspective might see EBP as the governmental co-option of independent and sometimes critical research. Sparrow made this point as early as 2011 in his Governing Science paper for the Harvard Kennedy School and has since, along with others, elaborated upon the challenges posed when trying to weave academic science and police practice together using a limited range of methodologies (Sparrow, 2016; Williams and Cockroft, 2018; Wood et al., 2017).

Conversely, those with a more administrative perspective might see EBP as a continuation of the development of a crime science that was formed by the Home Office in the 1980s and continued with the police research series throughout the 1990s before slowly morphing into the What Works Centre for Crime Reduction within the College of Policing. Lastly though, we should not neglect cultural perspectives and the idea that EBP is a vehicle or mechanism for change in a Police Service that is having to adapt to rapid social, political, and technological changes.

Ultimately, there are different and contested understandings of what EBP is or should be, and it is the new generation of police officers who are learning how to use these tools who will decide what the future looks like. Put simply, the purpose of EBP is to provide police officers with tools to help them make sense of policing problems and to provide twenty-first century democratic policing agencies with the transparency and accountability mechanisms that citizens of a digitalised and globalised society demand.

To conclude this chapter, we will return briefly to the earlier task on definitions. Have a look through the definitions below again and make notes on the key difference and distinctions in each perspective. Which one sounds like the evidence-based approach that policing needs?

"Evidence-based policing is the use of the best available research on the outcomes of police work to implement guidelines and evaluate agencies, units and officers using the best research" (Sherman, 1998: 3).

"Evidence-based policing means that research, evaluation, analysis and scientific processes should have a seat at the table in law enforcement decision making about tactics, strategies and policing" (Lum and Koper, 2017: 3).

"In an EBP approach, police officers and staff create, review and use the best available evidence to inform and challenge policies, practices and decisions" (College of Policing, 2020a).

In the following two chapters, we will explore how to make the best use of EBP. Chapter 10 focuses upon the College of Policing's desire for police officers and staff to create their own research and evidence, but, prior to this, we will look at the ways and means of reviewing existing evidence and utilising it to improve police practice.

References

Alderson, J. (1979) *Policing Freedom*. Plymouth: MacDonald and Evans.

Banton, M. (1964) *The Policeman in the Community*. London: Tavistock.

Bayley, D. and Shearing, C. (2001) *The New Structure of Policing: Description, Conceptualization and Research Agenda*. Washington, DC: National Institute of Justice. Available at: www.ncjrs.gov/pdffiles1/nij/187083.pdf

Bazemore, G. (2000) *Community Justice and a Vision of Collective Efficacy: The Case of Restorative Conferencing*. Washington, DC: National Institute of Justice. [Online]. Available at: www.ncjrs.gov/criminal_justice2000/vol_3/03f.pdf

Bittner, E. (1970) *The Functions of the Police in Modern Society*. Maryland: National Institute of Mental Health.

Bowling, B., Reiner, R. and Sheptycki, J. (2019) *The Politics of the Police* (Fifth Edition). Oxford: Oxford University Press.

Bradford, B. and Jackson, J. (2010) *Trust and Confidence in the Police: A Conceptual Review*. Available at: SSRN: https://ssrn.com/abstract=1684508

Chan, J. (1996) Changing police culture. *British Journal of Criminology*. 36(1): 109–134.

College of Policing (2020a) *Evidence-Based Policing*. Available at: https://whatworks. college.police.uk/About/Pages/What-is-EBP.ahspx

College of Policing (2020b) *Policing 2040*. Available at: https://whatworks.college. police.uk/About/News/Pages/Policing2040.aspx

Commission on the Future of Policing in Ireland (2018) *The Future of Policing in Ireland. Report of the Commission on the Future of Policing in Ireland. Dublin, Ireland*. Available at: http://policereform.ie/en/POLREF/Pages/PB18000006

Council of Canadian Academies (2014) *Policing Canada in the 21st Century*. Ottawa: Council of Canadian Academies.

Fielding, N. (1988) *Joining Forces: Police Training, Socialization and Occupational Competence*. London: Routledge.

Garland, D. (1996) The limits of the sovereign state. *British Journal of Criminology*. 36(4): 445–471.

Goldstein, H. (1979) Improving policing: A problem-oriented approach. *Crime & Delinquency*. 25(2): 236–258.

Goldstein, H. (1990) *Problem-Oriented Policing*. New York, NY: McGraw-Hill.

Goldstein, H. (2003) On further developing the problem-oriented policing: The most critical need, the major impediments, and a proposal. *Crime Prevention Studies*. 15: 13–47.

Hall, S., Critcher, C., Jefferson, T., Clarke, J. and Roberts, B. (1978) *Policing the Crisis: Mugging, the State and Law and Order*. London: MacMillan.

Harsanyi, J. (1983) Bayesian decision theory, subjective and objective probabilities, and acceptance of empirical hypotheses. *Synthese*. 57: 341–365.

Holdaway, S. (1984) *Inside the British Police*. Oxford: Blackwell.

Lentz, S. and Chaires, R. (2007) The invention of peel's principles: A study of policing "textbook" history. *Journal of Criminal Justice*. 35(1): 69–79.

Lipsky, M. (1980) *Street-Level Bureaucracy: Dilemmas of the Individual in Public Services*. New York, NY: Russell Sage Foundation.

Lum, C. and Koper, C. (2017) *Evidence-Based Policing: Translating Research into Practice*. Oxford: Oxford University Press.

Manning, P. (2010) *Democratic Policing in a Changing World*. Boulder, CO: Paradigm Publishing.

Mastrofski, S., Reisig, M. and McCluskey, J. (2002) Police disrespect toward the public: An encounter-based analysis. *Criminology*. 40(3): 519–552.

Mayne, C. and Rowan, C. (1829) Principles of policing. *The Morning Post*. Tuesday, September 29.

McCold, P. and Wachtel, B. (1998) *Restorative Policing Experiment: The Bethlehem Pennsylvania Police Family Group Conferencing Project*. Pipersville, PA: Community Service Foundation.

Moor, L., Peters, T. Ponsaers, P. Shapland, J. and van Stokkom, B. (2009) Restorative Practices within community oriented policing, or meeting the needs of the officer on the beat. In L. Moor, T. Peters, P. Ponsaers, J. Shapland, and B. van Stokkom (ed.) *Restorative Policing*, 7–18. Antwerp: Maklu.

Moore, D. and Forsythe, L. (1995) *A New Approach to Juvenile Justice: An Evaluation of Family Conferencing in Wagga Wagga: A Report to the Criminology Research Council*. Wagga Wagga: Centre for Rural Social Research, Charles Sturt University-Riverina.

National Police Chiefs' Council (2020) *Policing Vision 2025*. Available at: www.npcc. police.uk/documents/Policing%20Vision.pdf

Paterson, C. and Williams, A. (2018) Towards victim-oriented police? *Journal of Victimology and Victim Justice*. 1(1): 85–101.

Pease, K. and Laycock, G. (2018) Realist evaluation and Bayesian statistics: A marriage made in heaven? In G. Farrell and A. Sidebottom (eds.) *Realist Evaluation for Crime Science*. London: Routledge.

Reith, C. (1938) *The Police Idea: Its History and Evolution in England in the Eighteenth Century and After*. Oxford: Oxford University Press.

Reith, C. (1956) *A New Study of Police History*. Edinburgh: Oliver and Boyd.

Reuss-Ianni, E. and Reuss-Ianni, F. (1983) Two cultures of policing: Street cops and management cops. In M. Punch (ed.) *Control in the Police Organization*, 251–274. Cambridge, MA: MIT.

Roach and Pease (2017) How to morph experience into evidence. In J. Knutsson and L. Tompson (eds.) *Advances in Evidence-Based Policing*, 84–97. London: Routledge.

Schein, E. (1992) *Organizational Culture and Leadership*. San Francisco, CA: Jossey-Bass.

Scottish Institute for Policing Research (2020) *60 Second Briefing*. Available at: www. sipr.ac.uk/assets/files/60%20second%20briefing%20&%20opportunities.pdf

Sherman, L. (1998) Evidence-Based Policing. Ideas in American Policing Series. Washington, DC: Police Foundation. Available at: www.policefoundation.org/wp-content/uploads/2015/06/Sherman-1998-Evidence-Based-Policing.pdf

Sherman, L. (2013) *The Rise of Evidence-Based Policing: Targeting, Testing and Tracking*. Available at: https://cebcp.org/wp-content/evidence-based-policing/Sherman-TripleT.pdf

Skogan, W. (2008) Why reforms fail. *Policing and Society*. 18(1): 23–34.

Skolnick, J. (1966) *Justice Without Trial: Law Enforcement in a Democratic Society*. New York, NY: Wiley and Sons.

Smith, M. and Tilley, N. (2005) *Crime Science: New Approaches to Preventing and Detecting Crime*. Cullompton: Willan.

Sparrow, M. (2011) *Governing Science*. Executive Session on Policing and Public Safety. Available at: www.ojp.gov/pdffiles1/nij/232179.pdf

Sparrow, M. (2016) *Handcuffed: What Holds Policing Back, and the Keys to Reform*. Washington, DC: Brookings Institution Press.

Sutton, M. (2010) *Stolen Goods Markets: Problem-Oriented Guides for Police*. Available at: https://popcenter.asu.edu/sites/default/files/problems/pdfs/stolen_goods.pdf

Sweeney, T., Turnbull, P. and Hough M. (2008) *Tackling Drug Markets and Distribution Networks in the UK: A Review of the Recent Literature*. London: Institute for Criminal Policy Research.

Tilley, N. and Laycock, G. (2018) Developing a knowledge base for crime prevention: Lessons learned from the British experience. *Crime Prevention and Community Safety*. 20: 228–242. Available at: https://link.springer.com/article/10.1057/s41300-018-0053-8

Vitale, A. (2017) *The End of Policing*. New York, NY: Verso.

Waddington, P. A. J. (1999a) *Policing Citizens*. London: Routledge.

Waddington, P. A. J. (1999b) Police (canteen) sub-culture: An appreciation. *British Journal of Criminology*. 39(2): 287–309.

Weisburd, D. and Neyroud, P. (2012) *Police Science: Towards a New Paradigm*. Washington, DC: National Institute of Justice.

Weitekamp, E., Kerner, H. and Meier, U. (2003) Community and problem-oriented policing in the context of restorative justice. In E. Weitekamp and H. Kerner (eds.) *Restorative Justice in Context: International Practice and Directions*, 304–325. Cullompton: Willan.

Wood, D., Cockroft, T. and Tong, S. (2017) The importance of context and cognitive agency in developing police knowledge. Going beyond the police science discourse. *The Police Journal*. 91(2): 173–187.

Wycoff, M. and Skogan, W. (1994) *Community Policing in Madison: Quality from the Inside Out; An Evaluation of Implementation and Impact; A Final Summary Report Presented to the National Institute of Justice*. Rockville, MD: U.S. Department of Justice.

Chapter 8

Doing Research on Crime and Policing

Introduction

Having observed and reviewed the evolution of evidence-based policing, we can now broaden our research lens to incorporate the wider fields of criminological and social scientific research. As Chapter 7 noted, evidence-based policing is a new idea, and it builds upon hundreds of years of research science and the development and use of a range of different types of research evidence. Our choice of preferred research evidence is influenced by what we want to know, or need to know, and what we value as authentic knowledge. If we have little faith and trust in official statistics, then we may pursue conversations with front-line professionals or offenders to find what we perceive to be a more valid source of knowledge. Conversely, if we think that the views of people bring problematic bias to the generation of knowledge, then we may prioritise the objectivity of statistics. Either way, we make both implicit and explicit decisions when we use and review research on crime and policing, and this chapter provides some context to help inform your methodological decision-making and to help you develop research skills and attributes.

The academic discipline of criminology introduces students and police officers to the potential use of social scientific data in supporting and quality assuring problem-solving methodologies and the decision-making used to address these problems. This chapter critically appraises what is considered to be useful evidence and identifies key public sources of evidence that students can use. The chapter also provides a critical appraisal of the research sources that are often given preference by policing institutions and encourages the reader to focus upon how to use research and data alongside their professional knowledge and personal experiences. Finally, the chapter concludes with an overview of key terminology used in the field of applied research such as effectiveness, impact, and evaluation to help guide students through the sometimes disorienting landscape of evidence-based policing and criminological research.

DOI: 10.4324/9781003081012-8

Useful Evidence?

Let's get started with some fundamentals and consider what we mean when we use the term research. Here is the formal definition of "research" from the Oxford English Dictionary:

> The systematic investigation into and study of materials and sources in order to establish new facts and reach new conclusions.

- So, research is not indiscriminate it involves a *systematic investigation*
- Research has a clear purpose: *to establish new facts and reach new conclusions*
- It involves the use of *materials and sources*

To take the last point first, research involves the study of materials and sources (i.e. evidence). In criminological and policing contexts, these materials and sources tend to be a mixture of *primary sources* such as case materials, interviews, letters, speeches, research articles, or case studies and *secondary sources* such as journal articles, textbooks, dissertations, and commentaries. Furthermore, research has a clear purpose. Most obviously for this book, evidence-based policing is research that seeks to improve police practice, yet wider criminological and social scientific research may seek to question police practices, to interrogate the police organisation, and to compare it with similar institutions in different jurisdictions. So, as we noted in Chapter 7, there are different schools of thought and different academic perspectives that co-exist at any one time in all academic disciplines. Thus, while evidence-based policing prioritises research that improves police practice, it does not mean that you need to limit yourself to this tight definition.

When we undertake research, we are seeking initially to collect, observe, and review data to inform our perspective on a particular issue (Bryman, 2015). We may also continue to the point where we create our own data (which is the focus of Chapter 9). There are several textbooks available which will introduce you to the full research process, and we will summarise some of the insights from these texts across the next two chapters. Please use the reference list as a guide to further interrogate specific research issues that are of interest or use to you. But, before we even consider research generation and creation, we need to review information that is already available to us. There are lots of answers to research questions already out there waiting for us to find them, and we need to review available data before generating anything that is new to ensure we are not just repeating work that others have already done. As the above definition states, the third key component of research is that it is undertaken as part of a systematic investigation. This will sound very familiar to anyone who works in the police profession. The next section provides a closer inspection of what a systematic research investigation might look like.

Reviewing Existing Research

As the practical use of research findings is so often specific to your own context, it is important for you to be able to undertake individual reviews of existing research evidence in a systematic manner. There are some basic tools and methods you can use to do this which will be covered in this section. In most academic textbooks, you will see that this process is referred to as undertaking a literature review, but with the arrival of the digital economy, this language often feels a bit dated. Useful data and information are now readily available from a panoply of multimedia sources, and the challenge for those reviewing this information is to develop a system for identifying what is useful and being able to check the validity, reliability, and credibility of this information against others sources. This section introduces some traditional approaches to undertaking a literature review before moving on to a discussion in the latter part of the chapter on the challenges of undertaking systematic searches of the internet.

You will all have read, watched, and interacted in some way with stories about crime and policing at some point. Everything that we interact with in this way is a potential source of research, and our assumptions about crime and policing are shaped by a mixture of our personal experiences and external sources of information. But, to develop our understanding of crime in a more sophisticated manner, we need to take a systematic approach to the investigation of crime problems, and we need to persistently question our own assumptions about why crimes occur and who commits them by looking for sources of evidence that both support and challenge our initial assumptions.

This next section will illustrate what happens when we research indiscriminately and, following on from this, how we should research in a structured and systematic manner. The rest of the chapter continues to highlight the importance of systematic approaches to research and how this logical and structured approach impacts upon what we find and how those findings are perceived and interpreted by others.

Task 1

1   Choose one specific crime type (anything that interests you; burglary, assault, riot!) and put this into an open access search engine to see what you find.

You will undoubtedly see a lot of search hits, and the tricky next step is to decide which ones to focus upon without being drowned in information. As one of the key challenges for researchers is finding relevant information, this will often require us to use more specific search criteria than we would if were just surfing the web. So, let's have a go at tightening our search criteria.

2   Find the "Advanced Search" option in the search engine you are using.
    You will now be able to narrow your search using date criteria and loca-
    tion criteria. You will also be able to refine your search to more specific
    words, phrases, and criteria. Try looking for a crime type in a specific
    location during a specific time period.

You should see that the number of search hits decreases quite dramatically
but that the relevance of those hits improves. This search process allows you
to narrow the focus of your research, to isolate information that is not of use,
and to work your way through the relevant information in a methodical and
systematic manner. You will often have to spend quite a bit of time refining
your search criteria before you get to the most useful terms and phrases as
well as any relevant dates and locations.

Researchers will often search through multiple databases to find the information they need. There are many databases that require you to have a commercial licence to access, but there are also a growing number of publicly
accessible databases that store information on crime and policing. For example,
the Global Policing Database emerged out of a British and Australian collaboration to improve access to evaluations of policing interventions. You can
access it with this link – https://gpd.uq.edu.au/s/gpd/page/about

Try using the advanced search option in this database and then narrow your
search using the available features. You should find that you uncover much
more useful information and that you can do this much more quickly than
when you used a commercial search engine. You should also be cognizant of
the potential challenges that arise when you use commercial search engines
due to the multiple criteria that influence the information that is returned to
you. Many organisations pay search engines to prioritise their brand and data
and the search engines also factor in your previous search histories to any data
returns. Many international jurisdictions will also limit the information you
can access for a mixture of reasons, including data sharing, user anonymity
and confidentiality, and national security. Most importantly, remember that
search engines are not objective entities and that they use algorithms which
will build bias into your searches.

Different databases are useful for different purposes. Some databases are
designed for public access, and there are other open access data resources
that you can use that are based within governmental resources and university
systems. Have a look at some of the examples below to see how much information you can find using freely accessible research tools.

- European Police Science and Research Bulletin
  www.cepol.europa.eu/science-research/bulletin
- Campbell Collaboration
  www.campbellcollaboration.org/website-search?searchword=policing
- Centre for Evidence-Based Policing

http://cebcp.org/evidence-based-policing/resources-tools/
- US Society of Evidence-Based Policing
  www.americansebp.org/
- The UK Society of Evidence-Based Policing
  www.sebp.police.uk/

Systematic and structured research involves researchers using the same or similar search terminology in multiple databases to ensure that they can find all of the relevant information they need. There is no way of shortcutting this process. It can take quite a long time to learn about your subject matter and to allow that learning to help you to develop the appropriate search criteria to use in the most appropriate databases. You might need to change or refine your search terms quite a few times before you find the ideal language to access the information you need. The good news is that this process gets easier and quicker with time and practice.

Task

Depending upon which resources you can access, try using the National Police Library at the College of Policing (www.college.police.uk/library) or a library at a College or University to test out this systematic approach to research. You should look for papers produced by governments and police organisations as well as academic articles and journals. This process will help you to become familiar with the different types of data and information that are available. While this initial search process can take quite a long time, you will eventually find yourself at a point which we call "saturation" (i.e. where you are no longer finding new information). You can then move on to the next stage of your research.

Once you have identified some useful information, you will need to start arranging this information in a manner you can make sense of. You should read the abstracts and introductions from what appear to be the most useful papers, reports, and articles. You can jettison those articles that end up not being much use but where you find very useful articles you should analyse them thoroughly to unearth further information and read through their reference lists to find further reading.

One of the key things that you will need to start identifying is what appears to be good-quality evidence. Researchers define good-quality evidence by criteria such as trustworthiness, credibility, and applicability to the chosen research project. Good-quality evidence can also be quality assured by finding other forms of evidence that confirm or validate the findings or, in some cases, which contest the findings and require you to do further checks. The quality of evidence increases as you find further confirmation and verification of the initial findings. This initial stage of the research process is essential to ensure that our own individual biases do not interfere with our choice of sources too much and that we are not ignoring or subtly rejecting research findings that do not align with our initial assumptions and perspective.

Once we have completed the search process, we need to organise the data according to the key themes that have emerged. This is the beginning of the analytical stage of the research where we break large amounts of research data into more manageable themes that we have identified during the search. We will return to this search and sort process in more detail in Chapter 9 and, for the moment, we will just look at how theory helps us to order and make sense of our research findings.

Connecting Theory and Research

A lot of criminological research focuses upon uncovering new knowledge to improve our understanding of the nature of crime in society, but our specific focus in policing is to understand how policing and criminal justice interventions work. This might include how we use an intervention to nudge or change an offender's behaviour or how we might choose an intervention or policing strategy that provides better protection for potential victims of crime. In order to understand how and why interventions and policing strategies or tactics work, we need to link together our theoretical insights from the first half of the book with the research insights that we are focusing upon in the second half of the book. This will provide us with some useful knowledge that we can apply to real-life problems.

Figure 8.1 shows the crime triangle which neatly summarises many of the insights from routine activities theory (Felson, 2018). Rather than focusing upon individual offenders or victims, routine activities theory

Figure 8.1 The Crime Triangle.

focuses upon the crime events and activities that take place when potential offenders and victims are brought together without capable guardianship. This theoretical perspective can therefore help us to understand how a police intervention might change the behaviour of motivated offenders or potential victims as well as the interactions between offenders and victims of crime.

Task 2

Consider what might assist motivated offenders to come together with suitable targets/victims in time and space in the absence of capable guardians. Where does the role of the police fit into this crime triangle?

Task 3

Think about your chosen crime type again within the context of the crime triangle and the opportunities for intervention that it presents. The table in Figure 8.2 contains 25 opportunity reduction techniques. Review the table and identify some of the techniques that could be used to manage your crime problem.

You should now be able to see how the combination of theory and research can come together to offer potential solutions to crime problems. As the researcher you just need to start off this research process by asking some basic questions:

- What do I need to know?
- Where can I find relevant and trustworthy information?
- What does this data source tell me that can be applied to my research problem?

Let's move beyond hypothetical ideas now and look at a case study:

Case Study 1

Kyle is a 14-year-old boy who has been arrested for possession with intent to supply a class A illegal substance. Kyle came into contact with police at an address in a town many miles from his home, having been missing for a significant amount of time. During this period, he has also been expelled from school. Since his expulsion, Kyle's mum has been working closely with his youth offending team case worker and other professionals to determine the best way to get him back into education. After contact with the police, Kyle is accepted into a pupil referral

Table 8.1 Risks and Evidence-Based Interventions

	Risk Factors	*Evidence-Based Intervention*
Individual		
Family		
Environment		

unit but just when things had been starting to look positive, he goes missing again. Three days later, Kyle is found and arrested again, this time for assaulting someone during an exchange of class A drugs. It appears to you that Kyle has got involved in some kind of organised criminal activity. All of the help that has been presented to Kyle so far has not worked and you are tasked with researching alternative ways of approaching this problem.

a   In Table 8.1, identify some of the evidence-based early childhood precursors that can expose children like Kyle to exploitation by organised crime groups and later offending. Use the resources from earlier in this chapter as well as those provided by the College of Policing to research this crime problem. You will need to propose interventions you deem to be most effective and, where appropriate, elaborate upon how and why these proposed interventions might work.

For the second part of this case study task, you have been asked to design and implement a developmental crime prevention programme focused on early interventions for young individuals vulnerable to criminal exploitation.

b   Think about:
   • The needs of your target population
   • The intended impact of the intervention
   • Who needs to be involved in the intervention
   • Any required staff and training
   • Potential ethical and moral dimensions
   • Any potential unintended consequences...

This is what applied research looks like in practice. There is no set time frame for undertaking most research. You just need to make the most of the time available to you, and once you have identified a structured way of undertaking research, you can use this as the starting point for other pieces of research.

Increase the Effort	Increase the Risks	Reduce the Rewards	Reduce Provocations	Remove the Excuses
1. Target Harden	**6. Extend guardianship**	**11. Conceal targets**	**16. Reduced frustrations and stress**	**21. Set rules**
• Steering column locks	• Take routine precautions	• Off-street parking	• Efficient queues and polite service	• Rental agreements
• Anti-robbery screens	• 'Cocoon' neighbourhood watch	• Gender-neutral phone directories	• Expanded seating	• Harassment codes
• Tamper-proof packaging		• Unmarked bullion trucks	• Soothing music/muted lights	• Hotel registrations
2. Control access to facilities	**7. Assist natural surveillance**	**12. Remove targets**	**17. Avoid disputes**	**22. Post instructions**
• Entry phones	• Improved street lighting	• Removable car radio	• Separate enclosures for rival soccer fans	• 'No parking'
• Electronic card access	• Defensible space design	• Women's refuges	• Reduce crowding in pubs	• 'Private property'
• Baggage screening	• Support whistleblowers	• Pre-paid phone cards for pay phones	• Fixed cab fares	• 'Extinguish camp fires'
3. Screen exits	**8. Reduce anonymity**	**13. Identify property**	**18. Reduce emotional arousal**	**23. Alert conscience**
• Ticket needed for exit	• Taxi driver IDs	• Property marking	• Controls on violent pornography	• Roadside speed display boards
• Export documents	• 'How's my driving?' decals	• Vehicle licensing and parts marking	• Enforce good behaviour on soccer field	• Signatures for customs declarations
• Electronic merchandise tags	• School uniforms	• Cattle branding	• Prohibit racial slurs	• 'Shoplifting is stealing'
4. Deflect Offenders	**9. Utilise place managers**	**14. Disrupt markets**	**19. Neutralise peer pressure**	**24. Assist compliance**
• Street closures	• CCTV for double-decker buses	• Monitor pawn shops	• 'Idiots drink and drive'	• Easy library check-out
• Separate bathrooms for women	• Two clerks for convenience stores	• Controls on classified ads	• 'It's OK to say no'	• Public lavatories
• Disperse pubs	• Reward vigilance	• License street vendors	• Disperse troublemakers at school	• Litter bins
5. Control tools /weapons	**10. Strengthen formal surveillance**	**15. Deny benefits**	**20. Discourage imitation**	**25. Control drugs and alcohol**
• 'Smart' guns	• Red light cameras	• Ink merchandise tags	• Rapid repair of vandalism	• Breathalysers in pubs
• Disabling stolen mobile phones	• Burglar alarms	• Graffiti cleaning	• V-chips in TVs	• Server intervention
• Restrict spray paint to juveniles	• Security guards	• Speed humps	• Censor details of modus operandi	• Alcohol-free events

Figure 8.2 Crime Prevention Techniques.

Framing Research

In the first half of this chapter, we have looked at different ways of reviewing research evidence in a systematic manner, and with this case study, you have started to explore how you might apply research findings to real-life problems. You should be able to see that different types of research are useful for different purposes, and it is important for you to be cognizant of these differences when you start a research project. Some forms of research are exploratory (i.e. you need to learn about something) and others are confirmatory (i.e. you think you know something and need to check whether your assumptions are correct). It is helpful to understand which type of research approach you are taking as this will inform how you read and interpret relevant literature.

You can learn more about deductive and inductive thinking by using these links from the East Midlands Police-Academic Collaboration (Coxhead 2020).

www.empac.org.uk/exploratory-research-looks-forward/

www.empac.org.uk/the-deductive-paradox-finding-what-you-look-for/

Table 8.2 Confirmatory and Exploratory Methods

Confirmatory Method	Exploratory Method
A top-down approach that tests an existing theory of how the world works:	A bottom-up approach that can lead to the generation of new findings and theories about how the world works:
Theory $\rightarrow$ hypothesis $\rightarrow$ empirical data $\rightarrow$ conclusions	Observation (not experiments) $\rightarrow$ empirical data $\rightarrow$ descriptions patterns $\rightarrow$ conclusions $\rightarrow$ and sometimes theory
This method uses **deductive** logic (the logic of **justification**)	This method uses **inductive** logic (the logic of **discovery**)

The EMPAC website is one of many local and regional policing research resources that you can use to learn more about the research that is going on in your area. These local and regional resources should be used as complementary resources to those provided by the College of Policing as they focus upon crime problems through a local or regional lens and may provide more context-specific data and information than sources provided by national or international organisations.

Using Research

The accumulation of a research evidence-base to support decision-making in the police profession has become known as evidence-based policing, but as the first half of this chapter and Chapter 7 have outlined, there are many other different types of research that might be useful to you. The key strength of evidence-based policing is that it incorporates different types of evidence and draws on the experiences of other professional bodies that have brought research and practical experience together through the language of evidence-based practice. The language that is most commonly used in relation to this type of research is "what works." All evidence-based professions have access to a body of knowledge that informs "what works." For example, in the nursing profession, this is the Royal College of Nursing, which was established in 1916, and for General Practitioners, it is the Royal College of General Practitioners which was established in 1952. In comparison to these longstanding professional bodies, the College of Policing was only established in 2013, so there is lots of catching up to do!

The Colleges that represent the various medical health and social care professions have a national institute that advises on what the best available evidence is which is called the National Institute for Health and Care Excellence. The College of Policing has started the process of developing a similar institute through the establishment of the What Works Centre for Crime Reduction, but as it is a young institution, we still need to draw on research evidence from other places to make sure we have a full appreciation of crime problems and potential policing responses. Most of the time, we do not need to generate our own research to address this issue. We can use existing resources that are available to us via criminal justice and police institutions, from universities and think tanks, or just via the World Wide Web. The challenge for researchers is to find good-quality evidence, and this process often involves engaging with a multitude of resources from different places and providing a critical assessment of those resources in the form of a summary report. Sherman's original 1998 definition of evidence-based policing refers directly to making the best use of available evidence so the key basic skills that any new researcher needs (after understanding where to find good research) is how to provide some level of quality control over the research that is being reviewed.

In democratic countries, state agencies provide easily accessible information about patterns of crime and state responses to crime, so this can be used as a way of improving your appreciation of crime problems and finding data that is reliable. For example, the United Kingdom Office for National Statistics produces up-to-date reports on crime and justice that can be accessed here – www.ons.gov.uk/peoplepopulationandcommunity/crimeandjustice

Similarly, if you want to look for resources that have been used to address crime and policing problems in the past, you can find them in resources such as the following:

Home Office Police and Crime Prevention Series – https://discovery. nationalarchives.gov.uk/details/r/C13431866

National Offender Management Service Risk of Harm Guidance – www. nomsintranet.org.uk/roh/

Independent Office for Police Conduct – www.policeconduct.gov.uk/ research-and-learning

There are lots of sources of information and searchable databases available like these. Training yourself as a researcher requires you to put in the hours of researching to work out which resources are most useful for you and over time it will become much easier to know which resources to use for which purpose.

The existence of these resources means that there is no excuse for using old data or information. To clarify this last point, the term data refers to the raw facts and statistics that are collected by researchers, and the term information refers to the point at which those data and statistics are re-purposed with a specific intent (Bryman, 2015). As researchers, we interrogate data to find out what it tells us about a specific problem. We then try to generate useful information to help us solve contemporary policing problems. Because of this, there are significant similarities between research generation and analysis and intelligence generation and analysis which we will explore in the final part of this chapter (Tekir, 2009). The dynamic and ever-changing nature of crime means that for research to be useful to police officers and organisations it needs to be up to date, rigorously tested, and context specific. Let's look at each of these issues in turn to better understand what makes good research evidence.

The Most Up-to-Date Evidence

For most of the twentieth century, criminal justice researchers were primarily concerned with the challenge of accessing useful information about criminal justice from criminal justice institutions that were not always keen to share information that they perceived as their own. Slowly, democratic institutions have matured to the point that transparency is seen as a positive quality and a key staging point on the route to effective institutional accountability. Outside of these democratic and institutional developments, the advent of the World Wide Web spun the challenge of gaining access to data on its head by releasing a momentous amount of information into easily accessible public spaces and led to new challenges in terms of deciphering what is useful research evidence and what is not. You will often hear about this challenge in relation to the term, *big data*, which refers to the ever-growing volume, variety and velocity of data available for analysis (Chen et al., 2012).

Research data can incorporate anything from official statistics and policy reports to news stories, social media, and citizen journalism that is made immediately available on the web. The questions that researchers need to ask relate to how useful the data is for the purpose of a project, how much the data can be corroborated by other sources, and how relevant the context you are researching is to your research question. Thus, the types of evidence that you might need to use will change depending upon your circumstances and the types of research questions you are asking. As this chapter has demonstrated, there are lots of resources available to you with a single click of an electronic device and one of the interesting challenges for researchers is selecting what is both the most up-to-date and rigorously tested knowledge.

The College of Policing has developed in tandem with the What Works Centre for Crime Reduction to present the resources it recommends as being the most up to date for police officers and police institutions but you will also be able to find additional resources produced elsewhere. The advantage of using the College of Policing's resources is that they have been rigorously tested to make the process of research analysis easier and quicker for police officers and police researchers, thus hopefully saving you lots of time and effort. The opposing perspective to this is that the College of Policing is pointing you towards a very limited set of resources. Let's have a quick look at the What Works resource to see how the College of Policing define rigorously tested research and, as all researchers should do, test a few of the assumptions about this research.

Rigorously Tested Evidence

The College of Policing currently identifies randomised control trials as the gold standard of evidence-based policing research and presents a range of these resources on its webpages for police officers and staff to review. Randomised control trials are viewed by the College of Policing as the gold standard of research due to their ability to isolate causes and effects of crime and policing interventions and to determine which cause led to which effect. This knowledge and insight should enable police officers to choose evidence-based tools and interventions which they can apply to crime problems they are experiencing in their day-to-day work. But, and it is a big but, as patterns of crime have local peculiarities, it is always important to question how well some knowledge will transfer from one location to another. Social scientific knowledge is not underpinned by universal assumptions (like it is in, e.g., theoretical physics), so it is always important for police officers to integrate research-based knowledge with their own experiences of policing to test for flaws in research assumptions.

Task 4

Pick an intervention to review from the What Works Centre's crime reduction toolkit and make a note of the strengths and weaknesses of the research. You can find the crime reduction toolkit here – https://whatworks.college.police.uk/toolkit/Pages/Toolkit.aspx

You can add a localised focus to your research by choosing which project to look at according to geographical location. Click on the Policing and Crime Reduction Map and see how these projects engage with crime and policing from a more localised perspective – https://whatworks.college.police.uk/Research/Research-Map/Pages/Research-Map.aspx

These College of Policing resources provide useful reference points to quickly review existing best evidence, but they often do not fit the needs of police officers or policing agencies, and like all research evidence, they become out of date almost instantaneously. This top-down approach to the police organisational use of research has been challenged by other disciplines, most notably evidence-based health, where evidence-based practice has a longer institutional history. While the health profession still advocates for the use of randomised control trials and systematic reviews to assess the impact of clinical procedures, it also recognises the critical importance of decision-making from professionals in terms of how to use this evidence as well as the need for professionals to engage interactively with research to draw the best information out of it rather than ignoring or accepting findings uncritically.

Most obviously for police officers, answers are needed for immediate questions relating to persistent crime problems in their locality. Police officers themselves are critical sources of professional knowledge, and there is a need to integrate that professional knowledge with empirical findings from national and international studies to develop a research knowledge base that is specific to the context in which operational policing takes place. This next section looks at how we make research of use to our own personal research concerns.

Context-Specific Evidence

One of the key challenges for the implementation of evidence-based policing in England and Wales as well as other international jurisdictions has been the sense of alienness that has surrounded the term and concept on the frontline of policing (Telep and Somers, 2017). For police officers, who have been trained to understand that evidence means criminal evidence that goes to court, the language of evidence-based policing can seem counter-intuitive in that it implies that the work they have been doing is not evidence-based. Not only that, the perspectives from many of those on the front-line of policing has sometimes been to interpret evidence-based policing as science telling them what to do; that science presents universal answers and, at worst, is a way of telling you that you that you have been doing everything wrong (Kalyal, 2019).

This feels counter-intuitive for police officers as they know and see that crime changes shape across time and place. What everyone can agree on is that research evidence about crime and policing is context-specific and not immediately transferable. The challenge for policing bodies has thus been to find a way of integrating or assimilating the live and dynamic world of professional expertise with the colder and more static world of research evidence (Lum et al., 2012). In democratic societies, policing has often been characterised by the fierce independence of localised policing entities, and this requires evidence-based policing to be able to incorporate the real-time value of professional judgement and to integrate the positives of both scientific research approaches alongside craft-based knowledge. There is lot that can be learnt from the experiences of the medical profession in terms of the integration of evidence-based practice (Lehane et al., 2019), in particular, the role of reflective practice in helping to facilitate this organisational change and the need to widely disseminate relevant and up-to-date knowledge to busy practitioners in an easily digestible manner.

There are numerous examples of best practice approaches to generating evidence that delivers useful context-specific evidence. The types of research tools that are required are linked to the specificity of the question and the extent to which you need to demonstrate the impact or efficacy of an intervention. In many instances, it will be sufficient to simply demonstrate that crime occurrences have reduced or that there is less fear of crime in a community, but if you require further detail, then more sophisticated methodological approaches are required. The following are just examples of the types of questions you might be asked in relation to whether an intervention has been successful:

- Which quantifiable measures suggest that your initiative had the intended outcome/effect?
- How can you prove that your mechanism, and not another unseen variable, produced the intended effect?
- How could you measure how much the implementation of the selected intervention impacted on the outcome?
- How would you measure whether the outcome was worth the resources used to implement the chosen intervention?
- How would you predict whether the outcome was sustainable over a sufficient length of time to justify the investment in the intervention?
- Is the intervention transferable to other geographical places and or crime types?

As the questions grow in complexity then so do the methodological approaches and tools, we need to adopt to get answers. As we are all busy people, it is helpful to know that there are plenty of people out there already doing this work. The following section includes some examples of (relatively) accessible approaches to research using rigorous methodologies that you can use to review your assumptions about a proposed intervention. Each of the research tools provides a systematic approach to research and rigour in terms of how the evidence is generated.

Systematic Reviews

Systematic reviews provide overviews of the evidence-base on specific interventions so that professionals are able to get quick access to summaries of research to save time in assessing the relative effectiveness of a range of proposed interventions. Systematic reviews aim to provide exhaustive reviews of all available evidence on an intervention to support the decision-making of front-line professionals. Meta-analysis, a form of statistical analysis, can be used to synthesise quantitative data resulting from quantitative evaluation research on a number of similar interventions. The College of Policing publishes all of its systematic reviews on its website alongside rapid evidence assessments (REAs) – https://whatworks.college.police.uk/Research/Pages/Published.aspx

Rapid Evidence Assessments

REAs are less exhaustive than systematic reviews, and they can allow researchers to pull together key information for practitioners in a short time span. REAs synthesise evaluation research, on different or similar interventions, to extract evidence to support the development of evidence-based policy. It is argued that there should be a rigorous analysis of evaluation research to ensure all external and internal effects on any intervention are accounted for and to ensure that findings are not misused or misinterpreted. The objective of assessing evaluation research is to provide policy-makers with accurate and timely evidence about how and why something works (Pawson and Tilley, 1994). REAs cover a wide range of literature in a short space of time and produce synthesised evidence to inform new interventions. While some useful research can be missed due to the restrictions imposed by search techniques, the increasing amount of research recorded on the internet significantly reduces the risk. A narrative synthesis is often used for an REA as it synthesises evidence that answers the pre-set purposive supplementary questions

Open Source Intelligence Analysis

Most of this chapter has focused upon the role of research in developing an evidence-base that police professionals can use to help make decisions about existing interventions but another growing research area is in online investigations which are most commonly known as open source intelligence (OSINT) investigations. There has been slow take-up amongst academic research in terms of the use of open source evidence, but it is commonly used in the Police Service and the wider policing family. OSINT research is systematic research of publicly available information (Charmaz, 2014). OSINT approaches offer an alternative methodological approach when researching subject matter where there is limited access to data. OSINT is thus particularly useful when researching hard to investigate areas where a trawl of existing publicly available data might be useful. There is a fuzzy area here between systematic research approaches and web trawls which use tools such as data scraping to deliver insights on actions and behaviours based upon patterns of digital interaction in publicly accessible spaces (especially social media) that can be used for investigative or intelligence purposes.

As we have noted on several occasions the processes of research generation and intelligence collection have many similarities and require similar skillsets. Yet, the intersections between research (understood from an academic perspective) and intelligence (understood from a police/policing perspective) remain relatively unexplored. Cornish and Clark (2002) note the potential of OSINT to both assist in the investigation of complex crimes and to act as an important tool for academic researchers investigating rapidly changing crime areas. For example, wide access to the participants involved in organised crime and those who police it can be difficult and limited (Paterson et al., 2019; Severns, 2015), and the intersection between research and intelligence offers opportunities for improved evaluation and review of intelligence gathering methods as well as explorations of new practices (Tekir, 2009).

OSINT offers a potential avenue of future research development for the big data era where evidence is gathered and analysed from a variety of open sources, including the media, social networks, and police and government documents published on the internet. This approach to research is laden with ethical challenges, but growth is evident, particularly in the cybercrime arena, where there has been a conflation of social scientists and computer scientists into the new professional discipline of data scientists. It thus appears that OSINT is slowly being accepted as research data, despite some of the practical challenges and ethical obstacles highlighted in this section.

Initial resistance to the use of OSINT seems a little unfair once the mechanics of intelligence generation are reviewed. Intelligence is information from various sources that has been subject to a rigorous evaluation and risk assessment process to assist with decision-making (Harfield, 2009). OSINT is graded in terms of its quality and the methods used to gather the original information. This process enables anyone relying on the findings to judge the weight of the evidence before taking any decisions based on the findings, as they would do with academic research.

OSINT relies on a 3x5x2 system that puts a value on the strength of the intelligence and the extent to which it assists in decision-making. The original 5x5x5 grading system used a combination of the National Intelligence Model

Table 8.3 Open Source Intelligence Evaluation Criteria

Source Evaluation	Intelligence Evaluation	Handling Conditions
1. Reliable	A: Known directly to the source B: Known indirectly to the source but corroborated	P: Lawful sharing permitted
2. Not tested	C: Known indirectly to the source D: Not Known	C: Lawful sharing permitted with conditions
3. Unreliable	E: Suspected to be false	C: Lawful sharing permitted with conditions

5x5x5 system and the Maryland research evaluation scale but this has subsequently been simplified and can be presented as follows.

The work of a researcher has many similarities with that of a police detective (Severns, 2015). Detectives are trained to keep an open mind when gathering evidence and to follow multiple lines of inquiry. They gather the evidence in a logical and systematic way and analyse it as they go along. As a result, new lines of inquiry are identified, prioritised, and followed, and existing lines of inquiry are evidenced as much as possible to establish the facts of the case. There is therefore yet unexplored potential in bring together the worlds of evidence-based policing, academic research and OSINT.

Towards Contextualised Investigation

For many years, academic research and policing practices remained two distinct worlds, yet the advent of evidence-based policing pulls them together in a yet to be fully explored way. Sherman's initiation of evidence-based policing as the strategy to embed evidence-based practices into policing will undoubtedly lead to further police-academic collaboration with an as yet uncharted map to be drawn. Academics and practitioners alike would benefit from further conceptual modelling of the relationship between research and policing for the purposes of improving future policy and practice. The final section in this chapter on OSINT is included to provide one potential vision of future collaboration beyond the current focus of the College of Policing on systematic reviews and REAs. One of the challenges posed by evidence-based practice is that it understands policing through the lens of function rather than concept, and this can lead to a failure to ask critical questions about the fundamental assumptions that underpin thinking about policing and police interventions. Evidence-based policing needs to draw upon policing experience and rigorously test whether proposed policing outcomes are being delivered as expected and how they might be adapted (Pease and Laycock, 2018; Roach and Pease, 2017). This work needs to be undertaken at a speed that can align with the quick pace of policing environments and encourage innovation (Sparrow, 2016). Novel approaches in realist evaluation and Bayesian probability, amongst others, have the potential to increase the amount of experimentation and to avoid research and evidence-based policing becoming viewed as an activity of a privileged few.

Future policing research needs to extend beyond the current minimalist conceptualisation of policing, as directed from the College of Policing, which focuses primarily upon the unique authority and capacity of the police. Instead, a maximalist conceptualisation of policing, such as that found in the work of Bayley and Shearing (2001), should prove to be more fruitful. Such a maximalist approach would draw upon the full range of social control processes and statutory, civil, and informal bodies that perform policing functions and that contribute to order through a disparate range of social processes to maximise research and engage with the full breadth of policing potential in society.

References

Bayley, D. and Shearing, C. (2001) *The New Structure of Policing: Description, Conceptualization and Research Agenda.* Washington, DC: National Institute of Justice. Available at: www.ncjrs.gov/pdffiles1/nij/187083.pdf

Bryman, A. (2015) *Social Research Methods.* Oxford: Oxford University Press.

Charmaz, K. (2014) *Constructing Grounded Theory: Second Edition.* London: Routledge.

Chen, H., Chiang, R. and Storey, V. (2012) Business intelligence and analytics: From big data to big impact. *Management Information Systems Quarterly.* 36(4): 1165–1188.

Cornish, D. and Clarke, R. (2002) Analysing organized crime. In A. Piquero and S. Tibbetts (eds.) *Rational Choice and Criminal Behaviour: Recent Research and Future Challenges,* 41–62. New York, NY: Garland.

Coxhead, J. (2020) Exploratory Research Looks Forward. *East Midlands Police-Academic Collaboration.* Available at: http://www.empac.org.uk/exploratory-research-looks-forward/; http://www.empac.org.uk/the-deductive-paradox-finding-what-you-look-for/

Coxhead, J. (2020) The Deductive Paradox. *East Midlands Police-Academic Collaboration.* Available at: http://www.empac.org.uk/the-deductive-paradox-finding-what-you-look-for/

Felson, M. (2018) *Crime and Everyday Life (Sixth Edition).* London: Sage.

Harfield, C. (2009) *Defining and Defying Organized Crime.* London: Routledge.

Kalyal, H. (2019) One person's evidence is another person's nonsense. *Policing: A Journal of Policy and Practice.* Advance Access. https://academic.oup.com/policing/advance-article-abstract/doi/10.1093/police/pay106/5301662

Lehane, E. et al. (2019) Evidence-based practice education for healthcare professions: An expert view. *British Medical Journal of Evidence-Based Medicine.* 24(3): 103–108.

Lum, C., Telep, C., Koper, C. and Grieco, J. (2012) Receptivity to research in policing. *Justice Research and Policy.* 14(1): 61–95.

Paterson, C., Severns, R. and Brogan, S. (2019) *The Transnational Investigation of Modern Slavery.* Available at: http://shura.shu.ac.uk/25102/

Pawson, R. and Tilley, N. (1994) What works in evaluation research? *British Journal of Criminology.* 34(3): 291–306.

Pease, K. and Laycock, G. (2018) Realist evaluation and Bayesian statistics: A marriage made in heaven? In G. Farrell and A. Sidebottom (eds.) *Realist Evaluation for Crime Science.* London: Routledge.

Roach and Pease. (2017) How to morph experience into evidence. In J. Knutsson and L. Tompson (eds.) *Advances in Evidence-Based Policing,* 84–97. London: Routledge.

Severns, R. (2015) *One Step Ahead: The Police Transnational Firearms Network.* Available at: http://shura.shu.ac.uk/11142/1/PDF%20COMPLETED%20THESIS%20for%20%20library%20print.pdf

Sherman, L. (1998) *Evidence-Based Policing.* Ideas in American Policing Series. Washington, DC: Police Foundation. Available at: www.policefoundation.org/wp-content/uploads/2015/06/Sherman-1998-Evidence-Based-Policing.pdf

Sparrow, M. (2016) *Handcuffed: What Holds Policing Back, and the Keys to Reform.* Washington, DC: Brookings Institution Press.

Tekir, S. (2009) *Open Source Intelligence Analysis: A Methodological Approach.* Riga: VDM Verlag.

Telep, C. and Somers, L. (2017) Examining police officer definitions of evidence-based policing: Are we speaking the same language? *Policing and Society.* 29(2): 171–187.

Chapter 9

Doing Your Own Research

Introduction

Having discussed how to review research on policing and crime in Chapter 8 and the ways in which this approach to research creates linkages between police practice and criminological research, we can now move onto understanding how the research process works when you undertake your own research studies. Doing criminological research is much more interesting and intellectually stimulating than talking or reading about it. Furthermore, doing research need not be difficult. All we are doing is collecting data in a systematic manner about things we, or others, have done. This chapter thus aims to de-mystify the research process with an introduction to different ways of doing research.

Readers will be introduced to research philosophies and research design alongside ways to identify, justify, and use methodological knowledge to create a framework for research analysis. This will include explorations of quantitative and qualitative approaches as well as mixed methods. A brief introduction to other fundamental aspects of the research process will be provided such as sampling, analysis, and research ethics. The chapter will help students of policing and criminology identify, justify, and use an appropriate strategy for exploring research problems and critically explore the utility of a range of research strategies and methods. Students will then be able to assess the appropriateness of the use of these different strategies and methods to develop research skills that aid the collection of new empirical data or the analysis of secondary data collected by others. Let's start, of course, at the beginning, with the most important stage of the research process – asking the right question!

Asking Appropriate Research Questions

The most challenging point for any research project is the beginning. We normally start off with a problem we are trying to solve and a set of questions we are asking ourselves.

DOI: 10.4324/9781003081012-9

Why is crime x persistently recurring in area y or to group z?

Would change a to police tactics lead to a reduction in crime x?

How much more or less resource is required to successfully implement this change?

Consequently, we can understand research questions as a set of problem-solving questions that follow a method known widely as Socratic questioning in an attempt to uncover the truth behind a set of circumstances. The research process requires you to identify where the source of this truth or knowledge lies, so the most obvious starting point is to review what is already known about your problem.

What Do You Know About the Problem So Far?

The first stage of the research process involves collecting and assessing the information you have available to you. You should investigate what you need to know to develop your understanding of the problem. You might even have some ideas about what the missing information is and where you might find it. This growing sense of direction is called your hypothesis. A hypothesis will evolve and can sometimes completely change during a research investigation. It is rare in social science for a hypothesis to be found to be completely true or false, so researchers often use language that captures the fuzzy and complex nature of the social world and the ways that individuals and groups in that world interact with each other.

What Do You Need to Know That You Do Not Already Know?

This process is often referred to as a critical literature review (see Chapter 8 for more detail), and its purpose is to review existing knowledge about your problem, to test your initial hypothesis, and to identify any gaps in existing knowledge. The identification of the knowledge or research gap requires researchers to start to investigate more specific details about a defined problem. You may find answers that you do not want to find or a dearth of useful information. The early stages of research can be quite frustrating, so you need to keep considering your research question and hypothesis throughout this process. You may find that your investigation takes you down dead ends before you find more fruitful paths. The research process is not necessarily linear in terms of its development, so you need to keep records of your research and generate a systematic investigation process.

One way of providing a systematic and rational structure to your research is to use a logic model. This is an approach that is used across research disciplines, and you can find a short introduction to logic models as well as a range of other support tools on the College of Policing website – https://whatworks. college.police.uk/Support/Pages/Research-guidance.aspx

How Are You Going to Find the Information That You Need?

You will eventually get to a point which researchers call *saturation* where you feel you like you have used up all of your resources, time, and energy and can no longer find additional existing information about your problem. At this point, you need to consider additional methods of accessing or generating data and to consider the relationship between your hypothesis and your method(s) of data collection.

What Are the Potential Barriers to Achieving What You Need to Achieve?

You will also need to consider practical and logistical issues such as how much time you have to conduct the research, whether you are able to access the information you need to answer your question, and how much of that information is required to give you some knowledge that can be considered useful and reliable. If you are undertaking research within an organisation, you will normally need authorised permission from a line manager before you can proceed, and you may have to seek permission from other organisations too. Research takes up valuable time for the researcher and the researched, and you need to remain cognizant of any potential financial and other resource costs that your work might include.

It is at this point that researchers and investigators come into contact with issues of values and ethics through questions such as:

- *How do I obtain x piece of information and what are the ethical issues raised when doing this?*
- *Is there likely to be any harm caused by this research and the questions that are being asked?*
- *What is the most appropriate way of asking the relevant questions?*

Each stage of your research involves these types of questions, and each ethical issue needs addressing and resolving in a systematic manner. These early stages of the research process can be understood in similar ways to the police national decision model (NDM) as a sequence of questions and stages that are linked together by continued engagement with relevant ethical issues.

Researchers also use ethical frameworks to help guide and share their research and professional practice with the most commonly used framework for criminologists being provided by the British Society of Criminology – www.britsoccrim.org/ethics/

We will return to all of these practical and ethical questions in a little more depth throughout this chapter, but hopefully you can see that that there are clear linkages between doing research and police practice. Police officers are always required to investigate problems, to look at what they do and do

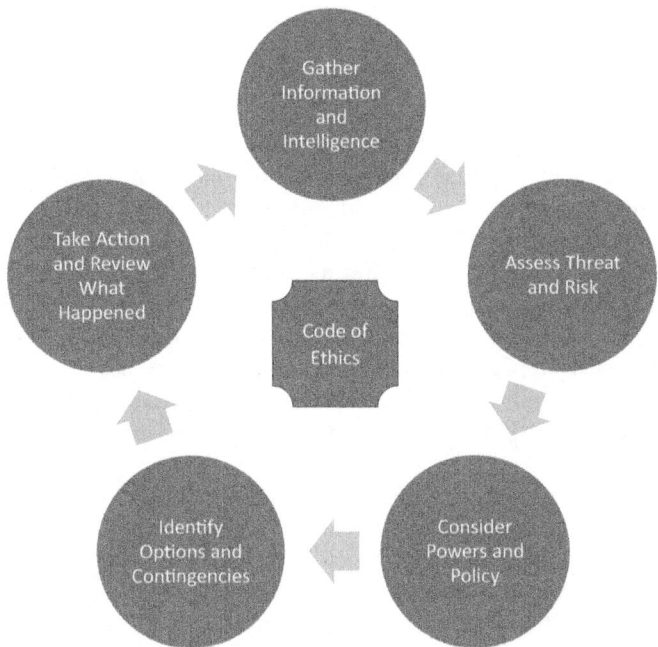

Figure 9.1 The National Decision Model.

not know, and to find ways of filling knowledge gaps. There are clear links between research methodologies, investigatory processes, and intelligence gathering methodologies, so research need not feel alien to police officers. It is just a case of learning the different organisational languages and ensuring that we reflect on our own role in the research process in shaping these research questions and methodological approaches.

Research Paradigms

A paradigm describes how we might look at a situation – our worldview and how it influences our interpretation of the world around us. For example, in a context where a child is described as being involved in criminal activity during the day, a police officer would ask about the type of criminality involved because the lens through which police officers are trained to understand the world around them is through the application of criminal law. A teacher would look at this differently and ask why the child was not in school if it was a school day, and a social worker might ask who is responsible for the care of the child. These are the paradigms or lenses through which we all understand our work. Researchers break our paradigms or world views up by using two key terms ontology and epistemology that have a significant influence upon how we approach research questions and the research methods we might use.

Ontology

In philosophical terms, ontology is the study of being and our interaction with the structure of reality that surrounds us. Ontology thus refers to the way we experience and interpret the world and the assumptions this provides us with to interpret and negotiate day-to-day social interactions. Our ontological sense of what policing means and its interface with crime and criminal behaviour is informed by many factors and a range of sometimes hidden or unexplored assumptions. This book has tried to highlight the multiple different realities through which individuals and societies interpret police and policing, so it is important as researchers not to drive the research process with our own assumptions and to encourage an openness to other viewpoints.

For example, modern post-enlightenment societies have been characterised by generic assumptions that invoke "the police" as an essential requirement for the maintenance of order, without which society would be, to some degree or other, reduced to chaos (Emsley, 1991). The rise of the Black Lives Matter movement coupled with academic post-colonial studies (Cole, 1991) and more critical reflections on the role of state and its police (Hall et al., 1978) all question the need for, or role of, the police, but there remains a consensus that some form of policing, in its wider conceptual sense, is needed. Thus, the collective ontological assumption is that there is a need within all societies for order and the imposition of rules, even if it is not necessarily in the form that currently exists.

The French sociologist Emile Durkheim (1912/2001) noted that as societies develop, religiously driven rule-making and enforcement evolve alongside other social and cultural changes. This societal genesis perspective is reflective of Durkheim's view that religion is important to the development of societies in supporting the coalescence of social units and class that establish and reinforce social cohesion. Thus, in the earlier stages of social development, policing may exist as an organic function rather than as the formally organised policing capability that are the norm in the wealthy western democracies.

Durkheim argues that as humankind forms larger social groups, a need emerges for the rules of society to be increasingly enforced by the community or tribal leaders; individually or in some form of grouping (Durkheim, 1893/1984, 1912/2001). In Europe, by the late fifteenth century, the French-Burgundian term *policie* emerges and reflect this evolving model of order maintenance and policing. Neocleous presents this ontological description of *policie* as follows:

The legislative and administrative regulation of internal life of a community to promote general welfare and the condition of good order and the
regimenting of social life.

(Neocleous, 2006: 22)

Fukuyama's (2012) *The Origins of Political Order* also reviews historic
and contemporary biological, sociological, and political literature to analyse
the formation of social systems. Like Durkheim, Fukuyama concludes that
societies, cognizant of the perpetual threat of conflict, are disposed towards
community building and evidences this with multiple examples of rules being
set and transgressors being held to account across the world and at different
points in history.

So, what has all this philosophising got to do with research?

Well, the decisions we make when developing research projects are informed
by our ontological appreciation of what policing means to us and our
assumptions about the role and function of police officers and organisations
in societies. Our interpretation of what makes good *policie* and what makes
good police is influenced largely by our experiences of policing as we grow
up and the assumptions that we form through personal experiences, our
kinship networks, and the various forms of externally mediated messages we
encounter.

Our experiences of good police or policing differ markedly depending upon
whether we are male or female, old or young, rich or poor, and in majority
white societies such as England and Wales, whether we are white or a member
of a minority community. Without an ontological appreciation of crime and
policing, there is a possibility that we will engage with crime and policing
problems without sufficient consideration of the perspectives of others,
particularly those vulnerable to crime or who have increased contact with
the police due to their vulnerabilities. Ontology encourages us to challenge
narratives about policing orthodoxies and widely held assumptions about
why crime takes place.

Thus, while there is almost universal agreement that societies require some
form of policing, there are diverging perspectives across societies about what
we all might regard as effective *policie* and who should deliver this. These
different perspectives on the role and function of police within society are
sometimes presented subtly and sometimes with ideological and political
energy. As you engage with more data that addresses policing issues, you
will see evidence of the different schools of thought about policing that we
discussed in Chapter 8 and which exist in diverging forms across policing
institutions, political institutions, think tanks, universities, and, of course, the
public.

Case Study

A young male is referred to Rescue and Response (R&R) following arrest in a county far away from home. He discloses that he is engaging in county lines activity under duress from a gang, and he is deemed by professionals to be susceptible to negative peer pressure. This young male has suffered traumatic experiences at an early age as a result of domestic abuse and began to associate with a gang two years ago. Following referral, the R&R caseworker meets with the young man and his social worker to discuss an intervention and he agrees to engage – a support plan that focuses upon his Emotional Wellbeing, Employment and Education is agreed. A referral is subsequently made to the National Referral Mechanism (NRM) which concludes that there are reasonable grounds to believe he is a victim of modern slavery. The young man raises a key challenge as being an absence of positive male role models to discuss the emotional strains he is experiencing. As a result, the R&R caseworker conducts a joint session with a Mental Health Specialist, and this leads to ongoing psychotherapy sessions. Despite this young man's willingness to engage, he continues to be at significant risk from the gang he associated with. During his period of engagement with R&R, he is kidnapped and forced to "work off" the debt he owes as a result of his arrest. This leads to another arrest, and further debt. The control held by gangs, and the debt bondage victims are trapped in, is consistently one of the hardest cycles to break.

a   Draw a thematic diagram or spider map that highlights the key risk factors that suggest this young individual is vulnerable to exploitation by organised crime groups.
b   What do you think is the role of law enforcement and other authorities in these circumstances?
c   Suggest potential initiatives for each vulnerable circumstance that may mitigate this individual's risk to exploitation.
d   Think about the intended effect of each initiative, its impact and the potential outcome.

Your responses to the question present a visualisation of your ontology of policing in this specific context.

Epistemology

The second underpinning strand of research philosophy revolves around epistemology. While ontology focuses upon our interpretation of what policing means to us as individuals and groups, epistemology is the study of knowledge and how we acquire and interpret that knowledge. In simple (!) terms, epistemology can be described as understanding how we know what we know.

As an example of this, Hills (2014) refers to "policeness" as one of the fundamental ways we know about what police means to us at a level that transcends individual nation states and their systems of police and policing. Policing provides a useful illustration of epistemology as police organisations are easily identified (or *known*) by citizens through their presentation (uniform, structure, societal presence) and their activities (beat policing, investigation, prevention, etc.). Historically, research on policing has adopted a narrow conceptualisation of policing that focuses primarily on the unique authority and capacity of the state police (Bittner, 1970), whereas a broader conceptualisation of policing, such as that found in the work of Bayley and Shearing (2001), draws upon a broader range of social control processes that present a very different image of policing to the public.

In modern societies, the police are often representatives of formal legal systems, and this provides them with the authority to resolve conflict and restore order in a variety of ways. In nomadic or proto-societies, the rule base may be more consensual and theologically-based where the scope and remit of "police" differs and renders it difficult to explain the activities of police in isolation from other modes of policing. Critically, policing is a fundamental part of the social contract agreed between polity and citizen, recognising a need to ensure that the rules of society are observed and that the society, its leadership, or other socially acceptable body are able to hold transgressors to account. Policing is thus an expression of power that is given shape and form in each social and political context. It is ever-changing, and police organisations need to continually develop to reflect the social, political, and cultural changes that are taking place around them.

Case Study (Part 2)

Now, have a look back at the assumptions you made about the risks presented in the previous case study and the decisions you made about proposed interventions. What image did you construct of the individual in the case?

Epistemology attempts to understand how we know what we know and how this influences our decision-making and the assumptions and knowledge that underpin that decision-making.

The Philosophy of Policing Research

Together, ontology and epistemology influence how we think about the world and, as a consequence of this, how we think about policing. When we undertake research, we call this our "research paradigm." This ontological and epistemological thinking shapes how we interpret the problems which we are tasked with confronting, and this can result in us designing very different strategies and tactics to assess and measure the impact of the same problem. It is therefore essential that we can provide clear rationales for our research choices to make our research paradigm clear. Drawing on the work of Guba and Lincoln (1994), here are the most prominent research paradigms that you are likely to encounter.

Positivism

The positivist research paradigm emerged out of the work of Auguste Comte (1798–1857) in the nineteenth century. Comte argued that any objective scientific understanding of reality needed to be based upon experimentation, observation, and logical reasoning to identify cause-and-effect relationships in the world around us. Positivism draws on the natural sciences and is underpinned by a belief that the social world can be understood through quantifiable observations and statistical analysis of these observations.

In its purist terms, positivist researchers should be separate from the social world and should act as objective observers of the data that has been collected. The positivist paradigm has had most influence over the evolution of evidence-based policing in England and Wales through, the work of Sherman, the What Works Centre for Crime Reduction and also Jill Dando Institute of Security and Crime Science which is based within University College, London. The reason for this, as we noted in previous chapters, is that evidence-based policing developed as a tool to support police decision-making through an assessment of outcomes in similar circumstances. With evidence-based policing, positivist paradigms often seek out independent and objective assessments of reality through experimental research methods such as randomised control trials (RCTs). We will look at RCTs in more detail later in this chapter, but it is important to acknowledge at this point that their value in researching the social world of policing is often contested (Roach and Pease, 2017; Wood et al., 2017).

Interpretivism

Interpretivists critique the positivist position that human behaviour can be fully understood from an objective position and instead focus research upon an understanding of the subjective world of human experience. Interpretivism requires the researcher to understand human motivation and how others interpret the world around them. Interpretivists encourage individuals to situate themselves within the research and place a greater emphasis upon the value of individual interpretations in making sense of research findings. This perspective is also often referred to as social constructionism as we are interested in how others construct their own reality (Bogdan and Biklen, 1998). Interpretivism leads researchers to view the social world as the product of personal and social constructs and, because of this, they place a value on the collection of qualitative data, as opposed to quantitative data, which is drawn from engagement with people and their social world (Punch, 2005).

The positivist and interpretivist paradigms should be understood as two opposing ends of a spectrum of research philosophies. When you review police research, you should be able to see evidence of these paradigms in how the data is collected and the prevalence of quantitative or qualitative perspectives. Academics spend many hours arguing the case for one research paradigm presiding over the other and, different disciplines, may have a preference for one perspective over another. Evidence-based policing certainly emerged out of a positivist paradigm, but it has evolved over the past two decades to a more pragmatic position that sometimes involves a combination of the two paradigms.

Pragmatism and Realism

Pragmatists view research paradigms and methods of data collection as being decided by each individual research question. In these circumstances, researchers can draw on quantitative, qualitative, and mixed methods approaches depending upon the object of study. The challenge for any researcher is that mixed methods approaches can potentially add both additional time and complexity to the research process. Importantly for scholars of policing, Feilzer (2010: 8) argues that pragmatism recognises the need for research to solve practical problems. Realists favour a mixture of research methods as they realise that human interpretation can be inaccurate and unreliable and also that statistical interpretations may offer only partial insight into a problem. Importantly, for both realists and pragmatists, the combination of methods must be complementary (see Bhaskar, 1975, 1979) for more on this and the critical realist philosophy).

It is not necessary to worry too much about the language of research paradigms and philosophies, but it is important to reflect upon which sources of data you might place most value on and how this can unconsciously direct the type of background information you might undertake during research projects and in policing investigations. We encounter a common ground here between police investigation and academic research where there is a need to both keep an open mind in terms of the direction you might pursue and to ensure that you critically reflect upon any potential biases and subjectivity that might influence the outcome of your investigation.

Let's try applying these ideas to another case study.

Case Study: Part 1

You are first on the scene at what has been reported as a domestic dispute. There is no visible conflict taking place between the two adults as you arrive but there is a child present who seems extremely upset.

What are your priorities as you arrive at the scene?
How are you going to ensure you have as much as information as you need to manage this situation?
What are you going to do after you have finished the initial management of this incident?

There is no correct or incorrect answer to the questions in the case study above. The correct answer can only be made by an individual on the scene who engages with the people present and learns as much about the circumstances as possible. Once you have the relevant information, you can make informed decisions. In some instances, the incident will be resolved immediately, but there are other times when you will need to undertake your own background research on the problem to help you develop a more informed decision.

Case Study: Part 2

After ten minutes, all is calm at the house. The two adults are claiming that this was a malicious complaint, and the child has gone quiet. You verify the identity of each individual and confirm that the two adults are partners who live together and that they are looking after the son of a relative who is at work.

Where will you be able to access information that might help you address any concerns you have as you leave the scene?

Which sources of information might help you generate a better understanding of the situation?

So, what type of information did you look for in the case study? This will give you some clues about what your preferred research paradigm might be. It is important for all of us to recognise that we might intuitively drift to a preference for particular approaches to understanding a problem whilst also recognising that we might sometimes also need to challenge our intuitions. It is important to have as wide an appreciation as possible of the information that is available to you to understand a specific problem. In the next section, we will introduce you to the different types of evidence that you can access to help you make decisions about which methodological options you might pursue.

Prior to getting into too much detail about research processes though, it is important for us to introduce some key terminology related to different types of research evidence.

What Is Evidence?

Why is this an important question? Well, when police officers talk about evidence, they are most commonly referencing issues of law and proof; the necessity to prove an argument in court. When academics talk about evidence, they are most commonly referring to research data. Although academics often have very specific ideas about what research means to them, research is a normal component of all businesses, including policing. When we are faced with complex challenges, we have to explore why those challenges have emerged and look for solutions. Research is thus an essential component of problem-solving as we illustrated in Chapter 6.

Goldstein's (1979) work on "Problem-Oriented Policing" provided the first detailed explanatory framework for police officers to make sense of complex problems and to formulate context-specific solutions to those problems. It is the testing of these solutions and recording of that testing that brings together police problem-solving and criminological research. When you get academics talking about research, they tend to favour very different approaches to doing research and the use of different types of evidence. So, let's address this first challenge by defining what evidence is.

When we hear about evidence being used in relation to a crime, most people's first thoughts are of evidence presented in a court room. This evidence can include witness testimonies, physical objects (e.g. stolen goods), or documentation (e.g. mobile phone data) as well as circumstantial evidence which can support or challenge the assumptions which infer meaning upon other evidence. It is this final point where connections can be drawn with criminological understandings of evidence (e.g. the mobile phone data indicates that someone was in the area where a theft took place) as decisions about proof are made based upon the accumulative impact of evidence. In similar ways, social scientific evidence is drawn out of the accumulation of data and information to support or refute a theory or hypothesis. In policing terms, this hypothesis might relate to contentious debates such as whether stop and search tactics lead to less crime or, more precisely, what type of approach to stop and search might be most effective.

Case Study

The first study focuses upon a very general question and hypothesis which is difficult to prove – Does more stop and search mean less crime?
   https://whatworks.college.police.uk/Research/Documents/SS_and_crime_report.pdf

In the second document, the question and hypothesis is much narrower in its focus, and this means it becomes easier to provide a strong supporting argument for the hypothesis. Read the executive summary on page three which summarises the impact of the introduction of body worn video upon the number of detections that result in a criminal charge.
   https://whatworks.college.police.uk/Research/Documents/BWV_Report.pdf

---

So, evidence does not necessarily provide certainty when it comes to decision-making nor should it. Our assumptions in the physical sciences are periodically confounded. From Galileo to Newton and Einstein to contemporary debates about string theory, we are continually challenged as existing hypotheses and assumptions about the universe that surrounds us are contested by the emergence of new evidence or data. New criminological data might take the form of new types of criminality, new patterns of crime, new demographics of offenders, and the effectiveness of police responses to these issues. Given the constantly changing nature of crime, it is important that we continue to test our assumptions about how and why crime occurs, and which types of policing responses are needed. In order to do this testing, we need to start by observing the data that is available to us.

Data represents the building blocks of new knowledge. Data sources include substantive records such as those held on the police national database and in intelligence logs, as well as data that can be drawn from individual experience, policy documents, and the application of legislation in courts. Pieces of data are then put together to prove or answer specific questions, to prove or disprove hypotheses, and to generate new ideas and thinking about potential responses to crime. Research knowledge on crime and policing is dynamic and always changing, so it is important that you are using up-to-date data when you are doing your research.

Researchers generate new data all of the time, and this means that hypotheses and theories are challenged and, in some instances, new hypotheses and theories emerge. Researchers test hypotheses through research and produce findings from that research which constitute "evidence." This complex hypothesis testing process means there are a multitude of perspectives on what constitutes good and bad evidence for any profession. This is why the

College of Policing in England and Wales advises police organisations to "use the best available evidence to inform and challenge policing policies, practices and decisions."

So, what constitutes the "best available evidence"? Well, academic norms suggest that good evidence is peer reviewed and transparent about its methodological approach. The best available evidence also emerges from professional forums and may be anecdotal or partial before it is tested. Thus, the experiences of people working on the front-line of policing provide as valuable evidence as official police and government statistics. The key to developing good research is to bring these different types of evidence together in a systematic way to address specific problems. The most important point here is that the types of evidence we need to inform decision-making about policies, practices, strategies, and tactics differ depending upon the question you are asking and the subject matter you are interrogating. So, let's move on to an introduction to different types of research evidence. We will look first at quantitative research evidence, then at qualitative research evidence before looking at the benefits of combining or mixing both forms of research evidence.

Quantitative Research Evidence

Quantitative data is made up of numbers and thus draws on traditional scientific methodologies used in mathematics, economics and theoretical physics. This scientific method seeks to develop impartial and objective data that is collected in a consistent manner so that it offers a purely scientific form of knowledge that is, in theory at least, devoid of human bias. As we discussed earlier in the chapter, this quantitative approach is often referred to as positivism, a philosophy of knowledge with its roots in the Enlightenment period, which is underpinned by the belief that that there is a consistent and identifiable scientific reality that can be identified and analysed through the use of the scientific method.

The aim of quantitative-based forms of research is to uncover potentially unseen patterns related to crime and policing and, where appropriate, to try to establish causal links between policing and crime (like in our case study where we looked at whether the introduction of body worn cameras would lead to an increase in crime detections). As is the case in the previous case study, evidence can demonstrate that a specific strategy or tactic is or is not effective but when we are weighing up whether to use a specific strategy or tactic additional questions are raised such as what might be the most appropriate strategy or tactic in a given set of circumstances. This requires much more evidence to make decisions with a sense of certainty. So, for example, we might ask for statistical data related to the previous use of a tactic in a specific location.

The following case study illustrates this point:

Case Study

Let's look at the "Does more stop and search mean less crime?" study again https://whatworks.college.police.uk/Research/Documents/SS_and_crime_report.pdf

This broad question is very difficult to answer, but when we focus the question on to specific crime types, we start to access more useful operational information. Chapter 2 of the report presents the detailed findings of the research study. Page 14 presents the evidence, and from page 15 onwards, the report presents interpretations of the data that are potentially useful for police officers tasked with assessing what might be the best use of stop and search. Review pages 15 to 18 and make some notes on what you think would be the best use of police stop and search powers in this region.

This case study provides an example of how quantitative data can be used to test a hypothesis (or assumption). Research thus acts as a tool for testing your own assumptions. You can then reflect on the findings of this research and adapt your assumptions or day-to-day practice accordingly. We all do this as part of our daily lives as we make mistakes and correct our actions or behaviour in response to this, but research provides an extra scientific dimension to this process (methodology) to ensure interpretations of the findings can be justified when they are subjected to rigorous scrutiny.

Quantitative research can involve observations of statistics over periods of time to generate knowledge about crime patterns and the efficacy of different policing responses. This type of work is undertaken in police organisations by analysts to help inform police decision-making and the appropriate deployment of resources to specific geographical areas or crime types. At a more sophisticated level, quantitative research can also help police organisations answer complex questions such as what is the most appropriate intervention to use for a specific type of crime. The College of Policing supports this process by providing evidence reviews for police officers to access which identify the most up-to-date scientific evidence available on policing interventions.

You can have a look at some of these evidence reviews here: https://whatworks.college.police.uk/Research/Systematic_Review_Series/Pages/default.aspx

You will see that the College of Policing prioritises sources of quantitative data ahead of the qualitative data that we will introduce in the next section. The most widely recognised methodological measurement tool in the English-speaking world of policing is the Maryland Scientific Methods

Table 9.1 The Maryland Scientific Methods Scale

Level 1	Observed correlation between an intervention and outcomes at a single point in time. A study that only measured the impact of the service using a questionnaire at the end of the intervention would fall into this level.
Level 2	Temporal sequence between the intervention and the outcome clearly observed; or the presence of a comparison group that cannot be demonstrated to be comparable. A study that measured the outcomes of people who used a service before it was set up and after it finished would fit into this level.
Level 3	A comparison between two or more comparable units of analysis, one with and one without the intervention. A matched-area design using two locations in the UK would fit into this category if the individuals in the research and the areas themselves were comparable.
Level 4	Comparison between multiple units with and without the intervention, controlling for other factors or using comparison units that evidence only minor differences. A method such as propensity score matching, that used statistical techniques to ensure that the programme and comparison groups were similar would fall into this category.
Level 5	Random assignment and analysis of comparable units to intervention and control groups. A well conducted Randomised Controlled Trial fits into this category.

Source: Sherman et al., (1997).

Scale (Sherman et al., 1997). The Maryland Scale is an evidence-based tool which identifies how robust an intervention evaluation methodology is; Level 5 being the most robust and Level 1 the least.

Confused?

I thought so.

The RCT represents the gold standard of this type of experimental research. RCTs are complex, costly, and resource intensive, so the majority of research that takes place does not resemble this. Nor should it. Research can take a multitude of forms, and research design should always be based upon the demands of the question you are asking.

To return to our earlier point, the type of research question that is being asked should influence the choice of methodological approach. RCTs represent the gold standard of research that seeks to establish a causal link between two variables, i.e. the introduction of street lighting into a dark crime hotspot will often directly lead to a reduction in the number of victims of crime in this area. As such, the lighting is understood to have caused the reduction in victimisation (see Welsh and Farrington, 2008, for an overview).

As research has only recently become a core component of initial police training, it is understandable that there are quite stringent controls on what should be regarded as high-quality evidence. But if we look at other scientific and professional fields where there is a longer history of evidence-based practice, you will see that debates about what constitutes good evidence to support the development of professional practice incorporate a wider range of research methodologies (see NICE, 2015, for one example). In the next section, we address the second and much more contested area of criminological research, qualitative research data.

Qualitative Research Evidence

As we have commented throughout this chapter, different types of research evidence are more or less useful for answering different types of research questions. Although researchers may often favour different types of approaches to research, you should develop your methodological approach in response to the needs of the question and the values that underpin the research. Qualitative research methods are most commonly utilised to ask "why" and "how" questions. As Harfield (2009) extrapolates, qualitative research attempts to identify the "who, what, why, where, when and how" of policing interventions and their impact upon crime and criminal networks. Xu and Hsinchun (2005) promote network analysis as a method for gathering and analysing information to highlight *"regular patterns about the structure, organization, operation and information flow in criminal networks"* (Xu and Hsinchun, 2005: 102). Thus, as we have highlighted throughout this book, there are similarities in processes such as the gathering of police intelligence and the collection of qualitative research data.

Grounded theory is one of the most widely used, and broadly interpreted, qualitative methodological approaches in the social sciences. Grounded theory works on the premise that all knowledge and understanding of a subject matter is derived from data. As such, researchers can only start to make sense of theory and explanation after they have worked in the field. Grounded theory draws on the seminal work of Glaser and Strauss (1967), but it has since taken different directions. Strauss and Corbin (1990) developed grounded theory using a precise coding paradigm (see analysis section), whereas authors like Charmaz (2014) developed much more flexible approaches towards grounded theory.

The key principle that underpins grounded theory is the same as that which underpins any police investigation and attitudes towards evidence. All researchers must approach their investigation with an openness to the prospective findings. The evidence that we collect needs to be arranged and made sense of in a systematic manner prior to any analysis. Adaptive grounded theory (see Bulawa, 2014) approaches have a neat alignment with police investigative training and the methods and skills required to gathering information to be used as evidence or intelligence. Investigative training encourages officers to keep an open mind when gathering and analysing evidence and to retain a critical and reflective mindset.

So, qualitative evidence can provide a rich picture of the dynamics (who, what, where, when, why, and how) of crime patterns, networks of victims and offenders, and the impact of police operations, but this requires police and researchers to develop the technical skills to use a range of methodological tools. The next section briefly introduces some of the most commonly used data collection methods. The selection of data collection methods is based largely upon the simplicity of their use. Each method can be developed in a range of different ways, and you should consult social research textbooks to learn more about the nuances of each method. Bryman's Social Research Methods remain one of the most comprehensive textbooks on this subject matter although there are several textbooks that situate research methods specifically within the context of crime and policing (see, e.g., Brunger et al., 2016). We'll start by looking at surveys.

Surveys

Surveys are data collection tools which can be used to collect quantitative and/ or qualitative data. Surveys that focus upon the collection of quantitative data tend to use closed questions which require rigidly structured answers such as yes/no, multiple choice options, or scales from one to five that capture a spectrum of responses (e.g. strongly agree, agree, no opinion, disagree, strongly disagree). Quantitative surveys can thus be given rigid structures and be deployed online to ask specific questions and collect lots of data quickly. There is lots of freely available software out there to support you with this work although this ease of design and implementation means you need to be cognizant of any potential ethical or data security issues. This speedy process generates quite descriptive data which is easily translated into quantifiable date with generalisable findings which allow you to learn a lot about, for example, public attitudes towards an issue and how these attitudes might differ across social groups.

For example, if you wanted to learn about coffee drinking habits across different social groups:

- Age:
- Gender:
- How often do you drink coffee?
- How many cups of coffee do you drink per day?
- Do you drink more or less coffee than your work colleagues?

It is easier to provide some guidance on some of these answers rather than leave some confusion that leads to an inaccurate or missing answer. To support this process, you can use a Likert scale like the one below.

	A lot more	A bit more	About the same	A bit less	A lot less
Do you drink more or less coffee than your colleagues?					

Surveys are helpful in identifying answers to who and what questions but are more limited in terms of explaining why attitudes and/or behaviours may exist. Surveys are therefore useful tools for testing assumptions and hypotheses and providing quick and up-to-date snapshots of data during a specific period of time. Surveys can also be used to collect qualitative data by using open-ended questions that measure perspectives, attitudes, and interpretations, but their relative rigidity means it is not possible to probe respondents further about specific issues and to really understand our answers to why questions. If we want to learn more about why the data emerges with the patterns that it does, then we need to dig deeper and most commonly turn to observations, focus groups, or interviews. We will address each of these in reverse order.

Interviews

Interviews have many similarities with surveys and may even ask the exact same question, but they differ in providing a much more personal level of engagement that helps to facilitate follow-up questions and what is often referred to as a conversation with a purpose (Burgess, 1991). Interviews purposefully engage with an individual's emotions and feelings about a subject and are much less rigid in structure than surveys. Indeed, interviews are often understood to be exploratory and can be structured according to the purpose of the interviews. The most commonly utilised interview form is the semi-structured interview, but interviews can also be undertaken in a highly structured manner or through long unstructured conversations (often known as narrative interviews). Most interviews sit somewhere in between these two extremes, and the design of interviews should be influenced by the aims of the research project and the researcher's own ontological and epistemological positions.

For example, if you are engaged in a project which seeks to raise the profile of marginalised voices (e.g. victims of crime), then you would provide a loose structure to your interview to enable the participant to direct the subject matter of the discussion. Conversely, if you were exploring how police officers used a piece of legislation in their day-to-day work, you would have a clearly structured question schedule so that each officer was asked the same question and the answers could be compared during the analytical stage of the research.

Interviews are able to provide researchers with the opportunity to explore views, values, and lived experience in a depth that surveys struggle to achieve. Interviews can be time-consuming. You always need to factor in the time it will take to transcribe data, and this can limit the number of interviews you might include in a project. For dissertation students, interviews provide an excellent tool for understanding a small world and then exploring how well you might generalise these findings. You might want to speak to a specific shift at work, a small group of community members, or specialists in an area when you can learn lots from this small group within a limited period of time.

One of the key issues that you need to address when embedding interviews into your research design is how you might choose your sample population and manage any potential researcher or respondent bias that could be consciously or unconsciously built into the research findings. Bryman (2021) describes this process as purposive sampling whereby interviewees are chosen for their relevance to the research question. Purposive sampling is a non-probability form of sampling and is determined by the needs of the research and is widely used in police research where it is often difficult to gain access to large interview samples due to competing work priorities. The use of knowledge of the subject and the range of people involved who can supply the best information is a useful aid to purposive sampling (Denscombe, 2010).

To learn more about interviewing and other research methods, you should utilise the UK Data Service research support tools which provide all sorts of useful help for those who are new to interviewing. You can access these materials using this link – www.ukdataservice.ac.uk/teaching-resources/interview.aspx

For time reasons, it can be helpful to conduct multiple interviews at one time or in one place, and researchers will sometimes manage competing priorities by bringing a group of people together at one time to provide multiple perspectives in one setting. This is called a focus group.

Focus Groups

Focus groups tend to take the form of a group interview with an interview schedule as described above that is used in a group setting. Focus groups can provide a pragmatic solution to the time-consuming challenges of undertaking multiple one-to-one interviews or obtaining access to hard-to-reach populations. Focus groups can also differ to interviews as their purpose is to allow the group to provide answers and to generate meaning and understanding of situations through their interactions. Focus groups thus allow the researcher to identify group norms and provide insights into the cultural dynamics through which people understand this work. This is what Schein (1993) refers to as the deeper values and assumptions demonstrated by members of an organisation, or more simply, "the way we do things around here." All of these data collection tools can be used in isolation or alongside each other to help you get to the point where you have sufficient data to support your needs. The more data that you collect, the more likely you are to develop a more sophisticated and nuanced understanding of your research environment although there are challenges presented too as research is time-consuming, and there is always the danger of going native amongst your research populations and losing the objective detachment that you will have started with. The most immersive form of research is ethnography which allows you to become an observer inside your research environment and sometimes even a participant too.

Ethnography

As a rule, the longer a research project goes on, the more a researcher should be able to understand about the environment they are researching through the processes of immersion in data and reflection on this qualitative inquiry. This approach is often called ethnography (see Hammersley and Atkinson, 1995, for more detail). Post-World War II, policing studies emerged from break-through studies such as Inside the British Police by Simon Holdaway (1983) that built upon the insights of earlier North American classics from Bittner (1970) and Skolnick (1966) and that have been referenced in more detail in previous chapters. Due to the time required to immerse yourself in an often difficult-to-access policing environment, the number of contemporary eth-nographies is quite limited, and this method of data collection is sometimes simply described as observation due to it being difficult to undertake research without some observations of the environment taking place.

Observation can facilitate a deeper understanding of organisational systems and processes as well as occupational cultures that develop within the organ-isation. This type of research can draw a picture of an organisation from the bottom-up which offers valuable insights beyond the more tightly controlled remit of structured surveys, interviews, and focus groups. This type of analysis is open to accusations of bias and subjectivity due to how close the researcher gets to the research environment, but it also offers important challenges to the top-down visions of crime and policing that are produced in statistical datasets.

Participant observation "involves social interaction between the researcher and informants in the milieu of the latter" (Taylor and Brogden, 1984: 15). The arrival of new policing degrees and the requirement to complete a research dissertation presents the prospect of participant observations where an individual operates simultaneously as a police officer and researcher with valuable appreciative insight into how narratives about crime and policing are constructed through informal and formal discourses and occupational culture. The usefulness of participant observation in organisational research, and particularly within policing, arises from its potential to *emphasise the importance of human meanings, interpretations and interactions with an insider perspective* (Jorgensen, 1989: 108).

All types of research have strengths and weaknesses and the most notable issue with all of the above methods is subjectivity. How do we know that the researcher is not just manipulating the process to serve their own purposes? Even if the researcher is trying to manage their own bias out of the process, is it really possible for the findings to be presented as valid knowledge? It is at this point that we introduce triangulation to our understanding of good research.

Triangulation requires researchers to analyse multiple sources and to tri-angulate the findings from each of the sources. For example, a researcher might combine documentary analysis with interviews and some observations to triangulate and verify their findings. While participant observation and qualitative interviews provide an insight into the "inner world" of policing, particularly as it operates in the "backstage" region (Goffman, 1959), documentary or textual analysis provides a contrast with this through its study of official or formal language and generates a more holistic understanding of the subject matter as it operates in both the "front" and "back" regions. Ultimately, it is the accumulation of different types of evidence that strengthens, tests and proves (or otherwise) a hypothesis or theory.

A Short Note on Mixed Methods Research

This desire to accumulate evidence and test different sources alongside each other to improve the rigour of the research process leads us to an extensive and complex area of contemporary methodological development which is neatly captured under the title, "mixed methods research." Mixed methods approaches to policing and criminological research seek to draw on the strengths of both quantitative and qualitative approaches and to minimise the limitations of each approach by developing these methodological approaches in a complementary or integrative manner (see Bryman, 2021, for more). As such, a mixed methods approach seeks to find a middle ground in which multiple viewpoints and perspectives can be considered simultaneously and encourages researchers to continue to develop their skills in alignment with the needs of research questions rather than to rely on those research skills we have already developed.

Any mixed methods approach needs to be carefully thought out at the initial research design stage to identify the need and rationale for such an approach and to identify the specific methodological tools that will complement each other in delivering the research findings. For example, a survey may generate lots of responses although without obvious depth, and this quantitative approach could be complemented by interviews which explore key themes in more detail. It is also important to take into consideration the time and resources available so that research can provide appropriate amounts of attention to each of the research design, data collection, data analysis, and write-up stages. There will always be some degree of trade-off between the time and resources available and the desired quality and utility of the research. Two of the key terms that we use to summarise this position in terms of the quality and utility of the research product are reliability and validity.

We would argue that there are lots of different types of evidence which are useful for different sets of circumstances and, which importantly, can be self-generated without the need for extensive time and resources. The key terminological reference points that are used to define the quality of the chosen research approach are reliability and validity. Reliability is ensured through a consistent methodological approach to the evidence gathering and analysis process and relates to the likelihood of replication of results in a different context. Validity relates to the accuracy and appropriateness of measurement. Validity is ensured by showing there is a good match between the evidence extracted from the research and the theory applied (Bryman, 2021). Bryman provides a much more in depth articulation of validity and reliability than we have space for here for those who want to explore this issue in more detail.

Craft and Science/Ethics and Values

You will have seen in the various case studies that we have used throughout the book how ethical issues and tests of your own values naturally emerge while you are undertaking research. Ethics and values guide the way we do research and collect evidence and how we might interpret and utilise the findings. The College of Policing in England and Wales already provide a starting point for thinking about research with the Code of Ethics which seeks to be "at the heart of every policy, procedure, decision and action in policing" (College of Policing, 2021). Similarly, the British Society of Criminology has its own statement of Ethics which you can access here: www.britsoccrim.org/documents/BSCEthics2015.pdf

The College of Policing code of ethics takes priority for serving police officers and seeks to promote self-awareness and personal reflection to support police officers in making ethical judgements in all aspects of their day-to-day work. The Code of Ethics is underpinned by nine policing principles which are implicit in the criminological ethics statement too:

Accountability: You are answerable for your decisions, actions, and omissions
Fairness: You treat people fairly
Honesty: You are truthful and trustworthy
Integrity: You always do the right thing
Leadership: You lead by good example
Objectivity: You make choices on evidence and your best professional judgement
Openness: You are open and transparent in your actions and decisions
Respect: You treat everyone with respect
Selflessness: You act in the public interest

(Home Office, 2014)

These principles should underpin how police officers think about research and its relevance to their role and the decisions they make. It thus follows that these principles should also underpin how we think about policing research. As you interrogate more research, the knowledge-base that underpins your actions becomes increasingly objective and can withstand rigorous quality and ethical review. Research should play a prominent part in any review process as you assess what might have been best practice or try to capture some innovation that produced a positive outcome. Consideration of ethical issues throughout the research process is thus a core element of developing reflective practice whereby you learn from both positive and negative experiences at work and continually test the assumptions that underpin your day-to-day work. The Code of Ethics simply provides a framework through which you can do this with support from the NDM to help embed ethical reasoning into policing practice. Put simply, the NDM situates the Code of Ethics at the heart of all police decision-making including research reviews and the generation of research.

Conclusion

The learning from the last two chapters can feel overwhelming at first, but by using the tools introduced in the chapter, you will quickly get used to the research process. Below is a table that will help with your first research project. Your task is to complete the following methodology table, making sure

Table 9.2 Research Planner

Central Research Question	
Research Philosophy	
Research Strategy	
Research Design	
Sampling	
Ethics	
Access	
Data Collection Method(s)	
Critique	
Other Methodological Considerations	

that you can explain and justify all of your decisions. The combination of this table and the College of Policing logic model (https://whatworks.college.pol ice.uk/Research/Documents/LogicModel.pdf) provides you with a template to develop your research ideas whether it be in a research dissertation project or with research you are undertaking in the workplace. Best of luck!

References

Bayley, D. and Shearing, C. (2001) *The New Structure of Policing: Description, Conceptualization and Research Agenda*. Washington, DC: National Institute of Justice.

Bhaskar, R. (1975) *A Realist Theory of Science*. Brighton: Harvester Press.

Bhaskar, R. (1979) *The Possibility of Naturalism*. Brighton: Harvester Press.

Bittner, E. (1970) *The Functions of the Police in Modern Society*. Maryland: National Institute of Mental Health.

Bogdan, R. and Biklen, S. (1998) *Qualitative Research for Education*. Michigan: University of Michigan.

Brunger, M., Tong, S. and Martin, D. (2016) *Introduction to Police Research*. London: Routledge.

Bryman, A. (2021) *Social Research Methods* (Sixth Edition). Oxford: Oxford University Press.

Bulawa, P. (2014) Adapting Grounded Theory in Qualitative Research. *International Research in Education*. 2(1): 145–168.

Burgess, R. (1991) *In the Field: An Introduction to Field Research*. London: Routledge.

Charmaz, K. (2014) *Constructing Grounded Theory*. London: Routledge.

Cole, B. (1991) Post-colonial systems. In R. Mawby (ed.) *Policing Across the World*. London: UCL Press.

College of Policing (2021) *Code of Ethics*. Available at: https://www.college.police.uk/ethics/code-of-ethics

Denscombe, M. (2010) *The Good Research Guide: For Small-Scale Social Research Projects (Open UP Study Skills)*. Maidenhead: McGraw-Hill.

Durkheim, E. (1893/1984) *The Division of Labour*. Basingstoke: Palgrave MacMillan.

Durkheim, E. (1912/2001) *The Elementary Forms of Religious Life*. Oxford: Oxford University Press.

Emsley, C. (1991) *The English Police: A Social and Political History*. London: Harvester Wheatsheaf.

Feilzer, Y. (2010) Doing mixed methods research pragmatically: Implications for the rediscovery of pragmatism as a research paradigm. *Journal of Mixed Methods Research*. 4(1): 6–16.

Fukuyama, F. (2012) *The Origins of Political Order*. London: Profile Books.

Glaser, B. and Strauss, A. (1967) *The Discovery of Grounded Theory: Strategies for Qualitative Research*. Chicago: Aldine.

Goffman, E. (1959) *The Presentation of Self in Everyday Life*. London: Penguin.

Goldstein, H. (1979) Improving policing: A problem-oriented approach. *Crime and Delinquency*. 25(2): 236–258.

Guba, E. and Lincoln, Y. (1994) Competing paradigms in qualitative research. In N. Denzin and Y. Lincoln (eds.) *Handbook of Qualitative Research*, 105–117. London: Sage.

Hall, S., Critcher, C., Jefferson, T., Clarke, J. and Roberts, B. (1978) *Policing the Crisis: Mugging, the State and Law and Order*. London: MacMillan.

Hammersley, M. and Atkinson, P. (1995) *Ethnography: Principles and Practice* (Second Edition). London: Routledge.

Harfield, C. (2009) *Defining and Defying Organized Crime*. London: Routledge.

Hills, A. (2014) What is policeness? On being police in Somalia. *British Journal of Criminology*. 54(5): 765–783.

Holdaway, S. (1983) *Inside the British Police*. Oxford: Blackwell.

Home Office (2014) *Code of Ethics Launched*. Available at: www.gov.uk/government/news/code-of-ethics-launched

Jorgensen, D. (1989) *Participant Observation: A Methodology for Human Studies*. Newbury Park: Sage.

National Institute for Health and Care Excellence (2015) *Research Recommendations Process and Methods Guide*. Available at: www.nice.org.uk/Media/Default/About/what-we-do/Science-policy-and-research/research-recommendation-process-methods-guide-2015.pdf

Neocleous, M. (2006) Theoretical foundations of the new police science. In M. Dubber and M. Valverde (eds.) *The New Police Science*, 17–41. Stanford, CT: Stanford University Press.

Punch, M. (2005) *Introduction to Social Research: Quantitative and Qualitative Approaches*. London: Sage.

Roach, J. and Pease, K. (2017) How to morph experience into evidence. In J. Knutsson and L. Tompson (eds.) *Advances in Evidence-Based Policing*, 84–97. London: Routledge.

Schein, E. (1993) *Organisational Culture and Leadership*. New York, NY: John Wiley and Sons.

Sherman, L., Gottfredson, D., Mackenzie, D, Eck, J., Reuter, P. and Bushway, S. (1997) *Preventing Crime: What Works, What Doesn't, What's Promising*. Washington, DC: Department of Justice.

Skolnick, J. (1966) *Justice Without Trial*. London: John Wiley.

Strauss, A. and Corbin, J. (1990) *Basics of Qualitative Research: Techniques and Procedures for Developing Grounded Theory*. London: Sage.

Taylor, S. and Brogden, R. (1984) *Introduction to Qualitative Research Methods*. New York, NY: Wiley.

Welsh, B. and Farrington, D. (2008) *Effects of Improved Street Lighting on Crime. Campbell Collaboration Systematic Review*. Norway: Campbell Collaboration.

Wood, D., Cockcroft, T., Tong, S. and Bryant, R. (2017) The importance of context and cognitive agency in developing police knowledge: Going beyond the police science discourse. *The Police Journal: Theory, Practice and Principles*. 91(2): 173–187.

Xu, J. and Hsinchun, C. (2005) Criminal network analysis and visualisation. *Communications of the Association of Computing Machinery*. 48(6): 100–107. Available at: https://dl.acm.org/doi/fullHtml/10.1145/1064830.1064834?casa_token=vTEdXlUljxAAAAAA:MLT8_luIuAlRfP-PpWkB_1WxjApuzAWi5ISjdOL2f_OvvWxUAwn4z_LVjBg5F8-V3ktBLNh0aBqTn2M

Chapter 10

Conclusion

Introduction

We will finish this book where we started by asking the question, what is the purpose of criminology for the police?

In simple terms, criminology offers new forms of academic and professional learning development in terms of theoretical analysis and research that can be used as part of a problem-solving toolkit in the workplace. Criminological understanding should help enhance the capability and capacity of individuals and, in consequence, police organisations. In this way, the integration of criminology into police models of education represents a continuing lineage that extends back to August Vollmer's work on police professionalism in the United States one hundred years ago and has made its way through the past century via the critical inputs to police thinking from historians like Charles Reith, problem-solvers like Hermann Goldstein, and social scientists like Lawrence Sherman. Therefore, the purpose of criminology for police is to encourage you to reach out to a range of novel ways of thinking about policing and to encourage the police profession to continue to develop in alignment with the needs of an ever-changing society.

In short, criminology should bring more voices to the table for discussions about how societies are policed. Like other social sciences, criminology seeks to support, develop, and, to some degree, inculcate critical thinking to encourage people to ask *why is that the way we do things around here?* This is important at a time when popular calls for police reform are echoing across the world and states are co-opting, and sometimes coercing, police organisations for their own policing purposes. It is ever more important for all police officers to question what they see around them.

In Spring 2020, the death of George Floyd was witnessed retrospectively by millions as he was held down by a police officer in the city of Minneapolis in the United States and choked to death. The camera phone footage of this police brutality quickly travelled around the world. This very public killing re-invigorated already strong calls for radical reform of policing in the United States and added further dynamism and energy to the Black Lives Matter

DOI: 10.4324/9781003081012-10

movement that has been established after the killings of Trayvon Martin in Florida in 2013 and Michael Brown in Ferguson, Missouri in 2014.

Despite the obvious differences in how policing by consent works in the United Kingdom, politicians and the public still draw significant social, political, and cultural influence from the United States, and these global stories travel and impact police officers in their own localities. In truth, this call for reform could have come from many countries. At the time of writing, some of the most significant economic and political forces across the globe, including countries such as India, Brazil, and China, are drawing their police into an increasingly authoritarian climate whereby minority groups are being targeted for harassment and persecution by state agents, including police. The independence of police from government remains important for this exact reason.

The United Kingdom has its own history of policing that has retrospectively been subjected to significant critique. Since the end of the Second World War, the authority of the police in the United Kingdom has been met with periodic protests over the policing of minority groups and multiple crises of legitimacy that are often aligned with wider political and economic crises (Hall et al., 1978). Most notably, police forces have faced consistent criticism about statistical disparities in stop and search rates and the impact this has on disproportionately negative outcomes for black males throughout the criminal justice process. The 2017 Lammy Report on the treatment of, and outcomes for Black, Asian, and Minority Ethnic individuals in the criminal justice system had highlighted the racial disparities that are endemic through every stage of the criminal justice process in the United Kingdom, yet the persistence of these challenges for policing and other state agencies continues to be evident with none of the report's 35 recommendations, at the time of writing, having been implemented.

There are similar questions to be asked about disparities in gender justice. In 2019–2020 convictions for rape hit their lowest point since tracking and recording of these crimes was started by the Crown Prosecution Service (CPS, 2020). While the key end point challenge has been a low proportion of successful court cases, there are also fewer cases being passed on by the Crown Prosecution Service to go to trial, and fewer cases being put forward by police forces. Despite four decades of policy reform, there are still multiple obstacles faced by women in relation to access to justice in cases of sexual harassment, domestic abuse, and sexual violence. In addition to this, the past decade has given significant profile to child exploitation cases that had historically escaped the attention of state services. The challenges faced by police and society remain manifold and complex at a time when the justice system in England and Wales is visibly creaking.

The police are key social actors within these complex examples of racial, ethnic, and gender injustice and the consequences of persistent injustice are low trust and confidence in police forces. It is here that criminological research has a clear role for police forces as more detailed analysis is required of precisely where these injustices occur and, most significantly, why they occur in such a disproportionate manner for specific societal groups. During these times of political and social crisis, we are all required to question the role of state power and how each individual, organisation, and nation state might conceptualise the purpose of police during times of social conflict. Criminology's contribution to these debates is incomplete. For example, there is little written in British academic criminology about the ways in which police organisations resist state power and exert their independence during times of conflict and insecurity. Much of academic criminology's contribution thus far is found in an administrative focus on efficiency and effectiveness or more critical analyses of front-line policing. There is much more work to do. The rest of this chapter reviews some of the immediate challenges faced by the police profession before articulating a summary of the key areas where criminology and the new model of police education can contribute. The chapter closes with some consideration of potential new horizons for police-focused criminological research.

Policing Futures

Policing is not just about the administration of law but the pursuit of justice and police education, rather than training, is about finding just outcomes and not just lawfully compliant ones (Taylor, 2012). A consistent message has been presented throughout this book about police needing to align itself with the social, political, economic, and legal needs of democratic society to deliver policing by consent and a sense of justice. Criminology has a potential role in developing this more nuanced appreciation of the aspiration for justice and the relationship between justice and good policing, but it needs to engage with state agencies such as the police to have a meaningful impact and to move quickly to engage with the big topics of any given time.

For example, the excessive use of force against minority groups by police officers in the United States has provoked significant debate which includes questions about the continued existence of the police as an institution (Vitale, 2017). These arguments have had a ripple effect into other jurisdictions and raised recurring questions about future police legitimacy. Vitale argues that the police in New York no longer meets the needs of society and his argument reflects those of late eighteenth and early nineteenth century commentators in England such as Henry Fielding (1757) and John Colquhoun (1800) who recognised that societies in fundamental transition need to re-imagine their police and policing accordingly. Fielding and Colquhoun laid out the groundwork for the development of a de-militarised and depoliticised London Metropolitan Police and Peel's principles of policing that still echo through discussions about underpinning philosophies of policing in democratic societies today (see Lentz and Chaires, 2007, for a discussion about the origin of Peel's principles).

These fundamental reforms, which unravelled across the nineteenth century, represented a re-configuration of our conceptual understanding of policing through attempts to meet the needs of the newly industrialised society (Paterson and Williams, 2018). The emergent industrialisation and urbanisation that drove the police reforms of 1829 is closing in on 200 years of history and perhaps requires some re-visitation at a point when society is once again reimagining itself in alignment with geo-political shifts and the digital information revolution. The UK government is already using technology to radically re-shape how it works under conditions of globalisation, transnationalism, and internationalism and police strategy is moving into alignment with this digital first agenda (APCC, 2020; College of Policing, 2020). Similarly, offenders and victims are no longer necessarily co-located, and modes of communication are increasingly virtual and, at times, anonymous. The skill set of offenders has changed dramatically, and police have yet to fully re-configure to align with this threat.

The demand for innovative thinking and empirical research to interrogate existing assumptions will undoubtedly continue. As we noted earlier in the book, the role of criminological study of the police has historically been separated into distinct categories which can all make potential contributions to improving understandings about the relationship between police, crime, and society:

- Administrative analysis that focuses upon policy development and performance enhancement
- Sociological analysis of the role of police and policing in society
- Cultural analysis of the meaning of police institutions and policing actors
- Marxist critique of the police role and function and their underpinning philosophies and strategies

Analysis of the professional challenges faced by police organisations requires us to engage in critical criminological and sociological scholarship of the police and policing. The sociological study of policing retains a broader focus on policing as a social process which aims to maintain order unlike the administrative studies which retain a narrower focus on evidence-based policing strategies, problem-solving, and policy evaluation. These administrative studies provide a framework for analysing the public role of the police and its position as a formal state institution within an inter-linked network of formal and informal policing providers. Administrative studies also provide a mechanism for the evaluation of the effectiveness of the state police in maintaining order, providing reassurance, and controlling crime. With this administrative approach, the analytical emphasis is directed towards the implementation of policy and the professional role of the Police Service, whereas analyses of the changing landscape of policing, the evolving role and function of the public police and the identification of the future shape of policing points us towards a very different future for the criminological study of the police and policing.

Critical perspectives on policing question the structural foundations of policing as much as their role in society and are subsequently concerned with questions surrounding police governance and legitimacy ahead of the efficacy of different policing strategies. Post-modern developments in policing scholarship will ensure that different criminological schools of thought flourish in the future and continue to embrace the divergent consensus and conflict perspectives on the role of policing that have been introduced in this book. This provides a further opportunity to reflect on your own thinking about the police and policing.

Competing narratives about community-orientation, national security, and public accountability make it increasingly difficult to answer the question – what is the role and the function of the police? An ever-changing policing landscape coupled with tension between policing, security, and order maintenance at the local, national, and international levels has made it more difficult to police a more demanding British public and simultaneously address the global complexity of twenty-first century threats to security and order.

Clamp and Paterson (2016) argue in their book, *Restorative Policing*, that there is a need to broaden and lengthen the conceptual lens through which police are analysed, and the wider concept of policing situated. This argument builds upon the work of Bayley and Shearing (2001) and their recognition of significant shifts in the governance and delivery of policing as we entered the new millennium. Analysis of this argument is given further urgency during a historical period where digital and information innovations are extending possibilities at the same time as geo-political shifts are also generating new uncertainties. The next section picks up these challenges with a summary framework that seeks to align the contributions of criminology, the new models of police education, and contemporary social, economic, and political policing needs in England and Wales.

Criminology, Policing, and Police Education

The arrival of mandatory degree-level qualifications for new police officers in England and Wales in January 2020 has been accompanied by much debate and conjecture within professional policing and across wider society. The potential strengths and weaknesses of introducing degree-level education have been argued vehemently by opposing sides and there is, as yet, insufficient empirical evidence to support either side of the for or against debate conclusively. Despite this, it is possible to provide a theoretical framework that explains where this new model of criminology and police education might be able to contribute to the future alignment of policing services with the contemporary needs of society. The themes that we will use to develop this framework are drawn from Marenin's (2005: 109) requirements of democratic policing which emphasise the importance of police professionalism, public accountability, and consequent trust and legitimacy. These categories have been used previously to build a framework for analysing the relationship between higher education and the learning needs of policing organisations (Paterson, 2011) and, in this instance, these three categories will be used to identify where criminology can potentially bring benefits to police education and the delivery of police goals.

As the previous sections in this chapter have already recognised, policing services are delivered in twenty-first century democratic societies against a socio-political and cultural backdrop that is characterised by social (in) justice, inequity, and a recognition of the need for clear legal and regulatory frameworks that support and protect vulnerable people. In response to this, the College of Policing has put values at the forefront of police education to support the development of a clearly articulated moral compass that should underpin future police practice. It is already recognised that the effective use of police discretion enhances police performance by improving police–community relations and bolstering perceptions of police professionalism (Paterson, 2011). It is this *professionalism* when engaging with the public combined with clear and transparent public *accountability* that generates police *legitimacy*. These three categories provide the framework for the rest of this chapter which addresses each of the three categories and then leads into a short conclusion.

Professionalism

Police professionalism relates to the giving of recognition and authority to a body of people to police. Images of professional policing are often iden-tified by the public in the form of a specific uniform although, in govern-mental terms, professionalism arises from education and training, status, and accountability to civil society. We can draw here on the work of the French sociologist, Emile Durkheim, and his work on order and change (1912) as well as Alice Hill's (2014) more recent work on the defining aspects of "policeness" across jurisdictions as relating to ownership of the knowledge, skills, and power required to fulfil societal or political expectations about the management of crime and disorder. Professionalism is thus often deemed to separate formal state police bodies from the myriad of other policing bodies (bouncers, parking attendants, city ambassadors, commercial security guards, private investigators) that exist in societies who do not meet these unwritten requirements to take professional responsibility for order maintenance and crime prevention.

The characteristics of professions are often understood to be degree-level qualifications, a governing authority, and a public body of knowledge that underpins decision-making in the profession. Professionalism is thus already an underpinning characteristic of many of the professions with which police officers work and the advent of the College of Policing in 2013 further aligned police with these professions by providing it with its governing authority and a public home for its evidence-base. Yet, unlike other professions, police do not yet have an extensive public body of knowledge to underpin strategy and decision-making. The College of Policing has started to collect and synthesise existing research, and it has commissioned and generated new research. Yet, the College requires the support of its members as well as embedded and independent scholars to help develop and test this evidence-base to give it the rigour, reliability, and validity of other professions. It is here that criminology has lots to offer.

Professionalisation means there will be externally recognised higher education qualifications available for all police officers and that an increasingly sophisticated evidence-base can be developed that underpins the evolution of policing strategies and tactics. The aspiration is that these changes will enable all police officers to manage enhanced complexity and increasingly diverse challenges; to be community leaders from the front-line. Embedded higher education can help student officers develop deeper learning which encourages professional reflection and autonomy in the field. In terms of the delivery of professionalisation, there is evidence that suggests that degree-level qualifications lead to the use of less force, fewer complaints, greater officer flexibility in managing diverse circumstances, and the consequent potential to enhance public legitimacy (Paterson, 2011). Whereas police training prioritises skills development for student officers, the educative element of criminology and social science prioritises softer communication skills, problem-solving, critical thinking, and reflection upon ethical issues with the aim of developing a culture of lifelong learning.

In addition to these ethics and values, the professionalism of police officers is also reflected in the knowledge and understanding of law and social problems that inform the judgements that police officers make in front of the public. Police officers are held to account through multiple mechanisms, including accountability to the law and courts, but it is the sense of justice being delivered amongst the public and in communities that is the source of their public legitimacy.

Legitimacy

The term police legitimacy is often used in conjunction with references to public trust in the police, but it is a more complex concept that incorporates a sense of obligations to abide by the law and its agents and a sense of fairness (or otherwise) that makes legitimacy a dynamic and fluid concept (Tankebe, 2012). For police officers, the challenge of maintaining public legitimacy can come into direct conflict with orders from police managers as the many purposes of policing (order maintenance, crime prevention, public protection) come into conflict. Police reforms thus face a challenge in meeting both the political imperatives of the state (order and control) and the needs of the citizenry (protection) that often leads to partly realised ideals and practice. It is for this reason that we have seen a slow evolution of community and neighbourhood policing into something more personalised and oriented around victim needs to help increase public confidence in the police and to enhance the legitimacy of the police institution (Bradford et al., 2009; Farrell, 2001; Kapoor, 2020). Policy trajectories across criminal justice agencies continue to raise the significance of embedding victims' interests into the criminal justice process, and this has led to the development of policies that emphasise the psychological and democratic benefits of situating victims at the heart of any police response (Ibarra and Erez, 2005; Taylor, 2012). It is therefore possible to re-configure the social relations through which police–community relations emerge, to increase public confidence in police action and to deliver more efficient and effective policing services (Paterson and Clamp, 2013). The potential implications for police legitimacy, effectiveness, and efficiency are significant. Community policing philosophies and problem-oriented policing strategies have infused contemporary policing with a renewed victim focus and an ability to respond to the diverse needs of complex societies.

One of the driving forces for the police educational qualifications framework has been the increasingly complex demands put upon police officers in their roles (HMIC, 1999, 2002) with a strong emphasis upon the importance of understanding and responding to vulnerability. Developments in our understanding of human behaviour and the social structures that produce crime and disorder mean that the challenges faced by new twenty-first century police officers do not simply relate to responding to crime to keep communities safe but also to proactively understand how the vulnerabilities of diverse communities may make some groups more vulnerable to specific harms.

Re-current harms may not be immediately visible, and some individuals and communities will resist engagement with police due to concern about as yet invisible threats and poor historic relationships with police, amongst other things. In all contexts, police are required to be proactive and to provide an equitable service, even in communities where their presence may not always be welcomed. Understanding the complex and dynamic context that surrounds police and policing should allow for a more nuanced and informed approach to social problems and more consistent decision-making that builds public trust. This is where knowledge, understanding, and evidence become essential components of the evolution of professional policing.

Some of the most significant criminological contributions to police practice have been in addressing repeat victimisation to improve crime prevention and build public trust at the community level. The successful repeat victimisation work in England and Wales in the 1980s and 1990s that initially focused upon property crimes used rational choice and routine activity-based theories to design target-hardening prevention activities that were aimed at repeat victims (Laycock, 2001). Police forces across England and Wales designed their own localised responses to localised patterns of burglary using accurate data to precisely identify the source of the problem. This work led to dramatic reductions in rates of property crime (Farrall, 2001).

Yet, although crime rates decreased dramatically during the 1990s and 2000s in England and Wales, police organisations were disappointed to find that public confidence in police did not improve significantly and, in some places, decreased. A clearer understanding of a further aspect of police legitimacy was emerging as although police were meeting the aims that they have been set by government and police leaders, they were not meeting the expectations of the public and especially the security needs of vulnerable communities. Criminological research has subsequently illustrated how important the way the police do policing is to the public (i.e. how they engaged with citizens and victims) and that this is a key factor in subsequent individual and organisational legitimacy in the eyes of the public (Bradford et al., 2009; Tyler, 2017).

In terms of police legitimacy, it is important for members of the public to understand that decisions are made with a rigorous grounding in the challenges of applying law to complex social problems. This is what we have expected lawyers, barristers, and judges always to do so why should the police officer, who is required to make split-second context-specific legal judgements, not be recognised as taking on equally complex challenges.

There has always been a fundamental tension between the core aspects of policing that address the need to manage threats to individuals and society through a bifurcation of techniques that target perpetrators of crime, potential and repeat victims of crime, and the criminogenic conditions that shape patterns of offending and victimisation across society. Over the past 30 to 40 years, we have seen a slow but incremental shift to more proactive community management strategies in policing, but public discourse about the police still focuses upon reactive calls for service and visible presence. The rationale and logic of policing is thus rarely clear to the wider public and a failure to articulate these changes can have a detrimental impact upon police legitimacy. It is this articulation and rationale to support decision-making that will be covered in the final section as we move on to discuss the role of police accountability in generating legitimacy.

Accountability

Police accountability systems seek to provide the machinery that builds trust in police institutions and police officers. Police officers and organisations are held to account for their actions by the formal machinery of the law and courts and a range of oversight bodies that include, most prominently, Police and Crime Commissioners, the Independent Office of Police Conduct, and Her Majesty's Inspectorate of Constabulary and Fire and Rescue Services. Police are also held to account by a range of horizontal forms of accountability that include community linkages, public confidence measures, and independent advisory groups. The multiple layers of police accountability systems have developed in response to enhanced demands for transparency and a recognition of the value external scrutiny can bring to how policing is delivered.

In most criminological textbooks, police accountability has historically been explored through interrogations of elements of organisational and individual accountability mechanisms. We provide some context for the governance of accountability mechanisms in Chapters 2 and 3 which leaves room for a more detailed interrogation of data and accountability in this final section, with a specific focus upon the rise in importance of evidence-based policing in shaping, measuring, and assessing police organisational management policing strategies. In this context, Chief Constables and Police and Crime Commissioners become the Chief Executives with responsibility for delivering agile and adaptive policing, crime and security plans at the regional level.

With reductions in police budgets being accompanied by the evolution of increasingly diverse communities that produce increasingly complex challenges, it has become ever more essential to understand the current state of the social world that immediately surrounds us all. This includes the traditional domain of publicly visible criminality that generates social anxieties as well as the less visible private and transient communities that, for many people, sit in the shadows of their everyday experiences. The role of good-quality data, drawn from a myriad of contributing agencies, can provide both effective oversight and accountability alongside an ever ready and up-to-date resource to support police decision-making at all levels in the organisation. Good decision-making in this context is what builds and maintains the public legitimacy of the police and remains the source of the organisation's professional prestige and social position as the primary contributor of protective services to the citizenry.

The best practice evidence from across the world indicates that collaborative models of learning can help to address the challenge of complexity and to enhance police professionalism, increase public trust, and support the development of problem-solving strategies (Paterson, 2011). Collectively, this secures the position of the police officer and organisation as the primary sources of policing knowledge amidst an increasingly competitive field of people offering policing and security services. The public police retain a distinctive function to all other policing providers in that their alignment to the state provides a direct link to the protection of the democratic citizenry. Therefore, the aims and values of the police educational learning environment need to be, as much as possible, in alignment with the political, social, and cultural norms in society and, of course, the ethics and values of the police profession. The need to stretch agreement about the purpose of policing in such a broad manner places considerable challenges upon police leadership and an enhanced importance on the role of mentorship, socialisation, and the generation of collaborative leadership from all aspects of organisations and partnerships (Herrington and Colvin, 2016).

This book has drawn together these three strands of professionalism, legitimacy, and accountability in an attempt to articulate what a twenty-first century criminology for the police might look like. This includes the introduction of theory that directly informs practice; research that assists problem-solving; and knowledge that underpins consistent and evidence-informed decision-making that can be accounted for in fair, equitable, and transparent ways. This knowledge-base is essential as police officers and organisations make critical day-to-day decisions at all levels of the police hierarchy about how policing should be done. The media appetite for stories about crime and policing leads, directly and indirectly, to questions about why the police do what they do. The high profile of signal crimes (Innes, 2014) draws the attention of politicians who question why police makes the decisions they make. And they do this sometimes years after an event has taken place.

Developing Criminological Research for (and by) Police

As we bring the book to a close, it is perhaps useful to reflect upon what comes next. Thus far, this book has provided an overview of how the academic discipline of criminology has been integrated into the College of Policing's education qualifications framework. It has also been an aspiration of the authors to provide you with opportunities to further investigate specific areas of inquiry that align with your own academic interests and your own future professional career plans. The aim of the second half of this book has been to lay out the landscape of police research as it currently looks for those pursuing police, or policing-oriented careers. The nuts and bolts of research and evidence-based policing are all in here, but it is now up to you to decide what the future of evidence-based policing and criminologically oriented police research looks like in England and Wales.

Criminology has a long and varied relationship with the police institution and has been friend, critic, and cynic at different points in this historical relationship that extends back 100 years. The most obvious integration of academic theory and professional practice in England and Wales at the moment is evidence-based policing which remains in its infancy but is gaining traction across the globe. The idea of evidence-based policing emerged out of the more established practice of evidence-based health and transferred to England and Wales when Larry Sherman moved from the United States to the University of Cambridge and established an evidence-based policing hub and masters-level degree qualification to educate a new cadre of police professionals from across the world in evidence-based policing. Yet, Sherman was not the first to develop a more clearly articulated relationship between police learning and development and higher education institutions with the most prominent previous actor being the crime science work at the Jill Dando

Institute which drew in many of the academics who had previously worked on crime and policing projects in the Home Office Research Unit. Regionalised collaborations between police forces and universities to deliver police training through the old Initial Police Learning and Development programme were introduced after the 2002 Training Matters review highlighted limitations in historical modes of training and the Police Reform Act 2002 gave police forces more freedom to choose how to deliver training (Wood and Tong, 2009).

Scotland undertook similar developments ahead of England and Wales when it established the Scottish Institute for Policing Research in 2007 as a collaboration between Police Scotland, the Scottish Police Authority, and 14 Scottish universities (SIPR, 2021). The main point to take from this brief bit of history is that evidence-based policing is just one developmental strand in the evolving relationship between police institutions and universities and that criminology has a myriad of influences across education, research, evaluation, and, in the widest sense, organisational learning and development.

Co-operative international developments with evidence-based policing are still limited, but it is possible to see further internationalisation of ideas as a future trajectory with evidence-based policing and criminological societies and networks established in Australia and New Zealand, the United States, India, and in various forms across Europe and via the European Union Agency for Law Enforcement training (CEPOL). The current state of the art involves varying levels of integration of criminology and other subject matters into the police domain, but there is still comparatively little known about how to deliver the best impact for police and other public safety functions whilst retaining some degree of criticality and independence. It is to this issue we turn next.

Beyond Evidence-Based Policing

Larry Sherman (1998) noted in his original Police Foundation article about the potential impact of evidence-based policing that the concept was designed to provide both a way of integrating theory and practice alongside a mechanism for change that would deliver impact for policing agencies unlike criminology which provided a range of ideas that generally sat on the periphery of policing circles and were often influenced as much by key individual relationships as novel ideas and innovations.

Sherman's call to arms bore similarities with work being undertaken by David Bayley and Clifford Shearing on behalf of the United States National Institute of Justice at the same time in recognising current as well as future changes to the shape and delivery of policing. In 2001, David Bayley and Clifford Shearing laid out a new research agenda for policing scholars with an emphasis on both "auspices" and "providers" of policing services in order to capture the, numerically more significant, myriad of agencies that are tasked with policing functions but who are not police. The final section of this chapter aligns these two endeavours and updates them to support a short look into the immediate future.

For most of the nineteenth and twentieth centuries, the dominant mode of thinking about policing in western democracies had been that police solve and resolve crime and disorder issues through a predominantly reactive approach, and they do this with a monopoly of control over coercive power and the threat of physical force. This discourse has now been displaced by a more proactive and preventive approach to policing which seeks to stop crime occurring in the first place and re-prioritises the position of victims of crime in criminal justice responses. On the frontline, experiences of police officers will differ greatly, but there is sufficient international evidence available to argue that democratic policing has become increasingly proactive and victim-oriented even though these shifts have taken place within the existing institutional architecture of offender-oriented criminal law and criminal justice institutions (Paterson and Williams, 2018).

Yet, police organisations are more likely to successfully tackle crime when policing strategies are based within and informed by those who experience crime and harm (Paterson and Best, 2016). Such an approach creates a need for police to develop problem-oriented partnerships with other agencies (including probation, social work, education, housing, and community-based organisations) to identify and address underlying causes of crime. The next stage of criminological and police development needs to be a research agenda that aligns with these existing shifts around victimisation and vulnerability to design, develop, and deliver a scientific underpinning for the new generation of police officers who are being developed through the police education qualifications framework. The College of Policing is already putting an enhanced focus on the prediction of future trajectories, but it is essential that understandings of vulnerability and the successful management of the challenges this presents to societies come from those on the frontline who see these harms on a daily basis.

The limitations of criminology are no different to the limitations of police institutions or other organisations in that there is an organisational temptation to stick with the way we do things around here. The future of criminology for police needs to be guided by those with the relevant experience to ensure that it is methodologically rigorous, independent, and able to stand up to external scrutiny, but it needs to be driven by this new generation of police officers who will shape the research agenda based upon the needs of their organisations and the communities which they work in.

References

Association of Police and Crime Commissioners (2020) *National Digital Policing Strategy 2020–30*. Available at: www.apccs.police.uk/latest-news/national-digital-policing-strategy-2020-2030/

Bayley, D. and Shearing, C. (2001) *The New Structure of Policing: Description, Conceptualization and Research Agenda*. Washington, DC: National Institute of Justice.

Bradford, B., Jackson, J. and Stanko, E. (2009) Contact and confidence: Revisiting the impact of public encounters with the police. *Policing and Society*. 19(1): 20–46.

Clamp, K. and Paterson, C. (2016) *Restorative Policing: Concepts, Theory and Practice*. London: Routledge.

College of Policing (2020) *Policing in England and Wales: Future Operating Environment 2040*. Available at: www.college.police.uk/article/preparing-policing-future-challenges-and-demands

Colquhoun, J. (1800/2012) *A Treatise on the Police of the Metropolis*. Cambridge: Cambridge University Press.

Crown Prosecution Service (2020) *CPS Data Summary Quarter 4 2019–20*. Available at: www.cps.gov.uk/publication/cps-data-summary-quarter-4-2019-2020

Durkheim, E. (1912/2008) *The Elementary Forms of Religious Life*. Oxford: Oxford University Press.

Farrell, G. (2001) *How Victim-Oriented Is Policing?* International Symposium on Victimology, Montreal. Available at: www.researchgate.net/publication/28575311_How_victim-oriented_is_policing

Fielding, H. (1757) *An Enquiry Into the Causes of the Late Increase of Robbers: With Some Proposals for Remedying This Growing Evil* (Second edition). London: A Miller.

Hall, S., Critcher, C., Jefferson, T., Clarke, J. and Roberts, B. (1978) *Policing the Crisis: Mugging, the State and Law and Order*. London: MacMillan.

Her Majesty's Inspectorate of Constabulary (HMIC) (1999) *Managing Learning: A Study of Police Training*. London: HMIC.

Her Majesty's Inspectorate of Constabulary (HMIC) (2002) *Training Matters*. Available at: www.justiceinspectorates.gov.uk/hmicfrs/media/training-matters-2002 0101.pdf

Herrington, V. and Colvin, A. (2016) Police leadership for complex time. *Policing: A Journal of Policy and Practice*. 10(1): 7–16.

Hills, A. (2014) What is policeness? On being police in Somalia. *The British Journal of Criminology*. 54(5): 765–783.

Ibarra, P. and Erez, E. (2005) Victim-centric diversion? The electronic monitoring of domestic violence cases. *Behavioural Sciences and the Law*. 23(2): 259–276.

Innes, M. (2014) *Signal Crimes: Social Reactions to Crime, Disorder and Control*. Oxford: Oxford University Press.

Kapoor, V. (2020) *DEEP COP*. International Association of Chiefs of Police. Available at: www.policechiefmagazine.org/wp-content/uploads/IAC-413-July2020_F2_Web. pdf

Lammy, D. (2017) *Lammy Review: Final Report*. London: UK Government.

Laycock, G. (2001) Hypothesis-based research: The repeat victimisation story. *Criminology and Criminal Justice*. 1(1): 59–82.

Lentz, S. and Chaires, R. (2007) The invention of Peel's principles: A study of policing textbook history. *Journal of Criminal Justice*. 35(1): 69–79.

Marenin, O. (2005) Building a global police studies community. *Police Quarterly*. 8(1): 99–136.

Paterson, C. (2011) Adding value? A review of the international literature on the role of higher education in police training and education. *Police Practice and Research.* 12(4): 286–297.

Paterson, C. and Best, D. (2016) Policing vulnerability through building community connections. *Policing: A Journal of Policy and Practice.* 10(2): 150–157.

Paterson, C. and Clamp, K. (2013) Exploring recent developments in restorative policing in England and Wales. *Criminology and Criminal Justice.* 12(5): 593–611.

Paterson, C. and Williams, A. (2018) Towards victim-oriented police? *Journal of Victimology and Victim Justice.* 1(1): 85–101.

Scottish Institute of Police Research (2021) *About Us.* Available at: www.sipr.ac.uk/about-us/about-us

Sherman, L. (1998) Evidence-Based Policing. *Police Foundation: Ideas in American Policing.* Available at: www.policefoundation.org/wp-content/uploads/2015/06/Sherman-1998-Evidence-Based-Policing.pdf

Tankebe, J. (2012) Viewing things differently: The dimensions of public perceptions of police legitimacy. *Criminology.* 51(1): 103–135.

Taylor, C. (2012) *Policing Just Outcomes.* Perth: Edith Cowan University.

Tyler, T. (2017) Procedural justice and policing: A rush to judgement? *Annual Review of Law and Science.* 13: 29–53.

Vitale, A. (2017). *The End of Policing.* New York, NY: Verso.

Wood, D. and Tong, S. (2009) The future of initial police training: A university perspective. *International Journal of Police Science and Management.* 11(3): 294–305.

Index